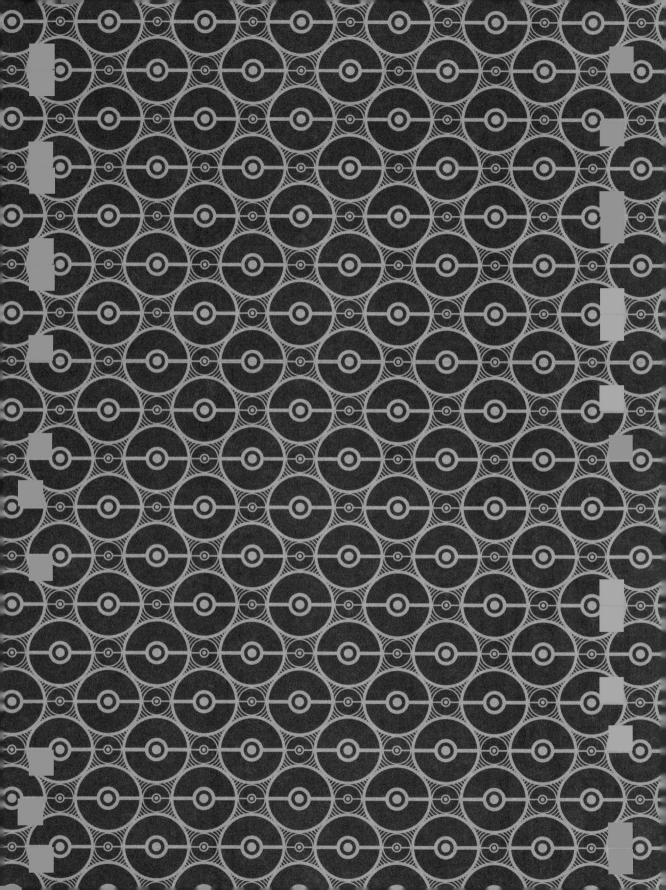

WELCOME TO A MOVIE THEATER IN A BOOK!

Are you a film buff? Is your mantra about Pokémon movies "Gotta catch 'em all?" Do you know everything about the adventures of Ash and Pikachu on the big screen? Well, there's only one way to find out! Put your Pokémon movie trivia skills to the test with this epic book. From cover to cover, in the pages of this definitive guide, you'll find awesome details on the people, places, and of course, battles in the Pokémon movies! It will put your Pokémon knowledge to the test and make you a true expert. So, turn the page if you're ready to prove you're the ultimate Pokémon movie fan!

FEATURED MOVIE RELEASES

POKÉMON:
THE FIRST MOVIE

POKÉMON 3: THE MOVIE

POKÉMON RANGER AND
THE TEMPLE OF THE SEA

1999　　2000　　2001　　2006　　2007　　2008

POKÉMON
THE MOVIE 2000

POKÉMON: LUCARIO AND
THE MYSTERY OF MEW

POKÉMON: THE RISE OF DARKRAI

● POKÉMON THE MOVIE: WHITE - VICTINI AND ZEKROM

● POKÉMON THE MOVIE: BLACK - VICTINI AND RESHIRAM

POKÉMON THE MOVIE:
HOOPA AND THE CLASH OF AGES

2009 ● **2011** ● **2014** ● **2015** ● **2016**

POKÉMON THE MOVIE:
VOLCANION AND THE
MECHANICAL MARVEL

POKÉMON:
ARCEUS AND THE
JEWEL OF LIFE

POKÉMON THE MOVIE:
GENESECT AND THE
LEGEND AWAKENED

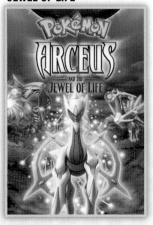

MEET THE MOVIE STARS

ASH KETCHUM

Hailing from Pallet Town in the Kanto region, Ash has one dream—to become a Pokémon Master! Along with his best buddy, Pikachu, Ash is on a journey to learn all about Pokémon. On the road, he's had so many adventures, made so many friends, caught so many wild Pokémon, and of course, has been up for every Pokémon Battle challenge. Ash works hard, and he plays even harder!

A FRIEND IN DEED

Ash is always there for his friends, both old and new. He can't stand by when he knows there's a Pokémon or person in trouble. He springs into action and will do whatever it takes to right a wrong.

TALK THE TALK, WALK THE WALK

Ash has a lot of bravado. Proud and confident, Ash likes to brag about his abilities. But win or lose, Ash is a good sport who's always ready for the next adventure, the next challenge, or the next opponent. He's never afraid to try, and he's an "all in" kind of guy. When Ash puts his mind to something, he really brings it!

PIKACHU

Height	1'04"
Weight	13.2 lbs
Type	Electric

Ash's First Partner Pokémon, Pikachu, can shock and amaze with its incredible Electric-type attacks. However, its true battle strength comes from its beautiful friendship with its Trainer, Ash. Pikachu opts to stay out of its Poké Ball and travels side by side with his pal. Perhaps Ash is so confident because he knows he has the best partner in Pikachu. Together, they have taken on every adventure, shared every meal, climbed every challenge, and they are ready for more! Ash and Pikachu are an unstoppable team.

SQUIRTLE
THE TINY TURTLE POKÉMON

Height: 1'08"
Weight: 19.8 lbs

WATER

BULBASAUR
THE SEED POKÉMON

Height: 2'04"
Weight: 15.2 lbs

GRASS	POISON

CHARIZARD
THE FLAME POKÉMON

Height: 5'07"
Weight: 199.5 lbs

FIRE	FLYING

LAPRAS
THE TRANSPORT POKÉMON

Height: 8'02"
Weight: 485.0 lbs

WATER ICE

SNORLAX
THE SLEEPING POKÉMON

Height: 6'11"
Weight: 1014.1 lbs

NORMAL

CYNDAQUIL
THE FIRE MOUSE POKÉMON

Height: 01'08"
Weight: 17.4 lbs

FIRE

CHIKORITA
THE LEAF POKÉMON

Evolves into…

Height: 2'11"
Weight: 14.1 lbs

GRASS

BAYLEEF
THE LEAF POKÉMON

Height: 3'11"
Weight: 34.8 lbs

GRASS

NOCTOWL
THE OWL POKÉMON

Height: 5'03"
Weight: 89.9 lbs

NORMAL FLYING

TOTODILE
THE BIG JAW POKÉMON

Height: 2'00"
Weight: 20.9 lbs

WATER

CORPHISH
THE RUFFIAN POKÉMON

Height: 2'00"
Weight: 25.4 lbs

WATER

PHANPY
THE LONG NOSE POKÉMON

Height: 1'08"
Weight: 73.9 lbs

GROUND

DONPHAN
THE ARMOR POKÉMON

Height: 3'07"
Weight: 264.6 lbs

GROUND

SWELLOW
THE SWALLOW POKÉMON

Height: 2'04"
Weight: 43.7 lbs

NORMAL FLYING

GROVYLE
THE WOOD GECKO POKÉMON

Height: 2'11"
Weight: 47.6 lbs

GRASS

SCEPTILE
THE FOREST POKÉMON

Height: 5'07"
Weight: 115.1 lbs

GRASS

AIPOM
THE LONG TAIL POKÉMON

Height: 2'07"
Weight: 25.4 lbs

NORMAL

STARAVIA
THE STARLING POKÉMON

Height: 2'00"
Weight: 34.2 lbs

NORMAL FLYING

TURTWIG
THE TINY LEAF POKÉMON

Height: 1'04"
Weight: 22.5 lbs

GRASS

MONFERNO
THE PLAYFUL POKÉMON

Height: 2'11"
Weight: 48.5 lbs

FIRE FIGHTING

GLISCOR
THE FANG SCORPION POKÉMON

Height: 6'07"
Weight: 93.7 lbs

GROUND FLYING

GROTLE
THE GROVE POKÉMON

Height: 3'07"
Weight: 213.8 lbs

GRASS

STARAPTOR
THE PREDATOR POKÉMON

Height: 3'11"
Weight: 54.9 lbs

NORMAL FLYING

SCRAGGY
THE SHEDDING POKÉMON

Height: 2'00"
Weight: 26.0 lbs

DARK	FIGHTING

OSHAWOTT
THE SEA OTTER POKÉMON

Height: 1'08"
Weight: 13.0 lbs

WATER

SNIVY
THE GRASS SNAKE POKÉMON

Height: 2'00"
Weight: 17.9 lbs

GRASS

LEAVANNY
THE NURTURING POKÉMON

Height: 3'11"
Weight: 45.2 lbs

BUG	GRASS

PIGNITE
THE FIRE PIG POKÉMON

Height: 3'03"
Weight: 122.4 lbs

FIRE	FIGHTING

NOIVERN
THE SOUND WAVE POKÉMON

Height: 4'11"
Weight: 187.4 lbs

FLYING	DRAGON

HAWLUCHA
THE WRESTLING POKÉMON

Height: 2'07"
Weight: 47.4 lbs

FIGHTING	FLYING

GRENINJA
THE NINJA POKÉMON

Height: 4'11"
Weight: 88.2 lbs

WATER	DARK

TALONFLAME
THE SCORCHING POKÉMON

Height: 3'11"
Weight: 54.0 lbs

FIRE	FLYING

BROCK

Pewter City Gym Leader and Pokémon Breeder Brock is a nurturer by nature. His life's mission is to care for his pals, both Pokémon and human. Knowledgeable Brock has the skills to mix up medicine to heal Pokémon and specializes in Rock-types. However, perhaps he's best known for his delicious recipes. Ash is a big fan of his talented buddy Chef Brock, who can improvise a yummy meal on the go.

Brock is the kind of person who knows a little something about everything, from training to geography to medicine to battle strategy. However, there's one subject he's obsessed with that he can't quite figure out—how to talk to girls. Much to the embarrassment of his travel companions, he goes completely gaga every time he sees a girl he has a crush on, and well, he likes them all.

VULPIX
THE FOX POKÉMON

Height: 2'00"
Weight: 21.8 lbs

FIRE

ONIX
THE ROCK SNAKE POKÉMON

Height: 28'10"
Weight: 463.0 lbs

ROCK | GROUND

MUDKIP
THE MUDFISH POKÉMON

Height: 1'04"
Weight: 16.8 lbs

WATER

ZUBAT
THE BAT POKÉMON

Evolves into…

Height: 2'07"
Weight: 16.5 lbs

POISON | FLYING

CROBAT
THE BAT POKÉMON

Height: 5'11"
Weight: 165.3 lbs

POISON | FLYING

MARSHTOMP
THE MUDFISH POKÉMON

Height: 2'04"
Weight: 61.7 lbs

WATER | GROUND

FORRETRESS
THE BAGWORM POKÉMON

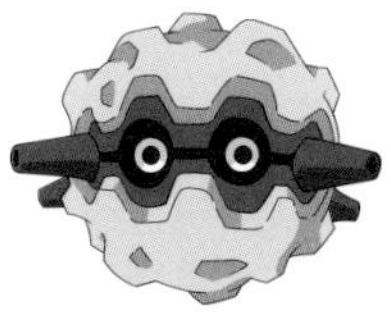

Height: 3'11"
Weight: 277.3 lbs

BUG | STEEL

BONSLY
THE BONSAI POKÉMON

Height: 1'08"
Weight: 33.1 lbs

ROCK

SUDOWOODO
THE IMITATION POKÉMON

Height: 3'11"
Weight: 83.8 lbs

ROCK

HAPPINY
THE PLAYHOUSE POKÉMON

Height: 2'00"
Weight: 53.8 lbs

NORMAL

CROAGUNK
THE TOXIC MOUTH POKÉMON

Height: 2'04"
Weight: 50.7 lbs

POISON | FIGHTING

MISTY

Sassy Misty isn't afraid to speak her mind and tell Ash exactly what she thinks of him, and really, everything. Outspoken and up for adventure, Misty left her sisters behind at the Cerulean Gym to make her own way in the world. She's on a mission to learn all she can about Water-type Pokémon.

TOGEPI
THE SPIKE BALL POKÉMON

Height: 1'00"
Weight: 3.3 lbs

FAIRY

STARYU
THE STAR SHAPE POKÉMON

Height: 2'07"
Weight: 76.1l lbs

WATER

PSYDUCK
THE DUCK POKÉMON

Height: 2'07"
Weight: 43.2 lbs

WATER

GOLDEEN
THE GOLDFISH POKÉMON

Height: 2'00"
Weight: 331.1 lbs

WATER

MAY AND MAX

This brother-sister duo from Petalburg City likes to travel together with their pal Ash. Although May wants to look out for her little brother, he wants to prove he's big and bright enough to be part of the team. But the truth is, May also has some growing up to do. She and Max are ready for all the adventure that awaits them when they join Ash on his journey!

May dreams of being a Pokémon Coordinator who competes in Pokémon Contests. She works with her Pokémon to make them as skilled, well-groomed, and graceful as possible in the hopes of earning ribbons.

Max is too young to be a Pokémon Trainer, so for now, he's studying up. However, he can read his sister May like a book. He knows all of her secrets and often embarrasses her with stories or jokes at her expense.

DAWN

Pokémon Coordinator Dawn is on top of her game. She loves dressing up and competing in Pokémon Contests, just like her decorated mother, Johanna. This stylish girlie girl would have brought her whole fabulous wardrobe on the road with her if she could have! She never likes a hair out of place and is just as detail-oriented in her Pokémon Contest appearances. Confident and caring, Dawn is a great travel companion.

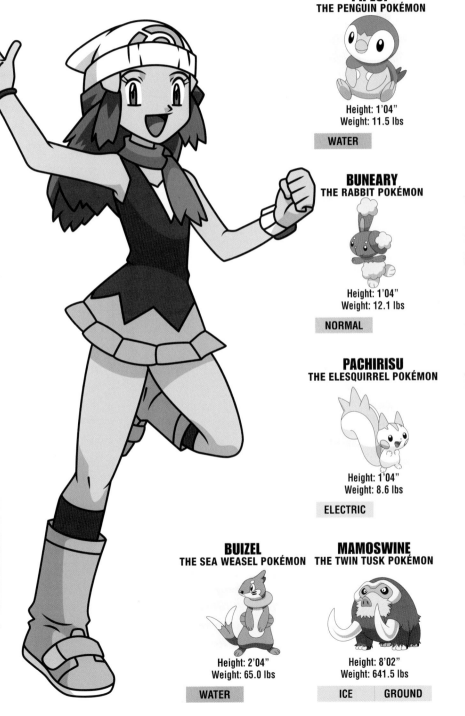

COMBUSKEN
THE GOLDFISH POKÉMON

Height: 2'11"
Weight: 43.0 lbs

FIRE   FIGHTING

SQUIRTLE
THE TINY TURTLE POKÉMON
Height: 1'08"
Weight: 19.8 lbs

WATER

MUNCHLAX
THE BIG EATER POKÉMON
Height: 2'00"
Weight: 231.5 lbs

NORMAL

EEVEE
THE EVOLUTION POKÉMON

Height: 1'00"
Weight: 14.3 lbs

NORMAL

PIPLUP
THE PENGUIN POKÉMON
Height: 1'04"
Weight: 11.5 lbs

WATER

BUNEARY
THE RABBIT POKÉMON
Height: 1'04"
Weight: 12.1 lbs

NORMAL

PACHIRISU
THE ELESQUIRREL POKÉMON
Height: 1'04"
Weight: 8.6 lbs

ELECTRIC

BUIZEL
THE SEA WEASEL POKÉMON
Height: 2'04"
Weight: 65.0 lbs

WATER

MAMOSWINE
THE TWIN TUSK POKÉMON
Height: 8'02"
Weight: 641.5 lbs

ICE   GROUND

IRIS

Sprite and spunky, Iris is from the famous Village of Dragons. Although she likes to tell Ash he's "such a kid," she is not exactly old and wise herself. She has a lot to learn when it comes to training Pokémon, not that she'll admit it. She loves the excitement on the road, traveling with Ash. However, her favorite mode of transportation isn't walking down the path—it's swinging from tree branches.

EMOLGA
SKY SQUIRREL POKÉMON

Height: 1'04"
Weight: 11.0 lbs

ELECTRIC   FLYING

AXEW
THE TUSK POKÉMON

Height: 2'00"
Weight: 39.7 lbs

DRAGON

DRAGONITE
THE DRAGON POKÉMON

Height: 7'03"
Weight: 463.0 lbs

DRAGON   FLYING

DRILBUR
THE MOLE POKÉMON

Height: 1'00"
Weight: 18.7 lbs

GROUND

Evolves into...

EXCADRILL
THE SUBTERRENE POKÉMON

Height: 2'04"
Weight: 89.1 lbs

GROUND   STEEL

CILAN

Cilan is a man of many talents! He is a triplet who runs the Striaton City Gym along with his two brothers. Cilan is also a terrific chef who often compares battle situations to food. But perhaps Cilan is best known as a Pokémon Connoisseur, or someone who can help Trainers build strong relationships with their Pokémon pals.

PANSAGE
THE GRASS MONKEY POKÉMON

Height: 2'00"
Weight: 23.1 lbs

GRASS

CRUSTLE
THE STONE HOME POKÉMON

Height: 4'07"
Weight: 440.9 lbs

BUG   ROCK

STUNFISK
THE TRAP POKÉMON

Height: 2'04"
Weight: 24.3 lbs

GROUND   ELECTRIC

CLEMONT AND BONNIE

Clemont is the Gym Leader of Lumiose City, but perhaps more notably, he's one of the area's greatest scientific minds. Clemont is always tinkering around on some technological breakthrough. He loves to spend his time building robots and machines better known as Clemontic Gear. You just never know what magical tool he can pull out of his backpack to try to save the day! Sometimes his creative inventions will do the job, but other times they'll just be an entertaining epic fail. Either way, Clemont is always there to find a way to help his pal Ash.

Bonnie isn't just Clemont's little sister: she's also his biggest fan. Bonnie looks up to her clever brother Clemont and follows him around wherever he goes, including on his journey with Ash. There's only one thing she loves even more than her brother—Pokémon. She just can't resist a cute Pokémon like Dedenne!

Bonnie nicknamed the amazingly powerful Legendary Pokémon that decided to travel along with her and the crew "Squishy." Although it seems to prefer to be carried in Bonnie's purse in its Core Forme, in its Complete Forme, it's almost four times taller than she is.

BUNNELBY
THE DIGGING POKÉMON

Height: 1'04"
Weight: 11.0 lbs

NORMAL

LUXRAY
THE GLEAM EYES POKÉMON

Height: 4'07"
Weight: 92.6 lbs

ELECTRIC

CHESPIN
THE SPINY NUT POKÉMON

Height: 1'04"
Weight: 19.8 lbs

GRASS

DEDENNE
THE ANTENNA POKÉMON

Height: 0'08"
Weight: 4.9 lbs

ELECTRIC   FAIRY

ZYGARDE
THE ORDER POKÉMON
Complete Forme

Height: 14'09"
Weight: 1344.8 lbs

DRAGON   GROUND

SERENA

An old friend of Ash, Serena might just be his biggest fan. She's always there with words of encouragement and positivity. Maybe it's because she's a fierce competitor herself. Serena loves to enter Pokémon Showcases where she can show off her talented Pokémon pals and her knack for baking delicious Pokémon Puffs. She is also known for her PokéVision videos showcasing her Pokémon, their interests, and even their acting skills.

SYLVEON
THE INTERTWINING POKÉMON

Height: 3'03"
Weight: 51.8 lbs

FAIRY

BRAIXEN
THE FOX POKÉMON

Height: 3'03"
Weight: 32.0 lbs

FIRE

PANCHAM
THE PLAYFUL POKÉMON

Height: 2'00"
Weight: 17.6 lbs

FIGHTING

NURSE JOY

For Pokémon that are sick, need rest after a match, or even want a little extra TLC, they have a friend in Nurse Joy—or rather, friends. There is a Nurse Joy at every Pokémon Center. They're all nearly identical, as they look alike, talk alike, and even dress alike. Most importantly, they offer the best treatment for Pokémon hands down in every town. So, if you or your Pokémon need to make a pit stop, look no further than Nurse Joy at your local Pokémon Center.

Depending on which Pokémon Center you visit, Nurse Joy can have a different Pokémon aide by her side.

WIGGLYTUFF
THE BALLOON POKÉMON

Height: 3'03"
Weight: 26.5 lbs

NORMAL   FAIRY

CHANSEY
THE EGG POKÉMON

Height: 3'07"
Weight: 76.3 lbs

NORMAL

AUDINO
THE HEARING POKÉMON

Height: 3'07"
Weight: 68.3 lbs

NORMAL

OFFICER JENNY

Luckily, every town has an Officer Jenny to protect and defend all the people and Pokémon. Just like Nurse Joy, they're all nearly identical. When duty calls, Officer Jenny is there to ensure justice is served! Sometimes, she'll even enlist Ash's help.

TEAM ROCKET

The trio of Jessie, James, and Meowth are obsessed with catching Ash's pal Pikachu. No matter where Ash goes, Team Rocket is one step behind causing trouble, make it double, errr, triple. But Jessie, James, and Meowth are just one small fraction of the whole Team Rocket operation. There are many more members wreaking havoc all over.

IN DISGUISE

Jessie, James, and Meowth often dress up in wild disguises so Ash and his friends won't recognize them. These outfits are often silly and require special accents. Jessie, James, and Meowth do their best to sell their fake identities, but Ash and his friends don't always buy it.

FOOD, GLORIOUS FOOD

Arguably, the only thing Team Rocket dreams of more than catching Pikachu is chowing down on a delicious meal. Their stomachs grumble louder than even their mouths. If only they cooked as much as they complained, they might be top chefs!

WOBBUFFET
THE PATIENT POKÉMON

Height: 4'03"
Weight: 62.8 lbs

PSYCHIC

MIME JR.
THE MIME POKÉMON

Height: 2'00"
Weight: 28.7 lbs

PSYCHIC	FAIRY

CACNEA
THE CACTUS POKÉMON

Height: 1'04"
Weight: 113.1 lbs

GRASS

WEEZING
THE POISON GAS POKÉMON

Height: 3'11"
Weight: 20.9 lbs

POISON

ARBOK
THE COBRA POKÉMON

Height: 11'06"
Weight: 143.3 lbs

POISON

CHIMECHO
THE WIND CHIME POKÉMON

Height: 2'00"
Weight: 2.2 lbs

PSYCHIC

MEOWTH:
THE SCRATCH CAT POKÉMON

Height	1'04"
Weight	9.3 lbs
Type	Normal

Meowth is an important part of Team Rocket and travels out of its Poké Ball. It possesses a special gift: the gift of gab. Meowth can talk to humans and its preferred manner of speech is funny wisecracks.

POKÉMON: THE FIRST MOVIE
THE STORY

A mix of strange liquid and broken glass spills across the floor as Mewtwo breaks out of the test tube where it was born. Mewtwo first opens its eyes in a gray lab surrounded by big machinery and a group of scientists led by Dr. Fuji. He has a scraggly, long beard on his chin and small glasses that make his eyes look even smaller. "What am I?" Mewtwo asks.

Dr. Fuji happily explains that after years of hard work, it appears he has successfully created a clone from the DNA of Mythical Pokémon Mew. But not just a clone, this clone is better, this clone is Mewtwo—a powerful Pokémon. But the experiment isn't over. Now, Dr. Fuji wants to keep Mewtwo in the lab so he can run tests on it. However, Mewtwo doesn't want to spend its life being studied. It wants its freedom, and as a powerful Pokémon, it has the strength to get it.

Mewtwo's eyes glow blue with power as it fires beams that destroy the lab. It's so strong its Psychic-type strength even slices through the very machine that made it. The scientists scramble as it all comes crashing down. Surrounded by rubble and fire, Mewtwo has succeeded in finding liberty and now it wants to find its purpose.

Just then, a helicopter lands on some rocks next to Mewtwo. A man emerges from the smoke—it's Giovanni, a Team Rocket boss in a business suit—and he offers to show Mewtwo how to control its incredible powers and take over the world. Giovanni vows that although the scientists saw it as an experiment, he sees Mewtwo as a valuable partner. But can Mewtwo trust Giovanni?

At Giovanni's secret lair, he gifts Mewtwo special shiny armor topped with a sleek helmet. Then, he shows Mewtwo its first battlefield. A giant Onix growls

at Mewtwo, whose instincts suddenly kick in. Mewtwo fires a single bright blue Psychic blast and tall Onix comes crashing down. Mewtwo is beginning to realize its Psychic power.

Giovanni continues training Mewtwo with delight as he watches it easily defeat a herd of Tauros, Alakazam, Magneton, even a duo of Arcanine and Nidoking. Team Rocket goons, standing on the sidelines of these battles, can't believe their luck or their eyes as they toss Poké Balls to catch all the Pokémon in Mewtwo's wake. At first, Mewtwo loves the excitement of the battle. But Mewtwo is still wondering what to do with its power, its life.

Meanwhile, our heroes Ash, Misty, and Brock have no idea the evil that Giovanni and Team Rocket have been up to. They are up on a grassy hill, taking a break from adventure to have lunch along with their Pokémon pals Togepi and Pikachu, when a stranger arrives at their picnic—a Pokémon Trainer named Raymond. He's looking to challenge Ash, who is always up for a Pokémon Battle.

"You were created to fight for me," Giovanni says, revealing his true intentions. "That is your purpose!"

Mewtwo is shocked to hear the truth. Giovanni never wanted to be its partner. It turns out that he is the one behind the scientists that created Mewtwo and he has tricked Mewtwo again. Furious, Mewtwo rips off his armor and destroys Giovanni's lair with a blast of beaming blue.

"Humans may have created me, but they will never enslave me. This cannot be my destiny!" Mewtwo cries out as it makes another great escape.

Feeling betrayed yet again by humans, Mewtwo rises into the sky leaving the lair in ashes. Mewtwo travels back to the ruins of the lab it was born in to reflect on its purpose in life. This isn't the last the world, and humans, will hear of Mewtwo.

Up on a nearby cliff, Jessie, James and Meowth are spying on Ash and their Pokémon obsession, Pikachu. But they're not the only ones. As Raymond and Ash battle, it seems someone else is also watching the match unfold, thanks to a Fearow flying above carrying a camera around its neck. Who has their eye on Ash and why?

Ash and Bulbasaur easily win the first round against Raymond and Donphan with a bright Solar Beam. In the second round, Ash and Squirtle cinch a win against Raymond and Machoke with a Bubble Beam blast. Raymond gets mad and like a bad sport unleashes three of his Pokémon at once—Venomoth, Pinsir, and Golem. But one big Thunderbolt from Pikachu ends the battle with a bang!

Suddenly, another visitor approaches from the sky. It's Dragonite bearing a very unique invitation for Ash. When he opens the card, a beam of blue light appears with a tiny hologram of a woman in a long dress and tall hat.

"Greetings, I bear an invitation," she says. "You have been chosen to join a select group of Pokémon Trainers at a special gathering. It will be hosted by my master—the World's Greatest Pokémon Trainer, at his palace on New Island."

To make the contest, the hologram tells Ash he must take a ferry this very afternoon. Although girl-crazy Brock is only interested in meeting the hologram in real life, Ash is itching to compete. So the friends immediately head to the local ferry dock.

On the way, a huge storm begins to brew and it seems to be caused by none other than Mewtwo! It is swirling its hands in the air causing wild winds, stirring the seas, and a hard rain falls from black clouds. It's a storm unlike any other. Ash, Misty, Brock, Pikachu, and Togepi arrive at the ferry dock completely soaked only to discover service has been suspended because of the weather. The place is filled with disappointed Pokémon Trainers who had received the same invitation to compete on New Island.

A few Trainers seem determined to sail the rough waters on their own, but the Ferry Manager and Officer warn them that if anything happens to their beloved Pokémon, there is no Nurse Joy around to help them. Apparently, she went missing from the local Pokémon Center about a month ago. But nothing will stop some determined Pokémon Trainers!

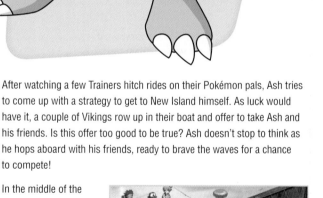

After watching a few Trainers hitch rides on their Pokémon pals, Ash tries to come up with a strategy to get to New Island himself. As luck would have it, a couple of Vikings row up in their boat and offer to take Ash and his friends. Is this offer too good to be true? Ash doesn't stop to think as he hops aboard with his friends, ready to brave the waves for a chance to compete!

In the middle of the ocean a massive tidal wave strikes the boat, soaking everyone on board and revealing the true identity of the Vikings—they're actually Team

Rocket's Jessie, James, and Meowth! Before Ash, Misty, and Brock can plan their escape another huge wave throws them off the boat and underwater. Struggling to swim to the surface, Misty and Ash think fast and call on their Water-type Pokémon Staryu and Squirtle to act as life rafts. Thanks to their Pokémon pals, they're able to ride out the storm by sticking together.

Squirtle spots a light in the distance and swims them toward it. A dark castle surrounded by gray clouds emerges in the distance. Its windows are glowing with light and its spires have windmills twirling in the breeze. They've arrived at New Island!

The very woman that was in the hologram greets Ash, Brock, Misty, Togepi, and Pikachu. But Brock has a hunch he's seen her somewhere else.

"I knew I recognized that face!" Brock says with a grin. "Aren't you the nurse who's missing from the Pokémon Center?"

"I fear you are mistaken. I have always dwelt on this island and have always been in the service of my master," the mystery woman replies without any emotion.

Brock, Misty, and Ash are beginning to feel that something strange is going on. The mystery woman asks them to follow her as she leads them through the dark cave  into a grand hall. It's a massive golden room with beautiful fountains, a spiral slide from floor to ceiling, and a luxurious dining table covered in delicious snacks.

There are three Trainers already there: Corey, a bold boy with black hair, who flew over on his Pokémon friend Pidgeot. Fergus, a Water-type expert who sailed along on his Pokémon pal Gyarados. And Neesha, a brave girl with a bob haircut who hitched a ride on her buddy, Dewgong.

The mystery woman admits that only the Trainers tough enough to make it to New Island in the storm have been deemed worthy by her master to compete. The storm was their first test. The Trainers are shocked to hear that weather was part of their contest, but the mystery woman promises her master will arrive shortly to explain.

Suddenly, the lights go off in the grand hall. A Psychic beam of blue light appears at the center of the spiral slide and a figure gracefully descends. The mystery woman introduces her master, the world's number one Pokémon Master and powerful Pokémon, Mewtwo.

"A POKÉMON CAN'T BE A POKÉMON MASTER! NO WAY!" —FERGUS

"Quiet human!" Mewtwo and the mystery woman say in harmony. "From now on, I am the one who makes the rules."

It's clear that Mewtwo is using its Psychic-type powers to control the mystery woman and even put words in her mouth. But, now that Mewtwo has an audience, it no longer needs her. So, it wipes her memory clean of the past few weeks and releases her from its control. Brock rushes to catch her as she faints. Her tall hat falls off revealing her pink hair and true identity. Brock was right all along, she is, in fact, Nurse Joy!

But Mewtwo isn't the only one with an evil scheme on New Island. It seems the Team Rocket trio of Jessie, James, and Meowth have snuck into the palace. However, they're not in the grand hall. They stumbled upon Mewtwo's secret laboratory. Inside, there are giant glass tubes filled with a strange liquid and three Pokémon: Venusaur, Blastoise, and Charizard. The tubes lead to a powerful piece of technology— the Pokémon Replication System.

Jessie accidentally triggers the massive machine to begin a sequence. It senses a Pokémon's presence in the lab. Suddenly, dozens of silver hands grab Meowth and throw it onto a conveyor belt.

"Put me down! Let me go!" Meowth yelps trying to run away.

Meowth is able to break through their grip, but the machine is able to pluck a few hairs off it. This gives it enough genetic material to clone Meowth. In seconds, the machine spits outs an exact replica of the Scratch Cat Pokémon into one of the giant test tubes.

Then, on the small computer screen, loud static breaks through the sequence. It begins to play a secret message from Dr. Fuji. He made it back while Mewtwo was destroying the lab to warn whoever found the machine next about its history. In the tape, he reveals that Giovanni funded the project to make even stronger super clones of Pokémon. From the DNA of an ancient fossil of Mew, the Pokémon Replication System made Mewtwo. However, no one anticipated how angry this clone would be.

Back in the Grand Hall, Ash and the other Trainers are experiencing Mewtwo's rage first hand. Mewtwo explains why it really brought all the Trainers to its palace. Mewtwo thinks all humans are evil and want to turn Pokémon into their slaves. Mewtwo explains that its goal is to rid the earth of all humanity, including all the Pokémon who have Pokémon Trainers because it believes they are weak for working for humans.

"Pika! Pika Pika!" Pikachu protests, explaining that it is Ash's best friend and teammate.

But Mewtwo doesn't believe Pikachu because it thinks humans and Pokémon can never be friends. Using its Psychic power it lifts Pikachu up in a Psychic blue beam and sends it flying. Ash jumps up, using his own body to break Pikachu's fall.

Upset to see Mewtwo's hate turn into hurt, Corey asks his Pokémon pal Rhyhorn to step in. It charges at Mewtwo with all its might, but the Legendary Pokémon stops it in its tracks with a single finger. Then, Mewtwo tosses it across the dining table.

"Fools! Your Pokémon attacks cannot weaken me. My powers are too great!" Mewtwo warns. "No Trainer can conquer me!"

"Then you won't mind proving it in a real match!" Ash snaps back.

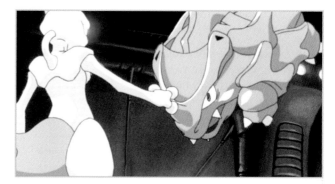

"YOU'RE NOT GOING TO GET PIKACHU!"
—ASH

"SOMEONE'S GOT TO TAKE A STAND. SOMEONE'S GOT TO SAY NO! AND REFUSE TO FIGHT JUST LIKE PIKACHU."—ASH

"Is that a challenge?!" Mewtwo asks.

"You bet it is!" Ash cheers.

Mewtwo calls on its own super clones of Charizard, Venusaur, and Blastoise.

They slide out of their tubes in the lab and walk onto a huge battle stadium behind the grand hall. Corey calls on Broo Broo, a Venusaur that is ready to fight with its friend. Neesha adds her Pokémon pal, a Blastoise so strong she's nicknamed it Shellshocker. Ash chooses Charizard, although it doesn't have a cool nickname, it's definitely fired up for battle. In fact, the minute Charizard steps onto the battlefield it shoots flames right in Mewtwo's face. Mewtwo doesn't even flinch, it's ready for the epic fight to begin!

Corey and Broo Broo start the battle by firing Razor Leaf, but Mewtwo and Venusaur throw it out of the ring and the round with Vine Whip. So, Neesha and Shellshocker step up and blast Hydro Pump. But Mewtwo instructs clone Blastoise to ram it into a wall with Rapid Spin.

The battle now rests squarely on Charizard and Ash's shoulders. Can they find a way to win the round against a team of unbelievably powerful clones, Mewtwo and Charizard? The two Charizard soar into the sky to wage their battle. Clone Charizard is so quick, it dodges all the Fire-type attacks Charizard shoots. Then, Clone Charizard surprises Charizard by jumping on its back and dragging it to the ground with Seismic Toss. Charizard hits the ground hard, but pops back up to let out a strong battle cry. Unfortunately, that yelp was its last gasp in the round. It's left unable to battle. Ash rushes over to his pal, now back on the ground.

Mewtwo wastes no time claiming the win and what it believes is its rightful prize— all of their Pokémon. They all try to run and scatter, but it's no use. Mewtwo tosses specialized black Poké Balls that chase down and catch every single one of Corey, Neesha, and Ash's Pokémon.

Back at Mewtwo's lab, the Pokémon Replication System is working on over-drive making clones of all the Pokémon Mewtwo captured. But Ash chases after his beloved buddy Pikachu, trapped in Mewtwo's Poké Ball. He throws himself down the same shoot that leads to Mewtwo's lab. He races down the conveyer belt to grab Pikachu's Poké Ball before it can be cloned. Dozens of mechanical arms reach out to grab the Poké Ball back. Ash uses all of his strength to rip it from their grip.

Ash is so determined he manages to hold onto Pikachu no matter what. Even robot arms are no match for the power of their friendship! As Ash runs against the machine, the Pokémon Replication System starts to short-circuit. Pulling against it with all his might, Ash falls down on the conveyer belt taking the Poké Ball that imprisoned Pikachu with him.

"Pika pi!" Pikachu cheers popping out of Mewtwo's trap.

Ash is so happy to see his best friend free! But before they can really celebrate, Team Rocket, who is still poking around lab, points out a problem. All the new clones are leaving the lab— Nidoqueen, Scyther, Gyarados, Vaporeon, and more!

"But where are the real ones?" Ash wonders what happened to all their Pokémon pals.

Suddenly the Pokémon Replication System circuits catch fire and it explodes in a big blast! Mewtwo's black Poké Balls fall like rain from the once-great machine. As they hit the ground, the original Pokémon are released. But before Ash can breathe a sigh of relief, there is a battle still to be won.

On the battlefield, Mewtwo is backed by its army of clones.

"The hour of my vengeance draws near!" Mewtwo threatens the Trainers. "With Pokémon and humans eliminated, the clones shall inherit the world!"

But Ash and all the Pokémon pals aren't going to let that happen! They march back onto the battlefield, ready to take a stand, together.

"It is useless to challenge me!" Mewtwo says, dismissing their effort.

"It's not going to end like this Mewtwo! We won't let it!" Ash replies.

Then, Ash charges toward Mewtwo. He tries to land a punch, but Mewtwo uses Psychic to send him flying. But just before Ash slams into the stadium wall, a pink bubble breaks his fall. And suddenly, a new challenger appears on the battlefield. "Mew!" it says as it swoops in.

It pops the pink bubble with a giggle. Then it blows a new one up and begins bouncing on it. Mew sure picked a funny time to have some fun! Mewtwo immediately sends a speedy Energy Ball to bursts its bubble. But nothing will get the playful Pokémon Mew down.

Mew soars down to meet Mewtwo face-to-face for the first time. Mewtwo is itching to battle Mew to prove that clones are superior, but Mew doesn't want to fight. Mewtwo chases it around the stadium. Then, Mewtwo fires a big blue blast that sends Mew up into the skies. The Trainers are all worried that Mew is hurt. But a few seconds later, Mew surprises Mewtwo by sending its attack right back at it! It's a direct hit that slams Mewtwo into the stadium wall.

Mewtwo seizes the chance to finally prove clones are superior. It lays out a battle challenge to Mew and the original Pokémon to take on its army of clones. But Mew argues that fighting doesn't show power, true strength comes from the heart. Mewtwo won't listen and instructs the army of clones to attack their Pokémon twins. To make it a fair fight, Mewtwo uses its Psychic powers to block their special abilities.

Ash and the other Trainers are sad to watch their Pokémon struggle against their clones. The battle wages on and on, but the Pokémon are so evenly matched no one is winning. Mew and Mewtwo continue their battle too in the sky above the stadium. They're all just fighting senselessly with no end in sight.

Pikachu decides to take a stand. It refuses to fight back, no matter how many times its clone strikes. Ash is worried about his best friend, but he's also inspired by it.

"Someone's got to take a stand. Someone's got to say no! And refuse to fight just like Pikachu!" Ash realizes.

But the fight between Mew and Mewtwo is just heating up. Their strong Psychic-type attacks caused a huge explosion in the stadium and the lights go out. All of the other Pokémon can't even continue to battle. However, Mew and Mewtwo look as determined as ever to keep at it. So Ash runs out in the middle of the battlefield to block their blows and stop the match. With a single hit, Ash falls to the ground.

"Pika pi!" Pikachu screams, racing to help its best friend, Ash.

Pikachu tries to use Thunderbolt over and over again to wake him up, but it's no use. Ash doesn't flinch. Pikachu begins to cry with worry. All of the Pokémon on the battlefield are so moved, they too begin to cry. The tears that fall from their eyes turn their heartfelt expression into powerful, healing magic.

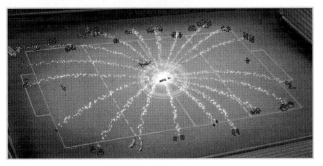

Somehow, the sky turns from darkness into bright daylight and bathes Ash in a glow that restores his strength. He stands up and smiles to see his best buddy, Pikachu, is right there for him. All of the Pokémon on the battlefield and all of the Trainers rejoice!

Mewtwo saw the miracle unfold on the battlefield and can't believe its eyes, or its heart. Ash and Pikachu's bravery have shown Mewtwo true friendship between Pokémon and humans. Mewtwo now understands that true power comes from one's character and is sorry for pitting Pokémon against Pokémon as a test.

"I see now that the circumstances of one's birth are irrelevant," Mewtwo says. "It is what you do with the gift of life that determines who you are."

Along with Mew, Mewtwo and the clones fly away together. Mewtwo plans to live in peace with its Pokémon pals and start learning its heart. Before the powerful Psychic-type leaves New Island, it decides to would be best to wipe the Trainers, Pokémon, and even Nurse Joy's memory of all that transpired.

Before they even know what's happened, Ash, Brock, Misty, Pikachu, and Togepi find themselves back at the ferry dock. Officer Jenny is busy warning all the Trainers of the terrible storm. But this time, Nurse Joy is there too to offer shelter at the local Pokémon Center.

"How did we wind up in this place anyway?" Ash wonders.

His friends shrug. Even stranger, the clouds suddenly part and the storm disappears. As Ash looks up at the sunshine, he sees something flying in the distance.

"Hey! What's that?" Ash says pointing to the sky. "The day I left home to start my Pokémon journey, I saw a really rare Pokémon. And just now, I thought I saw another one!"

"Maybe you're just seeing things, Ash," Misty says.

Whether Ash spotted a Mythical Pokémon in the sky, or whether he'll ever remember what transpired on New Island, the incredible bravery and friendship he and Pikachu displayed changed the course of the world forever. That kind of powerful heart is unforgettable and will serve them well.

LOCATIONS

THE LAB WHERE MEWTWO WAS CREATED

A state-of-the-art lab was built atop an island made of rock by Team Rocket boss, Giovanni. Its sole purpose was to create powerful Pokémon. Giovanni staffed it with top scientists and filled it with the most technologically advanced equipment— including the Pokémon Replication System that gave birth to Mewtwo.

GIOVANNI'S COMPOUND

Whisked away in Giovanni's helicopter, Mewtwo finds itself in his secret hideout. There, Mewtwo is given sophisticated armor Giovanni had made for it and shown its first Pokémon battlefield— for better or for worse.

THE GRASSY HILLSIDE

Here's where we first find Ash, Misty and Brock in the movie. Brock is cooking up some lunch, but a surprise visitor is ready to heat up something else— a battle with Ash. With his pals Squirtle, Bulbasaur, and Pikachu by his side, Ash secures a victory against the challenger. Ash is feeling proud and ready for another challenge. So, when a Dragonite approaches him with an invitation to a special match with the #1 Pokémon Trainer, it seems like too good an offer to pass up!

THE FERRY STATION

Ash, Misty, Brock, and Pikachu all hoped to hop a ferry to get to Ash's match with the #1 Pokémon Trainer. However, the weather was so bad, Officer Jenny and the harbor manager, Miranda, informed everyone that no ship would sail from the docks in these conditions. Well, no ship they had ever seen.

TEAM ROCKET'S VIKING BOAT REPLICA

The rough open waters were no match for skilled sailors, and yet Team Rocket wanted to seize the opportunity to trick the so-called twerps. They dressed up like Vikings and from a wooden ship, offered Ash passage to the Pokémon Battle. He couldn't resist the ride, but when the boat breaks in half, he and his pals will have to paddle themselves the rest of the way.

NEW ISLAND

Mewtwo's secret lair is an isolated floating island that acts as a foundation for its incredible castle. The massive mansion holds many different rooms in its wings.

THE LAB

Mewtwo's personal lab appears to be a modified version of the lab where it was born. It too houses the infamous Pokémon Replication System.

THE GRAND HALL

The room where Mewtwo's challengers are held has a series of fountains, a large dining table fit for a king, and a golden spiral slide so tall you can't even see to the top from the floor.

THE BATTLEFIELD

The massive arena where Mewtwo finally challenges the three Trainers could fit a huge crowd, but no one is there to cheer this epic battle on. It's open air, so beware, the Charizard clone has no problem using Seismic Toss there.

MEWTWO'S PRIVATE OFFICE

At the top of the castle is an office where Mewtwo devises his plans and keeps a watch through its windows. It is here, from his cozy chair, that Mewtwo first brews its storm.

CHARACTERS
ASH

When Ash faces a cunning and controlling opponent, Mewtwo, he relies on his friends to not only win the battle, but save the world!

PIKACHU

Ash's best friend uses both the strength of its attacks and its heart. Although Mewtwo, at first, doesn't believe that Ash and Pikachu are true pals, eventually seeing their bond is what changes Mewtwo's mind.

BULBASAUR

Along with Ash, Bulbasaur is excited to battle and visit the world's greatest Pokémon Master.

SQUIRTLE

When the crew finds themselves shipwrecked in a storm, Water-type Squirtle steps up to help its friends ride the waves to Mewtwo's secret lair.

CHARIZARD

Not one to shake hands, Ash's fiery pal introduces itself to Mewtwo by spraying it with flames.

COREY

Confident Corey is the first Trainer to greet Ash when he arrives at New Island. He is also the first one to stand up to Mewtwo. Corey braved the hurricane winds and flew in to New Island on his pal Pidgeot. Along with his Pokémon pals, he is ready to show his strength in battle, but Mewtwo didn't plan a fair fight.

PSYDUCK

VULPIX

MISTY

Impressed by the invitation, Misty joins Ash on his adventure to New Island with her Pokémon Pals.

BROCK

Ash's trusty travel buddy is excited to watch him battle the world's greatest Pokémon Master.

VENUSAUR

SCYTHER

PIDGEOTTO

RHYHORN

HITMONLEE

SANDSLASH

TOGEPI

STARYU

F RGUS

All of Fergus' Pokémon on hand are Water-types. So, he had no problem making his way across the wild sea on his great Gyarados! Once he hears of Mewtwo's plans, fearless Fergus is ready to fight back along with his Pokémon pals.

GYARADOS

GOLDUCK

NIDOQUEEN

VAPOREON

SEADRA

TENTACRUEL

I EESHA

When the ferry stopped running during the storm, top Trainer Neesha boldly rode on her friend Dewgong's back. Nothing was going to stop her from seizing her place at the contest against the world's greatest Pokémon Trainer! She made her way to New Island looking for the chance to show off her smart battle strategy.

DEWGONG

WIGGLYTUFF

BLASTOISE

RAPIDASH

NINETALES

VILEPLUME

I URSE JOY

When the local Nurse Joy goes missing from the Pokémon Center, Officer Jenny is on the case. However, Brock might just be the first one to solve the mystery. When Ash and his friends arrive at New Island, they're greeted by a woman in a dark brown dress— the same woman that appeared in the hologram invitation to the battle competition. Now that they're in person, Brock immediately asks if she's Nurse Joy. Although at that moment, she's under Mewtwo's trance, but once she's released from her slavery, her true identity is revealed.

MIRANDA

The harbor manager, Miranda, alerts the Trainers that the ferry service has been temporarily suspended. She tells them of the ancient legend of the winds of water— a storm so deadly it wiped out the land and the tears of the Pokémon survivors restored those lost in the destruction. However, unlike Officer Jenny, she understands that nothing, not even a natural disaster, can stop a determined Pokémon Trainer.

OFFICER JENNY

Although she tries to warn the Trainers waiting to hop the ferry that the worst storm ever is about to strike, four Trainers refuse to heed her warning when the glory of a Pokémon Battle is at stake.

RAYMOND

A Trainer looking for a battle knows he need not look further than Ash. Raymond challenges our hero to a battle, but doesn't like the outcome when Bulbasaur easily beats Donphan. So, Raymond challenges Ash again and like a bad sport, unleashes three Pokémon all at once. Still, Pikachu wins the round with a single Thunderbolt. Then, right afterwards Ash is invited to New Island to compete against the world's greatest Pokémon Master. Is it just a coincidence? Or is Raymond working for someone?

DONPHAN GOLEM MACHOKE PINSIR VENOMOTH

GIOVANNI

When Mewtwo burns down the lab it was born in to avoid becoming a slave to the scientists, Giovanni is right there, standing in the ashes, ready to make Mewtwo an offer it can't resist. Giovanni offers Mewtwo the power to become invincible through his special training and custom coat of armor. It is Giovanni who first introduces the concept of Pokémon Battles to Mewtwo. Giovanni tirelessly trains his new associate and Mewtwo loves the thrill of a good fight. But it's not a partnership Giovanni has in mind. When Giovanni's true motives are revealed and he tries to make Mewtwo work for him, Mewtwo breaks free of its armor, which had become its chains.

Only later, through a secret film left in the lab by Dr. Fuji, does it become clear that Giovanni was behind the birth of Mewtwo. It was he who funded the whole DNA replication of Mew and asked Dr. Fuji to create the world's most powerful Pokémon. So, it was no wonder Giovanni was there right after Mewtwo's birth with an offer it couldn't refuse. It was all part of Giovanni's evil plan.

PERSIAN

TEAM ROCKET

The trio of Jessie, James, and Meowth are always hot on Ash's trail. Desperate to purloin Pikachu to please their boss, Giovanni, they'll do almost anything to trick him. In this movie, the trio dresses up like Vikings and offers to row Ash and company through the terrible storm to New Island. Although the waves destroy their boat, they won't give up their dream of stealing Ash's best buddy. Jessie, James, and Meowth all manage to make their way to New Island. There, they discover Mewtwo's secret lab with the Pokémon Replication System.

DR. FUJI

The scientific mind behind Mewtwo, Dr. Fuji is the head of the lab where the world's strongest Pokémon was born. Dr. Fuji was very excited to begin his tests on Mewtwo, but he didn't consider that Mewtwo wouldn't want to spend its life being experimented on. Dr. Fuji succeeded in making Mewtwo so powerful, not even the machinery that made the mighty Pokémon could contain it. Dr. Fuji didn't account for Mewtwo's will to decide its own fate and that was a miscalculation that almost destroyed the world.

MEW VS. MEWTWO

You'd never suspect lively, little, wide-eyed Mew was such a powerful Mythical Pokémon. Because of its unique abilities, it's been in dangerous situations, but never lost its sweet playfulness. Nothing gets Mew down! Perhaps that's because it knows it's strong enough to stand up to anyone? Or maybe it's because it knows true strength is how you care for yourself and others?

This sensitive soul is so in touch with not just the feelings of others, but also the world. It can sense when the environment is in trouble and is deeply hurt. It cares about all living things, especially Mewtwo.

MEW
THE NEW SPECIES POKÉMON

Height: 1'04"
Weight: 8.8 lbs

PSYCHIC

I SEA YOU

Mew emerges from beneath the sea when it senses Mewtwo's presence. It soars up into the sky and towards New Island, no invitation necessary. Psychic-type Mew sees with everything in its being.

FUN

Mew just wants to have fun. Everything can be a game to the playful Pokémon. It won't just fly past the moon, it will circle its big round glow. When it arrives at New Island, it finds a ride— a windmill atop it and hops from blade to blade. When Mewtwo sends Ash flying, Mew breaks his fall with a bouncy bubble and then it pops it with a giggle. Even in a dramatic battle, it's never too busy to stop and smell the roses.

MEWTWO
THE GENETIC POKÉMON

Height: 6'07"
Weight: 269.0 lbs

PSYCHIC

Mewtwo is a one-of-a-kind Pokémon because it was made by humans from the DNA of the most rare Pokémon — Mew. Born in a lab, Dr. Fuji and his team of scientists had planned to experiment on their creation, Mewtwo. But Mewtwo was too powerful to live its life as a pawn. Like any other living creature, Mewtwo wants to be independent and determine its destiny. Unfortunately, it was so mistreated and manipulated by humans that Mewtwo's heart turned to hate. After the scientists and Giovanni tried to enslave it, Mewtwo decided it wanted to liberate Pokémon from humanity.

PSYCH 101

Mewtwo is one powerful Psychic-type Pokémon. Using its unique strength, it can control the bodies and minds of others. It can make Nurse Joy forget who she is and be its slave. It can lift itself and other Pokémon up off the ground and send them flying. It can make Pokémon fight each other for no reason. But it's not just living things it likes to toy with. Mewtwo, with the simple twist of its hand, can cause a fierce and unforgiving storm.

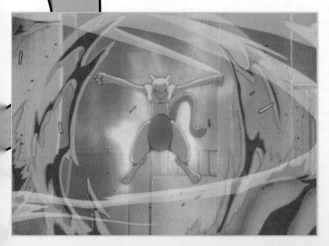

HEART OF IT

There is one thing even more powerful than Mewtwo's might—it's heart. But no scientist, human, or even Mewtwo itself tried to teach it morals and emotions. Through meeting Ash and his friends, Mewtwo sees that the true exploration of strength it needs to undertake is learning its own heart.

SPEAK UP

While Mewtwo's might is magnificent, it possesses another unbelievable gift. Mewtwo is able to communicate with humans. It can speak directly to them, no translation necessary. Its mouth doesn't move, but its words are heard thanks to its Psychic-type power. It can also make other humans speak for it, like Nurse Joy. Mewtwo's sentences might come easily, but as Ash and his pals learned, the conversation could be quite difficult. In fact, it could be argued that the hardest battle with Mewtwo is a battle of wits.

DON'T MIND IF I DO

Mewtwo can read minds. It knows what other Pokémon are thinking. Although, Mewtwo doesn't want to control other Pokémon, the way it feels humans do.

WHAT IN THE WORLD

Mewtwo has goals. Unfortunately, they're to destroy the Pokémon world and replace it with one of its creation. It wants nothing to do with Pokémon who have Trainers or even like humans. After its own experiences, Mewtwo doesn't believe Pokémon and humans can truly be trusted or even friends. Mewtwo wants Pokémon alone to rule the world and using the Pokémon Replication System it has an army of lab-created Pokémon to stand by its side.

INTERESTING ITEMS

THE INVITATION TO BATTLE

Who doesn't like getting an invitation?! Whether it's for a party or a competition, you want to make an unforgettable statement with the invite to be sure to attract participants. Mewtwo might not be a Pokémon Master, but it might be a master at invitations! It didn't use a stamp and wait around for a mailperson to deliver it. It sent a flying Dragonite messenger to hand deliver a personal card with a hologram of Nurse Joy to relay all the details. Needless to say, Trainers crowded the ferry station anxious to take Mewtwo up on its invitation!

DRAGONITE
THE DRAGON POKÉMON

Height: 7'03"
Weight: 463.0 lbs

DRAGON	FLYING

MEWTWO'S POKÉ BALLS

Mewtwo isn't just a one-of-a-kind Pokémon, the Poké Balls it tosses are quite unique too. Look out for these spheres that are black with yellow lining and a red center that looks like an eye, an eye that won't lose sight of its mission. Intelligent and determined, these Poké Balls will chase after any Pokémon across New Island, up high in the sky, and even through water. Nothing will stop them from catching Pokémon, even a Trainer. Well, that is, unless the Trainer happens to be Ash Ketchum.

NURSE JOY'S NEW ISLAND UNIFORM

Is it a uniform or a disguise? Mewtwo forces his brainwashed servant Nurse Joy to wear a dark, drab dress that comes up to her neck, runs down to her hands, and drops to the floor. The ensemble is topped off with a tall hat to cleverly conceal her well-known pink hairdo so no visitors will realize her true identity. Although, Mewtwo didn't bank on Brock being such a big fan of Nurse Joy's that he could see the real her, even through her disguise.

TOTALLY AWESOME TECHNOLOGY

THE POKÉMON REPLICATION SYSTEM

The cornerstone of Mewtwo's secret laboratory, the Pokémon Replication System can completely copy any Pokémon that crosses through its scanner. It appears that Pokémon, or even just the hair of a Pokémon, are put on a conveyer belt that carries them through a very sophisticated device that collects their DNA. With the Pokémon DNA data, the Pokémon Replication System spits out lab-created twins. The duplicate Pokémon are then dropped into tall columns filled with a strange fluid. While Mewtwo had to break the glass of his test tube to break free, in Mewtwo's lab, the lab created Pokémon can simply slide out of their columns. The lab-created Pokémon are loyal to Mewtwo. They heed Mewtwo's call and always stand by its side.

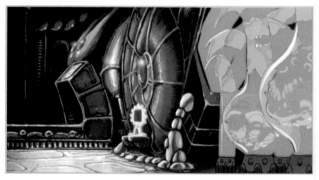

With the Pokémon Replication System, Mewtwo is able to duplicate all of Corey, Fergus, Neesha, and Ash's Pokémon. It's even able to copy Team Rocket member Meowth.

PICTURE THIS
TABLET OF MEW

A drawing of Mew appears to have been carved into stone a long time ago. Mewtwo first sees the Pokémon it is said to be created from on this simple stone slab, hanging in Dr. Fuji's lab. Although, no one knows the artist who made the portrait. Could it be ye olde selfie?

A VIDEO SHORT STARRING DR. FUJI

In the wake of Mewtwo's revolt, Dr. Fuji scrambled to leave a secret video message explaining the circumstances under which it was created. After the Pokémon Replication System copies Meowth, Team Rock discovers this short clip and the truth. In the video, Dr. Fuji explained that Giovanni, their boss, was behind it all.

Mewtwo reveals a giant battlefield. Then, it calls on its Clones, the evolved forms of the Kanto region's first partner Pokémon, Venusaur, Blastoise, and Charizard. Ash, Corey, Fergus, and Neesha are ready to prove their real Pokémon are better than any copies, but there's only one way— an epic Pokémon Battle!

MEWTWO AND CLONE VENUSAUR VS. COREY AND VENUSAUR

The first round finds Corey up first against Mewtwo. This time, he chooses his Venusaur buddy that he nicknamed Broo Broo. Corey calls out to Broo Broo to begin with a blast of Razor Leaf blades, but Mewtwo has Clone Venusaur throw Broo Broo off the field and out of the battle with a single Vine Whip.

MEWTWO AND CLONE BLASTOISE VS. NEESHA AND BLASTOISE

Neesha steps up with her buddy Blastoise that she nicknamed Shellshocker. Unfortunately, it's the one that gets shocked! Although Shellshocker makes a splash on the battlefield with Hydro Pump, Mewtwo has Clone Blastoise use Rapid Spin to knock it into a rock wall and out of the battle.

MEWTWO AND CLONE CHARIZARD VS. ASH AND CHARIZARD

Ash chooses Charizard, who is ready to battle, even if it isn't ready to listen to its Trainer. Ash asks Charizard to focus on using its speed, but it wants to fight fire with fire. The two Fire-type sore up into the night sky and no matter what Charizard does, it can't seem to land or dodge an attack. Clone Charizard swoops in close and jumps on Charizard's back in midair. Clone Charizard holds Charizard by its neck as it launches into Seismic Toss, forcing Charizard to fall from the sky and down to the ground. Clone Charizard lands on top of Charizard as they hit the battlefield hard. Clone Charizard soars right back up into the sky, while no one on the ground can believe their eyes as Charizard stands up and lets out a fierce final yelp. It gave the battle its all, but it's clear Charizard is unable to continue the fight as it falls back down.

But this is no ordinary battle, and this is no ordinary foe. With its win, Mewtwo doesn't waste a single second executing its plan. It unleashes its evil Poké Balls that chase and capture all the Pokémon, even though they are not wild. Then, they are all taken to the Pokémon Replication System to be duplicated into a special army for Mewtwo.

Mewtwo might have won this battle, but Ash isn't done fighting for what's right!

POKÉMON THE MOVIE 2000

THE STORY

According to an ancient Pokémon writing carved into a stone tablet, three Legendary Pokémon live in three small islands in the Orange Islands. Moltres, the Titan of Fire, calls Fire Island home. Zapdos, the Titan of Lightning, lives on Lightning Island. Articuno, the Titan of Ice, resides on Ice Island. At the heart of these three important islands is Shamouti Island. There is a sacred harmony between these Legendary Pokémon that keeps the world in balance.

One greedy man seeks to capture them all—Lawrence III. From his flying fortress, the tall, blond madman is plotting.

"Moltres, Zapdos, and Articuno. Any one of them would be a priceless addition to my collection, but together they are the three keys that unlock the ultimate treasure," Lawrence III explains.

His computer informs him that he is close to Moltres on Fire Island.

"Good," Lawrence III says as he prepares his attack. "Now, the chase is on."

From his command center, Lawrence III fires at the volcano's rock until Moltres is forced to evacuate from its secret hiding place. It flies up into the air, screeching with anger. Charged

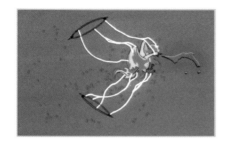

hoops are tossed from Lawrence's flying fortress and surround Moltres, trapping it.

"Well, I've taken the first piece without much difficulty," Lawrence celebrates.

He plans to capture Zapdos, then Articuno. Together, those three Legendary Pokémon are the only ones that can tame "the beast of the sea" that controls the world's water. The Legendary Pokémon that lives deep in the oceans to guard that beast is Lugia, and Lawrence has his eyes set on it as his prize.

Meanwhile, Ash, Pikachu, Misty, Togepi, and Tracey happen to be nearby enjoying a boat ride with their friend Maren. It's a beautiful day, the kind that seems perfect for setting sail. However, a sudden storm turns the sky gray and the sea rocky. The waves steer their ship way off course to Shamouti Island. Even stranger, they're surrounded by a school of Magikarp headed in the same direction. However, one of those Magikarp is actually a submarine with Jessie, James, and Meowth of Team Rocket inside.

Weirder still, back in Pallet Town, Ash's mom, Delia, is experiencing a similar phenomenon. While gardening with Mr. Mime, she and Professor Oak are puzzled when a wild storm sweeps in. Heavy rain pours down for a few seconds, followed by a short snowfall. This is weather unlike any they've seen in the middle of the summer.

When the clouds break, hundreds of Pidgey fill the sky, flying in one direction. On the ground, dozens of Diglett come racing down the road. In their haste, they take Professor Oak's bike right out from under him. Mr. Mime jumps up and down to let Delia know that it's also upset by something—but what?

"Pokémon are more in tune with nature than we are. When something goes wrong, they can sense it," Professor Oak explains. "And I'm afraid something somewhere is going terribly wrong."

On Shamouti Island, Ash, Misty, Tracey, and Maren have just parked their boat. A group of islanders in amazing headdresses and costumes greets them. Maren knows one of them, Carol, a woman with big earrings and a brown bob haircut. She tells them that they couldn't have picked a better day to visit because it's a special local holiday: the Annual Legend Festival.

"This is my favorite island holiday!" Maren says excitedly. "Are you gonna be the star of the show again, Carol?"

Carol explains that she has passed the honor of being Festival Maiden to her little sister, Melody. Melody is wearing sunglasses even though it's dark out and says exactly what she's thinking. Although she seems too cool to be excited about the festivities, Melody is definitely not playing cool when she meets Ash. But she's not the only one who's glad he's there. In fact, the entire group of villagers cheers when Maren introduces him. Apparently, a Shamouti Island elder explains that there is an ancient local legend that proclaims that a Pokémon Trainer named Ash will save the whole world.

"Only with you can the Guardian of the Waters vanquish the great Titans of Fire, Ice, and Lightning. In your hands, oh Chosen One, rests the world and its fate," the elder says.

"It does?" Ash says, completely confused.

Melody, the Festival Maiden, approaches him with a smile.

"Here's your traditional welcome kiss," Melody says, planting a smooch on his cheek.

Then, she invites Ash to watch her perform at the Legend Banquet that night. Misty's cheeks turn pink, and she looks totally jealous. This isn't lost on outspoken Melody, who teases Misty for having a crush on Ash. It seems everyone is focused on the Chosen One, as he is now called.

The crew follows the villagers as they dance in their costumes and play their instruments all the way to the festivities. The city is covered in lights and filled with locals in traditional costumes. Misty, Togepi, Ash, Pikachu, Tracey, and Maren catch the parade and ritual dance before making their way to the Legend Banquet.

As they dine in a painted hut, the show begins. Wearing a veil and an orange flower crown, Melody steps onto the stage. She plays a beautiful song from a special flute that seems to be made of seashells. Then, as the audience applauds, she approaches Ash, the Chosen One, and tells him some important instructions.

"WAIT A MINUTE. TRAINING POKÉMON'S TOUGH ENOUGH, BUT SAVING THE WORLD IS WAY TOO HARD."
—ASH

"All you have to do is get these glass balls from three islands—one from Fire Island, one from Ice Island, and one from Lightning Island. And you bring them to the shrine back here, and then I celebrate by playing this song," Melody instructs.

Excited to impress his pretty new friend, Melody, Ash replies, "Okay! Get me a boat and I'm ready!"

Maren offers to take Ash around to the islands. Ash asks Misty to come, too, but it's clear she's a little jealous of Melody's ability to charm him.

"If you want somebody to do whatever you want, whenever you want, you should find yourself a girlfriend," Misty replies.

But before Ash can respond, Pikachu grabs Ash's hat and runs out of the banquet, all the way down to the boat. It has a need for speed, but Ash is left wondering why his best friend is acting so strange. Suddenly, the weather starts acting even crazier. A heavy rain falls, and the huge waves rock the boat.

Back at the banquet, Melody is worried about Ash in the storm. She borrows her sister's speed boat to check on him. When Misty catches wind of her trip, she runs out to join Melody. Then, Tracey decides to go, too. But little does Melody know that three more people have stowed away on her boat—Team Rocket. What they won't do to steal Pikachu!

People all across the globe tune in to the news that night and see a shocking weather report. The Village Elder, Carol, Ash's mom, and even Professor Oak can't believe the weather disasters all over the globe that day—lightning, blizzards, and flooding. Apparently, an underwater river coming from a force in the Orange Islands is causing the extreme weather. It appears both weather and Pokémon are behaving quite strangely. Tens of thousands of Pokémon are flocking to Shamouti Island. Professor Ivy is so concerned that she calls Professor Oak to discuss the patterns they're seeing.

Meanwhile, Maren is trying to steer her boat around rocky waves and even bigger rocks. But when a wave throws them into the air, the rudder is broken, and the ship is tossed onto Fire Island.

The second they land, Pikachu jumps off the ship. It hurries up the steep stairs that lead to the local shrine atop the mountain. Ash chases after his buddy. Pikachu leads him to a stone shrine dedicated to the Bird of Fire, Moltres. Pikachu then points out the ancient red sphere nestled in the rock bird's beak. Ash grabs the first of three glass balls he needs to fulfill his duty as the Chosen One. In his hand, the red orb glows with a light that mimics fire.

On the speed boat, Melody is steering on the waves, riding them like a surfer. She's confident she can handle the storm, but the ocean is in charge of her. A wave picks up the boat like it's a ball and throws it onto Fire Island. They land right next to Maren and her boat. She tells them Ash and Pikachu are at the shrine.

Rather than climb the stairs, Melody pulls a lever that turns her speed boat into a sailboat. Then, she guides the vessel up the stairs. But she's not the only arrival at the shrine. Just then, Zapdos swoops in. It flies around, sending shocks. Then, it lands on the shrine, bathing the area in a blue glow and electric charges.

Pikachu sends messages wrapped in electricity to Zapdos. Meowth translates their meaning, explaining that Pikachu is wondering what Zapdos is doing on Moltres' island.

Zapdos squawks back, proudly proclaiming that since Moltres is gone, this island now belongs to it. This is the first anyone has heard of Moltres' disappearance, and it means the delicate balance of fire, lightning, and ice has been upset. Before Ash can even wonder how, Lawrence III's flying fortress appears above the shrine.

Zapdos' strength, the electricity, and the blue glow begin to be sucked up into Lawrence III's ship. Zapdos is puzzled, then powerless.

"Drained of its power, Zapdos will be too weak to resist capture," Lawrence III boasts.

Zapdos flies away to escape, but it leads Lawrence III's hoop cages to instead catch the crew and their boat. As they are pulled up into the ship, a second pair of hoops swirls around Zapdos, sealing its capture, too.

Trapped inside the flying fortress, the crew is trying to make sense of who would do such a terrible thing to Legendary Pokémon. Soon, it becomes clear when Pokémon Collector Lawrence III enters to show off his success with Moltres and Zapdos.

"I began my collection with a Mew card, and now I have all this," Lawrence III brags to Ash and his friends. "And soon my collection itself will be legendary."

He has set his next mark—Articuno. His computer has located the Legendary Bird of Ice nearby, who is freezing over all the local islands with its icy attacks. Articuno's marking its territory and turning the area into a tundra. So, Lawrence III exits to his command center.

In a nearby helicopter, Professor Oak, Professor Ivy, Ash's mom, and a couple of journalists are braving the storm to investigate what exactly is going on. Professor Oak explains that ancient writings consider the area to be the source of all the waters of the world. If the delicate balance of fire, ice, and lightning has been disturbed, it could be what is causing the powerful "beast of the sea." Ultimately, this weather pattern could flood the entire planet. It's clear that the well-respected scientist isn't the only one sensing the possible doom. Professor Ivy adds that Pokémon are in tune with nature, and they could all be gathering to try to save the world.

However, according to the ancient myth, the world will turn to Ash. And he is not wasting a moment! He tries to run into the charged hoops caging Moltres, but he alone isn't strong enough. So Ash calls on his pals Pikachu, Charizard, Bulbasaur, and Squirtle to try to break through. Inspired by Ash, even Team Rocket asks Weezing and Arbok to help free Zapdos. Amazingly enough, Ash and his Pokémon pals' combined attacks cause an explosion that tears through the hoops. Smoke billows out the side of the flying fortress, and Moltres is free. It immediately busts Zapdos out.

Then, the pair of Legendary Pokémon takes to the skies to destroy Lawrence III's flying fortress. Zapdos zaps the propellers. Moltres sets the hull on fire. But Ash, Pikachu, Misty, Melody, Tracey, and Team Rocket are all still on board. Lawrence III steers what's left of his ship to a crash landing. Part of his ship smashes right into the shrine on Lightning Island.

Up in the sky, Zapdos, Moltres, and Articuno are all locked in an epic battle. The crew braces for cover from a blast when a glass ball rolls right in front of Ash. It's the yellow orb from Lightning Island! He is now in possession of two of the three balls he needs to fulfill his duty as the Chosen One.

But there's no time to celebrate. Ash and his crew run for cover on a nearby boat from the Legendary Pokémon Battle raging above. A giant zap from Zapdos sends the boat downstream and over the edge of a steep waterfall. Just when it seems like the boat is doomed for a crash landing, a strange current leaps out of the ocean and lifts the boat into the air. It carries the boat all the way through the frozen ocean to Shamouti Island's shrine.

There, Slowking awaits them: "So, you're Ash."

Ash is amazed that Slowking can talk and even knows his name! But Slowking is surprised Ash is still missing one glass ball from Ice Island. The path to Ice Island seems blocked by the epic battle ensuing among Moltres, Zapdos, and Articuno. Suddenly, the current rises again from the ocean and reveals that Lugia is inside it.

"The Great Guardian, Lugia!" Slowking says in awe of the giant Legendary Pokémon before them.

Ash and his friends can't believe their eyes. Then, Lugia begins to sing.

"That sound!" Melody says, realizing where she's heard it before.

The special flute she played at the Legend Festival sounds exactly like Lugia's song! While the tune has calmed the three Legendary Birds, it's only temporary. Instead of fighting each other, Zapdos, Articuno, and Moltres band together to battle Lugia. Together, they send Lugia plunging from the sky, through the ice, and back down into the ocean. Who will save the world now?

"There's only one hope. Only the Chosen One can bring together the treasures to help the waters' great Guardian," Slowking says.

"But the legend says its song will fail," Melody cries.

"And thus the Earth shall turn to Ash!" Slowking replies.

Ash suddenly realizes it's really up to him, but is he up to it? It's not like Ash to doubt himself in battle, but saving the whole world is no ordinary challenge.

"I know it doesn't sound easy, Ash," Misty says.

"But you're the only one who matches the legend perfectly!" Tracey adds.

Melody begins to play her special flute again. The sound travels and reaches Lugia, which is still sinking beneath the sea. The Legendary Pokémon is suddenly bathed in a rainbow glow that helps it regain its strength. It begins to rise, and soon it appears in the sky before our nervous hero, Ash.

"When the treasures of fire, ice, and lightning are aligned, my song shall harmonize with their powers and tame the beasts both above and below the sea," Lugia explains. "But this can come to pass only with the help of the Chosen One."

"But what can I do that somebody else can't?" Ash wonders, nervous that he might not be the right person for the job.

"Pikachu!" it says, knowing its best friend will always rise to the challenge.

Then, Ash's other Pokémon friends—Charizard, Bulbasaur, and Squirtle—let themselves out of their Poké Balls to rally their Trainer. They're there to support him. In fact, Ash doesn't have to do it all alone because they vow to be there every step of the way to help their buddy!

"You can do it!" Misty cheers.

"We know you can!" Melody agrees.

Ash is so touched by his pals' support that he feels ready to find that final glass ball, even if it means making it through a snowstorm and three Legendary Pokémon locked in battle.
To set out on their way across the frosty ocean to Ice Island, Pikachu cleverly suggests Ash use a piece of the smashed boat to create a makeshift sled. Then, his Pokémon pals Charizard, Squirtle, and Bulbasaur help pull it through the snow to Ice Island. Lugia flies close behind them.

Zapdos, Articuno, and Moltres spot Ash and his Pokémon pals on the horizon. They can tell that Ash is on a mission to stop them, so the Legendary Birds turn their attention to stopping Ash.

Zapdos and Moltres attack in unison. Charizard and Pikachu fire back. Lugia flies out front to bear the brunt of the battle. But with a single zap, the ice that's been covering the ocean is cracked and swallows their sled. Now, Ash is stranded because the path to Ice Island has turned to freezing cold water. He's up the creek without a paddle—or a boat.

"We'll never get there now," Ash moans, feeling defeated.

Vrrrrrrrooooooooom! Just then, an unexpected ride has arrived with even more unexpected drivers. Team Rocket has combined an emergency raft and propeller fan to create a speedy airboat that soars over the snow and water. Ash can't believe his eyes. Are Jessie, James, and Meowth being the good guys?

"Though it's way outside our usual range," Jessie admits.

"We're going to do something nice for a change," James proclaims.

With no choice but to trust them, Ash hops in their makeshift airboat. Lugia continues to protect them from the trio of Legendary Birds as they head to Ice Island.

"Up there!" Ash says, showing them the way to the ancient shrine.

Team Rocket steers Ash right up to the frosty stone bird statue. In its beak lies the final treasure, a blue glass ball. Ash grabs it and hops back in the airboat. But before they can head out, Articuno strikes, then Zapdos, then Moltres. They run away from the fight as quickly as they can to protect the blue glass ball.

Lugia swoops in to carry Ash and Pikachu back to Shamouti Island. Team Rocket jumps on, too.

"Hold on tight!" Lugia warns as it dodges Moltres' fiery blast.

The Legendary Birds chase Lugia, which is flying as fast as possible.

"We're slowing Lugia down! The three of us are too heavy!" Jessie realizes.

"Let's protect the world from devastation!" James adds.

With that, Team Rocket lets go of Lugia. For arguably the first time, they feel good for doing good. They land amid the tens of thousands of Pokémon that have flocked to the area to help.

"That just one Pokémon could help the world would be worth the journey for thousands of them any day. But this day, the one that can make all the difference is you," Lugia reminds Ash.

They can see the shrine on Shamouti Island in the distance. They're getting close! But someone else has gotten closer—Lawrence III. He fires four charged hoops that fly around Lugia, trapping the Legendary Pokémon, Ash, and Pikachu. They wail together in pain.

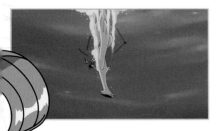

Lugia thinks fast and lunges back into the sea to weaken the charge. Then, it soars back into the sky. It is still surrounded by the charged hoops, but their strength has weakened. So, it opens its mouth to unleash a multi-stream Hyper Beam straight at Lawrence III. His grounded fortress is left in rubble, but the hoops still hold Lugia. It fires a bright Hyper Beam again to slash open the layer of ice on the ocean. Then, weak from the struggle, it dives back down into the sea. Lugia feels it has failed. An even stronger, darker storm is now tormenting the Orange Islands.

Ash and Pikachu have also fallen into the ocean, and worse yet, Ash has passed out from the impact. Misty thinks fast and jumps in to rescue her friends using a guide rope. Tracey helps reel them all back to the island, but Ash is still out cold.

"Come on, Ash! Breathe!" Misty pleads.

"You've got to!" Tracey worries.

Hearing the voice of his friends snaps him out of his slumber. Ash awakens and jumps right up. He knows there is no time to waste! He rushes to climb the snow-covered stairs to the shrine. He trips and falls, but he gets right back up. He places the final blue ball in place.

Instantly, a green glow flows out of the shine, through the floor, and up the columns, too. The ice melts away as Melody begins to play her special flute. Light breaks through the dark clouds. The battle-weary Legendary Birds hear Melody's song and soar back into the sky. The green glow flows from the shrine like a waterfall into the ocean. Lugia is restored and returns to the shrine. Ash hops on its back, and Lugia flies them through the sky, leading a rainbow made of a giant, glistening wave. Peace and harmony have returned.

All of the Pokémon of the globe, including the rivals Moltres, Zapdos, and Articuno, are celebrating the restored balance of the world. The rainbow wave drops back down into the ocean. The Legendary Birds return to rule their respective islands. The elder on Shamouti Island can't believe his eyes as the beautiful natural wonder of the world is back and better than ever.

"The fate of the world could not have been in better hands," Lugia says, thanking Ash as it drops him back off at the shrine on Shamouti Island.

Then, Lugia disappears back down into its ocean home. Hopefully, the world won't need to call on the Legendary Pokémon's aid again any time soon. But Ash knows no matter what lies ahead, he can conquer any challenge with the help of his friends!

LOCATIONS

MAREN'S POWER BOAT

Hunter green with an orange stripe, Maren's power boat is a fun way to travel through the Orange Islands. Ash, Tracey, Misty, and their Pokémon pals enjoy riding on her boat and soaking in the sun. Pikachu likes to stand right at the tip of the bow for the best view and the breeze. There is also a small cabin for taking a break. From the flying bridge, Maren steers her ship—well, until a terrible storm comes that throws it off course to Shamouti Island.

CAROL'S BOAT

Carol's sleek, silver speed boat can fly over rough water and is even stealthy enough to weave through waves. However, perhaps its most impressive feature is that it can also turn into a sailboat that can glide both on land and up stairs. After the boat is shipwrecked in the storm on Fire Island, Melody pulls a couple of levers to reveal a giant green and white sail. With a pull of the levers, it soars up the ancient stone stairs to the Fire Island shrine. Carol's sister, Melody, is an expert at steering this ship and doesn't hesitate to push its power to the max when the fate of the world is at stake.

LAWRENCE III'S FLYING FORTRESS

Part helicopter, part museum, part battle ship, Lawrence III's flying fortress is a force to be reckoned with. Inside, the spacious ship is refined. Paintings of cherubs in clouds decorate the ceiling, and copies of art depicting the myth from the Shamouti Island shrine are placed behind glass. A highly sophisticated computer controls the ship and also keeps Lawrence III informed of the Legendary Pokémon's whereabouts. A command chair attached to a retractable pole acts like an elevator, moving Lawrence III to the different decks of the unusually shaped ship. From the outside, the vessel is like a brick-red globe, with a ring of propellers to keep it floating in the air. At the bottom of the ship, a weapon extends that can fire a blast in a full 360-degree circle at a target. You can run, you can fly, but you can't hide from its firing range. The ship can also shoot charged hoops to capture a target, as it did to the Legendary Birds and even Ash and his crew.

THE HELICOPTER

Professor Oak, Professor Ivy, Ash's mom Delia, a cameraman, and a television reporter all head toward the troubling storm for different reasons, but they share a helicopter. Inside, the reporter interviews Professor Oak and Professor Ivy to uncover the science behind the supernatural event. However, Delia reminds the reporters that while they worry about the fate of the world, her whole world is her only son, Ash, who is caught up in this epic storm and battle.

THE LEGEND FESTIVAL LOUNGE

After catching the Legend Festival parade, Ash, Misty, Tracey, and Maren join the locals at Shamouti Island for a feast. They gather in a big hut with decorated walls and tables filled with food and festivalgoers. While they're enjoying the scene, the new Festival Maiden, Melody, performs on the stage, dancing with a special flute. She plays a beautiful song and then prances over to Ash. She announces to Ash and the audience that he is the Chosen One. Then and there, Ash learns that it is his responsibility to complete the task of finding a sacred glass ball at each of the shrines on Fire, Ice, and Lightning Islands. He must bring all three to the shrine on Shamouti Island. At first, he thinks it will be a fun adventure, but he soon learns this isn't just a game: the fate of the world rests in his hands.

FOUR OF THE ORANGE ISLANDS

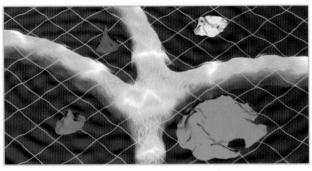

SHAMOUTI ISLAND

When Maren's boat is steered off course, Ash and his friends find themselves shipwrecked on the shores of Shamouti Island during the Annual Legend Festival. At first, it seems like a happy coincidence from a bad storm. But when the locals realize that Ash, our hero and the boy they call the Chosen One, has arrived, he seems to have crash-landed into fate. The lush island is decorated in lights, and the locals are dressed up in their traditional costumes, complete with masks for the Legend Festival. Shamouti Island is the larger island, flanked by Fire Island, Ice Island, and Lightning Island. It lies in the North Central region of the Orange Islands. Ancient writings say the source of all of the world's water lies around Shamouti Island and its three neighbors.

FIRE ISLAND

Home to the Legendary Bird of Fire, Moltres, this island is the first one Ash visits in his quest. At the shrine on Fire Island, Ash finds the glass ball of fire inside the beak of a sacred stone carving.

LIGHTNING ISLAND

Home to the Legendary Bird of Lightning, Zapdos, this isle lies between Fire Island and Ice Island. Ash accidentally reaches Lightning Island when Lawrence III's flying fortress crash-lands there and he and his pals are able to make their escape. However, it's not normally covered in ice and snow like it is when he arrives. Articuno seized the opportunity to stake its claim to the island while Lawrence III had captured its rivals Moltres and Zapdos. Ash knows he has no time to waste in restoring the balance between the three Legendary Birds. Luckily, he doesn't have to search far and wide for the glass ball of Lightning Island; it rolls right up before him in the snow.

ICE ISLAND

The third and final island Ash visits is the home of the Legendary Bird of Ice, Articuno. It appears to be a volcano, frozen over by its Legendary patron Pokémon. At the shrine atop it, Ash finds the final blue glass ball of ice. He nearly escapes with it when Articuno, Zapdos, and Moltres team up to stop him. Luckily, the Legendary Diving Pokémon, Lugia, swoops in to offer him a ride out of there.

THE SHRINE ON SHAMOUTI ISLAND

Located on a round cliff overlooking the ocean is perhaps the most sacred spot on Shamouti Island, a shrine to the local Legendary Pokémon. From this lookout point, one can see the three surrounding islands: Fire Island, Ice Island, and Lightning Island. Stairs lead up to the shrine's most famous fixture, a rock tablet carved with a myth that vows that only the Chosen One can help Lugia restore the delicate balance of the local Legendary Pokémon: Moltres, Articuno, and Zapdos. A circle of columns surrounds the tablet, which sits on a carved stone box. Inside the box are three containers for the ancient glass balls of Fire, Ice, and Lightning. The floor is also a circle, cut into slices and carved with a pattern. A priestly Slowking that can communicate with humans appears to be its custodian.

CHARACTERS

ASH KETCHUM

You might know him as a boy named Ash, but to the local people of Shamouti Island, he is called the "Chosen One." The fate of the world rests in our hero's hands as he is tasked with traveling through an epic storm and battle to find three important glass balls. Then and only then will the balance of the globe be restored. Luckily, he has the help of his Pokémon pals and even the Legendary Pokémon Lugia.

PIKACHU

Pikachu isn't just by Ash's side; it initially leads Ash out of the Legend Festival by stealing his hat. It senses the importance of his mission and helps Ash fulfill his destiny as the Chosen One.

SQUIRTLE, BULBASAUR, AND CHARIZARD

These three trusted Pokémon pals let themselves out of their Poké Balls to cheer Ash on when he seems to lose faith that he can save the world.

Then, they team up with Pikachu to pull his makeshift sled to Ice Island. Ash completes his crucial task with the help of his Pokémon pals!

TOGEPI

STARYU

PSYDUCK

GOLDEEN

LAPRAS

SNORLAX

MISTY

Misty doesn't like it when Melody suggests that she is Ash's girlfriend, and the two start off on the wrong foot. To prove Melody wrong, Misty decides not to join Ash when he first

sets out from Shamouti Island to find the trio of glass balls. However, when the storm sweeps in and Melody leaves to check on Ash in his quest, Misty is willing to join her rival to help her friend. No matter what she doesn't want to call it, Misty cares about Ash and will even jump into a freezing cold ocean to rescue him.

TRACEY SKETCHIT

Ash's pal is along for all the adventure in this part of the Orange Islands. He's there to encourage Ash and even help Misty's rescue mission. Although you can count on Tracey to be a pal, he's happy to stay out of the battles, whether they're between Misty and Melody or Legendary Pokémon.

VENONAT **SCYTHER** **MARILL**

MAREN

Maren has welcomed Ash, Pikachu, Misty, Tracey, and their Pokémon aboard her power boat. An experienced and well-known captain, she has traveled the Orange Islands a countless number of times. In fact, when they're shipwrecked on Shamouti Island, she runs into her old friend Carol and is thrilled to have arrived during the Annual Legend Festival.

DELIA

Delia is used to having her ambitious Pokémon Trainer son, Ash, traveling around the world looking for adventure. However, when she hears he's in the center of the epic storm and battle, she hops in the helicopter with Professor Oak to check on her boy. Although Ash saves the world, she reminds him that he is her whole world. She wishes he would be less daring, but if she had it her way and Ash didn't get involved, there would be no world. Still, you can't blame a mom for loving her son too much!

MR. MIME

PROFESSOR OAK

A tireless and respected Pokémon researcher from the Kanto Region, Professor Oak flies right into the eye of the storm in the hopes of understanding what is causing the unusual weather patterns. He experienced them firsthand back in his hometown, Pallet Town. A perfectly sunny day transformed into a rainstorm and then a snowstorm, and then a stampede of Diglett accidentally ran away with his bike in their haste. An important voice of science, Professor Oak is interviewed by the television news to try to explain the weather and Pokémon phenomena around the globe. It is his assumption that there must be some truth to the ancient writing claiming that this part of the Orange Islands is the cradle of the world's water.

TEAM ROCKET

In this movie, Jessie, James, and Meowth of Team Rocket are not up to their usual Pikachu poaching shenanigans (well, at least not once they realize the safety of the world is at stake). They are bonafide heroes. This is not a mistake. It's strange, but it's true. Perhaps their motivation will make this change of tune seem more believable. Team Rocket realizes that if there is no world, there will be no one left to steal from. So, they're out to help Ash save the globe! The trio calls on Weezing and Arbok to try to bust Zapdos out of Lawrence III's cage. They craft a makeshift airboat to take Ash to Ice Island. And perhaps even more shockingly, they selflessly and voluntarily blast themselves off of Lugia to lighten the Legendary Pokémon's load so it can help Ash get back to Shamouti Island faster. The only thing more upside down than the weather in this movie is Team Rocket's heroic behavior.

WEEZING

ARBOK

CAROL

When Maren's boat crash-lands on Shamouti Island, Carol is the local villager who greets them. Because she's wearing a special headdress for the Annual Legend Festival, her friend doesn't recognize her at first. Carol has been the Festival Maiden many times, but this year, she's passed the honor onto her little sister, Melody. Carol loves the Legend Festival and the island's traditions, but Melody is not as enthusiastic, to say the least.

MELODY

Melody is not thrilled that she has to be the sweet little Festival Maiden. Boldly steering fast boats straight into the eye of the storm is more her speed. Melody is always going full throttle, whether she's the captain of her sister's boat or just speaking her mind. Melody does not hold back. She isn't afraid of anything or anyone, not even the epic storm.

OH, BOY!

Melody names Ash the "Chosen One" as part of the island's traditions, but it seems she can sense he's the kind of boy who shares her sense of adventure. She immediately takes a liking to him and greets him with a customary welcome kiss on the cheek. Ash immediately blushes and seems to always want to impress Melody. When Misty seems upset by Ash's mushy behavior, Melody is bold enough to call her out for possibly having a crush on Ash. Melody might state the obvious, but she isn't one to pick a fight. She has better things to do than squabble over a boy! As Festival Maiden, she has a duty to help the Chosen One save the world.

PROFESSOR IVY

Professor Ivy is the leading researcher of the Orange Islands. A friend of Professor Oak, she immediately calls him when the Pokémon at her lab begin acting strangely to see if he's having a similar problem. Together, they decide to investigate the storm and the tens of thousands of Pokémon traveling toward Shamouti Island. She has a hunch that these Pokémon flocking to the area can sense some doom. She knows Pokémon are in tune with the balance of nature. So, if they're upset, she's ready to investigate why, even if it means taking a dangerous helicopter trip right into the heart of the problem.

BROCK

If you blinked, you might have missed Brock's cameo! He was helping Professor Ivy out at her lab when the storm struck. When Professor Ivy was on the video conference with Professor Oak, he was in the background trying to calm down a very scared Pokémon. However, it was hard to see him since he was running.

Not one to take most of the old island traditions too seriously, Melody nevertheless understands the importance of this part of her responsibility to her people, Pokémon, and the globe. Nothing will stop Melody on a mission!

IN TUNE

Melody is no misnomer: this girl can really wail! Her instrument is a ritual flute that mimics Lugia's song. Her skill is so strong, she can even dance while playing. Melody has perfect pitch. Every time she plays, the crowd is in awe, especially the Legendary Pokémon Lugia that is restored by the sound of that very flute.

VILLAGE ELDER

It is the Village Elder who first explains to Ash that they're excited for his arrival because he is, according to their island's myth, the Chosen One.

Although he wears a traditional headdress and garb for the Legend Festival, there's no mistaking his gray Mohawk and impressive facial hair when he's out of costume.

THE CAMERAMAN AND REPORTER

Hot on the beat of this epic battle and storm are a brave cameraman and reporter. They're bravely flying into danger to share the story as it unfolds so their viewers across the globe can understand the facts of the matter. These hard-hitting journalists interview the experts and get the story from all angles. After speaking with Professor Ivy and Professor Oak, they make time for the human interest story that involves Delia, a concerned mom worried about her son, the Chosen One.

LAWRENCE III

A man of refined taste, Lawrence III considers himself a Pokémon Collector. It all began with his first Pokémon Card featuring Mythical Pokémon Mew. Now, he has set his sights on collecting a real Legendary Pokémon, Lugia. He doesn't care who or what he hurts along the way—even the whole world. But then again, he doesn't even live in a city, a town, a village, or even on land. He lives alone, high above in his flying fortress. His only companion is a computer that does his bidding. To him, the globe is just a playing field for his game.

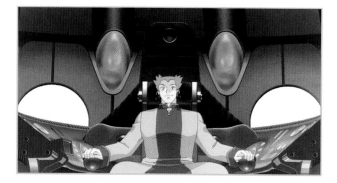

THE MORE YOU GET, THE MORE YOU WANT

Lawrence III might argue that he's a man who appreciates things of great value, like artifacts and Legendary Pokémon. His flying fortress

is filled with beautiful paintings and ancient treasures. However, he does not show anything or anyone respect. He wants what he wants because he wants it. He collects things with no purpose other than to please himself. Lawrence III just wants to possess things he doesn't have a right to own. Both Moltres and Zapdos weren't enough for Lawrence III and his collection; he had to complete the set with Articuno so he could get Lugia, too. Nothing is ever enough for that evil villain!

THE COMPUTER

Smart and precise, Lawrence III's computer keeps an eye on the ship and its surroundings. It's programmed to sense when a Legendary Pokémon is nearby and also when there's a security breach, like the accidental arrival of Ash and his friends. Lawrence III doesn't lift a finger; the computer carries out his orders.

LEGENDARY POKÉMON

ARTICUNO:
THE FREEZE POKÉMON

Height	5'07"
Weight	122.1 lbs
Type	Ice/Flying

With the mere flap of its wings in flight, Articuno can turn the air chilly and the weather forecast to snowfall. Known as the Titan of Ice, Articuno has the unique strength to manipulate ice and is associated with frosty Ice Island. It is one of the three Legendary Bird Pokémon that keep each other's power in check and the world in harmony. However, when Lawrence III catches Moltres and Zapdos, Articuno seizes the opportunity to rule over their islands. It covers Fire Island, Lightning Island, Shamouti Island, and the surrounding oceans in snow and ice, turning the area into its personal tundra.

MOLTRES:
THE FLAME POKÉMON

Height	6'07"
Weight	132.3 lbs
Type	Fire/Flying

Known as the Titan of Fire and part of the Legendary Bird Pokémon trio, Moltres lives on Fire Island in the heart of the Orange Islands. It is known for its fierce Fire-type attacks and its even more fiery personality. If it is ever injured in battle, it can supposedly heal itself with molten lava. However, it was no match for Lawrence III's charged hoops. It was the first Legendary Bird caught by the evil collector.

ZAPDOS:
THE ELECTRIC POKÉMON

Height	5'03"
Weight	116.0 lbs
Type	Electric/Flying

The Legendary Pokémon associated with Lightning Island in the Orange Islands, Zapdos is also known as the Titan of Lightning. One-third of the Legendary Birds that keep each other and the world in balance, it has the power to bend electricity to its will. While most people fear being zapped by lightning, Zapdos gains strength by being struck by the bolts. In fact, when Pikachu meets it on Fire Island, Zapdos grows stronger from its bright flashes of Thunderbolt. Zapdos also lets Pikachu know that Moltres is gone and that it claims Fire Island as its territory. But its power grab didn't last long, as Lawrence III had set his sights on Zapdos next.

LUGIA:
THE DIVING POKÉMON

Height	17'01"
Weight	476.2 lbs
Type	Psychic/Flying

Even bigger than this Pokémon's physical presence is its importance in maintaining the harmony of the world. It is tasked with keeping the three Legendary Bird Pokémon in check. To maintain this harmony, it possesses great strength. A single beat of its wings can blow a house down. It lives deep down in the sea and only surfaces when there is an emergency. That is precisely why Lawrence III began to capture the Legendary Birds: he was trying to lure Lugia out of its home so he could then try to capture it. Luckily, Lugia found a true friend and a brave partner in Ash.

FEATURED POKÉMON

Wise Slowking has a thirst for knowledge. Every day, it studies the mysteries of the universe. So, when the Slowking living by the shrine on Shamouti Island catches wind of the situation with the Legendary Birds, it is ready to help guide the Chosen One. Amazingly enough, this Slowking also happens to be able to communicate with humans and is thus able to keep Ash on track. Nothing gets by this Slowking: it even notices Team Rocket's good deed.

A school of dozens of Magikarp unwittingly swims alongside Team Rocket's Magikarp-shaped submarine. The real Magikarp are part of the Pokémon gathering around Shamouti Island to help.

Dozens of Diglett are in such a hurry to get to Shamouti Island that they don't even stop to skedaddle around Professor Oak. While he jumps up on the garden fence for safety, his bike isn't as lucky. His favorite two-wheel form of transportation gets carried off in the Diglett stampede.

One of the first signs of trouble, Professor Oak and Delia see a flock of hundreds of Pidgey flying over Pallet Town on their way to Shamouti Island.

"BUT WHAT CAN I DO THAT SOMEBODY ELSE CAN'T?" —ASH

THE BRAVE POKÉMON THAT GATHERED

By Professor Ivy's estimation, tens of thousands of Pokémon of all different species trekked over to the area around Shamouti Island by land, air, and sea, all in the hopes of being able to help restore balance to the world. Professor Ivy also pointed out that Pokémon are extra sensitive to the natural world and could tell that something disastrous might happen unless someone could stop it. Or, as Lugia explained, all the Pokémon came "Because they feel they must be here, in case they are needed... That just one Pokémon could help the world would be worth the journey for thousands of them any day." However, only one person could truly make a difference, according to the legend: the Chosen One, Ash.

THE LEGEND OF THE CHOSEN ONE

At the shrine on Shamouti Island, there is an ancient stone tablet carved with this poetic inscription:

"Disturb not the harmony of fire, ice, or lightning lest these Titans wreak destruction upon the world in which they clash.

Though the water's great guardian shall arise to quell the fighting, alone its song will fail lest the Earth shall turn to Ash.

Oh, Chosen One, into thine hands bring together all three! Their treasures combined tame the beast of the sea."

To translate the ancient text, let's first identify the key Pokémon, person, and thing. The Titans are the Legendary Birds: Moltres, Zapdos, and Articuno. The water's great guardian is Lugia. The "Chosen One" is Ash. The "beast of the sea" is the cradle of all the world's water that is found deep beneath the sea near Shamouti Island.

Lugia ensures that the rivals Moltres, Zapdos, and Articuno never overtake each other. They each have their own island, their own shrine, and their own glass ball. But when Lawrence III disturbs the harmony, the "beast of the sea" could flood the whole world. Lugia needs Ash's help to gather the three glass balls of Fire, Lightning, and Ice to renew the peace.

It's no wonder that the locals of Shamouti Island cheered when they heard that the Ash the ancient poem foretold had arrived. They had faith that Ash would fulfill the legend and restore the delicate balance of the world. And when he does, Lugia takes him on a ride while a rainbow made of water stretches across the sunny sky. The "beast of the sea" is restored.

INTERESTING ITEMS

THE WEIRD WEATHER PATTERNS ACROSS THE GLOBE

The day Ash arrived on Shamouti Island, the nightly news reported weather disasters all over the world. Massive floods in the middle of towns, snow in the summer, and lightning storms through cities all seemed to be caused by three underwater currents wrapping around Fire Island, Lightning Island, Ice Island, and Shamouti Island. Even Professor Oak was shocked to see what seemed like a sunny day in Pallet Town turn in less than a minute to a heavy rainstorm, to snow, then to hail, and then right back to a sunny day again.

ANNUAL LEGEND FESTIVAL

Locals and tourists alike flock to the yearly celebration on Shamouti Island, the renowned Annual Legend Festival. The area is covered in lights, and there is even an open market featuring delicious treats. Many Shamouti Islanders dress in colorful traditional costumes with headdresses and dance through the crowds. A fun parade that runs through town features a giant puppet Gyarados. In the evening, there is a special performance by the Festival Maiden, where she plays a flute that sounds like the Legendary Lugia's song.

THE THREE SACRED GLASS BALLS

Each of the three glass balls that Ash (the Chosen One) must find represents each local Legendary Bird. He alone can take them and place them at the shrine on Shamouti Island because he alone can unlock their full power.

THE FIRE BALL

The first glass ball Ash finds, the red ball, is located in the stone beak of a statue at the shrine on Fire Island.

THE LIGHTNING BALL

The yellow ball is the second glass ball Ash finds (or rather, it finds him). It rolls right over the powder-white snow covering Lightning Island and up to Ash.

THE ICE BALL

The final glass ball Ash must find, the blue ball, is located in the stone beak of a statue at the shrine on Ice Island.

LUGIA'S WATERY DISGUISE

Lugia can move ships and stop battles all under the cover of its trusty disguise, a wall of swirling water that looks like the ocean's turned into a tornado. Lugia's watery disguise helps it work in mysterious ways. The disguise can even help Lugia make a surprise entrance by popping out of it to break up a fight between the Legendary Birds.

> "THE CHOICE IS YOURS. YOU MUST GO ONLY WHERE YOUR HEART LEADS."
> —LUGIA

TH POKÉMON CARD THAT STARTED IT ALL

One item made Lawrence III want to be a collector: his beloved first Pokémon Card of the Mythical Pokémon Mew. Once he got a taste of collecting Pokémon, his evil mind wouldn't be satisfied with cards. All he desired was the real thing, and Legendary Pokémon, at that! Luckily, Ash and his friends were able to stop his cruel collection from growing. However, even though Lawrence III's flying fortress, computer, and plans were ruined, one thing survived it all—the Mew card. He plucked it from the rubble with a smile, happy to see his old friend. Let's hope Lawrence III learned his lesson and will stick to collecting Pokémon Cards.

THE FESTIVAL MAIDEN'S FLUTE

It's a tradition that the Festival Maiden plays a special song during the Annual Legend Festival on a unique instrument. The tune and the flute have been passed down through the generations. If played properly, this historic instrument sounds exactly like the song of the Legendary Pokémon Lugia. Melody learned the tune from her sister Carol, the last Festival Maiden. When it was her time to play it, she stood center stage, wearing a veil, a flower crown, and a traditional dress. Then, while she played, she danced.

TOTALLY AWESOME TECHNOLOGY
TEAM ROCKET'S MAGIKARP SUBMARINE

It looks like a Magikarp. It swims like a Magikarp. But it's actually a submarine! Powered and paddled by Jessie, James, and Meowth, it blends in perfectly with the Magikarp flocking to Shamouti Island.

LAWRENCE III'S CHARGED HOOP CAGES

To capture Legendary Pokémon, Lawrence III unleashes smart geometric-shaped hoops in midair. They can chase and surround any Pokémon he wants to catch, all the while buzzing with power. Once caught between a couple of them, even the strongest Legendary Pokémon is rendered powerless and taken back to his flying fortress. Unfortunately, with this technologically advanced cage, Lawrence III is able to capture Moltres, Zapdos, Lugia, and even Ash and his crew.

However, Lawrence III didn't realize he tried to cage a kid who would never ever give up! Ash calls on his Pokémon pals Pikachu and Charizard to break through the charged hoops and set Moltres free. Once freed, Moltres then sets Zapdos free, and they take Lawrence III's whole flying fortress down.

When the charged hoops get ahold of Lugia, it cleverly dives into the sea to weaken them so it can make an escape. The hoops might be powerful, but they're not waterproof.

> **"I'M THE CHOSEN ONE. RIGHT NOW, I FEEL MORE LIKE THE FROZEN ONE." —ASH**

ASH'S MAKESHIFT SLED

When Ash has a need for speed to get him to Ice Island, Pikachu thinks fast, suggesting that Ash make a sled out of a piece of broken boat. His Pokémon pals Charizard, Bulbasaur, Squirtle, and Pikachu all help pull it. Although Legendary Birds break their path and Ash is forced to abandon his sled, help is on the way.

TEAM ROCKET'S AIRBOAT

When Team Rocket sees Ash's sled become toast, Jessie, James, and Meowth are inspired to craft their own ride out of scraps to help him. Using the boat's emergency raft and a propeller from the crashed helicopter, they make a Franken-airboat. It's fast, it's light, it speeds over ice and snow and can turn on a dime. It's this magical machine that saves the day and brings Ash to Ice Island so he can find the final glass ball.

TEAM ROCKET'S MODIFIED, GOOD-IFIED MOTTO

JESSIE: If that kid thinks we're here for trouble …

JAMES: … we're certainly going to burst his bubble.

JESSIE: Instead of causing tribulation …

JAMES: … we've undergone a transformation.

JESSIE: Though it's way outside our usual range …

JAMES: … we're going to do something nice for a change!

JESSIE: Ha! Jessie!

JAMES: James!

JESSIE: Up till now, Team Rocket's been quite unscrupulous.

JAMES: Being good guys for once would be super-dupulous!

MEOWTH: That's right!

POKÉMUN 3: THE MUVIE

THE STORY

Atop a hill in lush and well-named Greenfield City lies a beautiful mansion with a red roof and a fountain in the garden. It's bedtime for one of the people who calls this mansion home, a little girl named Molly. Her father is reading one of her favorite books about the Legendary Pokémon Entei. But her dad knows even more about Pokémon than this book because he's Professor Spencer Hale, an important Pokémon Researcher who studied with Professor Oak.

"This is the one you're looking for, isn't it?" Molly says, pointing to her picture book that shows Unown.

"For a long time now," her father admits.

She turns the page to reveal a picture of Entei, one of Molly's favorite Pokémon because it's big and strong and it reminds her of her father.

"Then I am Entei! Raaaaaawr!" Professor Hale jokes, offering his daughter a piggy-back ride.

But their playtime is cut short when a video call from Schuyler comes in for the professor. Apparently, a hidden chamber with clues about the Unown has been discovered, and they need him to come take a look as soon as possible. So, Professor Hale tucks his daughter into bed, wishing her sweet dreams.

Then, he heads out to an ancient city in the middle of the desert. Schuyler leads him to his most recent find: a dark brick chamber where the walls are carved with some sort of message.

"I've never seen markings like this before, but they seem to be about the Unown," Schuyler says as he snaps reference photos.

Professor Hale takes a good look around and notices a small stone tile with a similar carving on the floor. He bends down to get a better look at it, but he doesn't see Unown materialize over his shoulder the second he touches it.

Nearby, Professor Hale spots a chest tucked into a decorative mantel. He opens the lid to find stacks of similar stone tiles. He takes out a handful, and suddenly, the markings glow blue and a charge flows through it. Before the professor can say a word, he's surrounded by Unown. A small portal opens up above him, and he is pulled into another dimension where all he can hear and see are Unown.

"It's the Unown!" he cries.

Professor Hale's computer and some loose tiles fall to the floor. Schuyler turns around to see what happened, but the professor has disappeared into thin air.

Back at the mansion, Molly comes running down the hall because she thinks her father has come back home. Instead, she finds Schuyler telling the butler that her father has gone missing.

"This is awful. Now the poor young miss is all alone in this world," David the butler says.

That night, Molly takes out her father's computer to look for clues about why he disappeared. She scrolls through photographs of the stone carvings and recognizes them as Unown. Then, she opens the chest and dumps all the tiles out on the floor. She begins to play with them like they're letters.

"I can spell our names with the Unown," she says, arranging them on the floor. "Papa and Mama, they're together with me."

"THEY KIND OF LOOK LIKE ALPHABET SOUP WITHOUT THE SOUP."
—MEOWTH

She begins to cry, her hands holding on to the tiles. A blue glow lights up the markings. Across the desert, deep in the ancient chamber, the portal reopens and Unown fly out. They soar up into the night sky and head straight for another portal over the moon.

Then, a portal opens up directly above Molly back in the mansion hall. Connected by a blue charge, the tiles swirl up from the floor and toward the portal. They transform into Unown, swirling around little Molly.

"Do you all want to play with me?" she asks the Pokémon.

They answer yes by covering the floor beneath her in a wave of blue crystal. It spreads across the room and up the walls. Then it ripples through the entire mansion, locking out her guardians, the butler, and even Schuyler. They're forced to run from the crystal as it flows down the hill and through the town, crystalizing everything in its path. The mansion itself is transformed into a giant, exotic crystal flower.

Molly opens her favorite book, the one she was reading with her father. The bittersweet memory of him pretending to be Entei fills her mind. Then, suddenly, the Legendary Pokémon Entei appears.

"Papa. It's you!" Molly cheers, giving the giant Pokémon a big hug. "You look just like the Entei in the storybook, but it's you!"

"Papa?" Entei wonders. "If that's what you wish."

Meanwhile, Ash, Pikachu, Misty, Togepi, and Brock are on the road just outside of Greenfield. They run into a Trainer named Lisa. While Brock is eager to be her boyfriend, she is eager to have a full Pokémon Battle with Ash. Ash chooses his Pokémon pals Totodile, Chikorita, Noctowl, Bulbasaur, Cyndaquil, and of course, Pikachu. Lisa calls on Granbull, Girafarig, Aipom, Butterfree, Mankey, and Quagsire. Although the battle ends in a draw, they have definitely found a new friend in Lisa. She offers to take them to the local Greenfield Pokémon Center to rest.

"Greenfield's supposed to be a beautiful little town with beautiful gardens and a beautiful mountain with a beautiful mansion right at the top!" Misty says excitedly.

But when they get to the garden hill that overlooks the city, they're completely surprised. Instead of seeing wildflowers and forests, before them lies a crystal wasteland. Everything is covered in strange dark shards.

Officer Jenny drives by on her way to investigate the disturbing transformation of Greenfield. Right behind her is a yellow TV station van. A reporter and cameraman hop out to report from the scene.

"Officials are baffled by this shocking phenomenon, which appears to have originated from the hilltop mansion of renowned Pokémon Researcher Spencer Hale, whose wife mysteriously disappeared two years ago," the reporter says into the camera.

"YOU CAN BECOME ANYTHING YOU WISH." —ENTEI

Back in Pallet Town, Delia is shocked to see the story unfolding on the news. Professor Spencer Hale is one of her close friends, and they went to school together. In fact, Professor Hale, Molly, and her mother even came to visit Ash and Delia not too long ago.

Over at the lab, Professor Oak is also watching the news with Tracey Sketchit. He can't believe one of his top students is missing!

"He recently sent me some of his latest research," Professor Oak says, pulling up the images of Unown that Professor Hale had emailed him.

Delia and Professor Oak decide to head to Greenfield to see if they can help. They pull up to the local Pokémon Center and are pleasantly surprised to see that Ash, Pikachu, Misty, Togepi, and Brock are all there.

What they don't realize is the cameraman is getting their every move onto the news. Molly is watching the whole broadcast back at the crystal mansion. When she sees Delia hug Ash hello, she feels a deep sadness.

"Papa, I want a mama too," she tells Entei.

"If that is what you wish," Entei replies, running out of the mansion and over the crystal wasteland to get her one.

Entei approaches Delia. The Legendary Pokémon hypnotizes her into believing that she is the mama that Molly so badly desires. Possessed, she asks Entei to take her to her child and passes out on its back. Entei runs off, but not before Pikachu stows away on it, too. Pikachu tries to stop Entei with a powerful Thunderbolt, but the Legendary Pokémon easily tosses it off.

"We can't let them get away!" Ash cries out, chasing after her.

Worried about their friend, Brock and Misty follow Ash. Just before he steps into the crystal wasteland, Brock grabs him before he also gets taken in.

Inside the mansion, Entei delivers Delia to Molly.

"Mama!" she cheers. "And I'm Molly, remember?"

Delia lifts Molly onto her lap and gives her a big hug, as if she were her real child. Molly wants Entei, Delia, and the crystal mansion to stay forever. Down in the great hall, the Unown are singing and swirling with delight. The crystal wasteland is growing stronger, swallowing more of the surrounding land. Looking out her window with her new papa and mama, Molly thinks the new world is so pretty! Entei is happy because Molly is happy.

News of Delia's kidnapping is being broadcast on televisions around the globe. Even over in Charicific Valley, Ash's old Pokémon pal Charizard gets wind of it. The locals are trying everything, but even a bulldozer can't seem to crack the crystal wasteland around the Hale mansion.

Back at the Pokémon Center, Professor Oak is busy trying to piece together the clues with Schuyler, Ash, and his friends. From the looks of it, they think this all might be the work of Unown. Just then, Professor Oak gets a video email from Molly warning them all to leave her, her mama, and her papa alone. But Professor Oak is confused because both her mama and papa are missing. What is going on?

Ash decides to take matters into his own hands. He and Pikachu sneak out of the Pokémon Center with plans to rescue his mom alone. However, he doesn't get very far before his buddies Brock and Misty insist they come, too! Then, their new friend Lisa shows up to give Ash her PokéGear so he can still communicate with the Pokémon Center. Humbled by all their kindness, Ash can't believe the fortune that good friends are.

With that, Ash, Pikachu, Brock, Misty, and Togepi set off down the only path to the mansion not covered by crystal—a little stream. However, Team Rocket thinks they've found another way to get to the Hale mansion as they pull up in their hot air balloon. But once Entei spots them on the horizon, it shoots them down with a single Shadow Ball blast. Team Rocket falls right though the crystal cover and into a strange corner of the mansion. Molly is happy to hear that Entei got rid of them. She doesn't want anyone breaking up her happy home.

They find a round tower entrance to the crystal mansion, but there's no door handle. They'll have to break through and then keep the crystal from sealing it back up. So, Ash comes up with a clever strategy. His Fire-type pal Cyndaquil teams up with Brock's Pokémon buddy Vulpix to shoot through the crystal with a fiery Flamethrower. Then, Ash's Water-type Pokémon pal Totodile and Misty's friend Staryu combine their Water Gun blasts to keep the crystal from being able to close up the hole Cyndaquil and Vulpix made. Pikachu is the first one to ride the wave and swim its way into the mansion. Brock, Misty, and Ash follow suit. Then, Ash runs in carrying Totodile and Staryu as they keep up their Water Gun blasts. The minute they make it through, the crystal swirls close, locking the kids inside the mansion.

Ash has his own strategy to get inside. He asks Noctowl to fly Chikorita and Bulbasaur up to the top of the waterfall. Then, they use their vines like ropes to help Ash, Brock, and Misty climb up. The camera crew catches Ash in the midst of the action. Molly is still glued to the news and sees the intruders. Entei offers to scare Ash and his friends away, but Molly admits she'd be excited to meet a real Pokémon Trainer and his Pokémon pals like Pikachu.

Just then, Professor Oak calls Ash on Lisa's PokéGear. He and Schuyler have been reading through Professor Hale's research on Unown. It seems the Unown have the ability of reading the thoughts of other life forms and altering the world to grant their wishes. Professor Oak thinks that Unown have tuned into Molly's imagination and are turning the world into her wildest dreams.

"That crystal fortress could be one of Molly's wishes made real by the Unown," Professor Oak explains.

Anxious to find his mother, Ash leads the way to the crystal mansion's great hall. As they climb the stairs, the surroundings turn into a network of glowing green veins with purple balls, and the steps turn into floating keys. It seems the Unown are creating a new reality.

Ash knows there's no time to waste. He has to get inside the crystal mansion and rescue his mother before it's too late!

Upstairs in her bedroom, Molly tells Mama Delia that she would love to be in a Pokémon Battle. So, she rides on Entei's back to greet her guests. However, along the way, she worries that she might be too young to battle since you have to be at least 10 years old to get your First Partner Pokémon and become a Pokémon Trainer. Entei tells Molly to just use her imagination and believe she can do it. Then, amazingly enough, Molly instantly transforms into a grown-up.

"WE ALWAYS BATTLE HARD, BUT WE ALWAYS STAY FRIENDS BECAUSE WE ALL LOVE POKÉMON." —ASH

Together, they ride down to a field of wildflowers with a pink sky, where Ash, Misty, and Brock await her. Grown-up Molly challenges them to a Pokémon Battle, but Ash doesn't recognize this grown-up and is focused on finding his mom. Brock figures out that the grown-up before them is actually Molly Hale, which proves she really can make anything come true in this world! Brock thinks fast and offers to take Molly up on her battle challenge to distract her while Ash continues on to look for Delia.

Out of thin air, a battlefield appears before them for the three-on-three battle. Brock chooses Zubat, while grown-up Molly chooses Flaaffy. With a single Thunder Shock zap, Zubat falls from the sky, unable to battle. So, Brock calls on his Fire-type pal Vulpix to heat things up. Grown-up Molly chooses Teddiursa, which might look cute but has a powerful Dynamic Punch and super-strong Fury Swipes. Vulpix is also quickly left unable to battle.

"Her dreamed-up Pokémon are tougher than real ones," Brock says under his breath.

For his next Pokémon, Brock brings out giant Onix, a force to be reckoned with for any Pokémon. Grown-up Molly responds by picking adorable little Phanpy, which is nearly 27 feet smaller than its opponent Onix. Yet, with one Roll Out tackle, Onix flies up into the air and is knocked out. Grown-up Molly giggles with delight at winning her first-ever Pokémon Battle. But it seems that the Pokémon weren't the only illusions: grown-up Molly was also dreamt up.

Back in Molly's bedroom, young Molly is lying down on Delia's lap.

"You're by yourself a lot, aren't you, Molly?" Delia asks. "Have you been lonely?"

"Maybe a little. But I don't feel that way anymore," Molly replies. "I have a mama and papa."

Next, grown-up Molly and Entei magically appear before Misty and Ash. So Ash can continue on to find his mother, Misty challenges her to a battle by bragging that she is the Cerulean City Gym Leader. Grown-up Molly is very surprised that someone so young

can be so important. Entei reminds her that she can be anything she wants. Suddenly, Molly instantly transforms into a girl about Misty's age right before their eyes.

Even more surprisingly, since Misty is a Water-type Pokémon expert, Molly decides to cover them all in a huge wave so they can battle underwater. At first, Misty is afraid she'll drown, but then she sees she can breathe even at the bottom of this ocean. Anything is possible when you're in Molly's dream world!

While Misty begins the battle, Ash finally finds his mother. Little Molly has fallen asleep on her. Ash takes the opportunity to explain the situation with the Unown to his mom. Delia realizes she can't go on lying to little Molly, even though she cares about her. Delia gently wakes up the small girl.

"I'm very sorry, Molly, but I'm not your real Mama," Delia admits. "You'll have to know the truth sooner or later. I'm really Ash's mother."

"Don't you remember when we played together, Molly?" Ash adds. "We were at Professor Oak's house in Pallet Town."

But Molly doesn't remember, and she doesn't want to leave the crystal mansion with them.

"I won't! I won't! I won't!" Molly cries out.

Her fear creates crystal spikes that shoot up from the floor and separate Ash from Molly and Delia. Ash tries to get her out, but Entei arrives to throw him out.

"Now she's Molly's mother," Entei commands. "Leave this place or you will be made to leave."

"I'm not going to lose to some illusion," Ash replies, calling on his Pokémon pals for backup.

Totodile tries a stream of Water Gun. Cyndaquil fires Flamethrower. Entei easily defeats them. But Ash won't give up because he knows he is just fighting Molly's imagination.

"You're wrong, Ash, you're wrong!" Molly whimpers.

A strong wind blows through the crystal mansion, and the spikes grow in anger. The scene, although scary, looks oddly just like a page out of her favorite book.

"I am this girl's father and I must protect her!" Entei vows.

Ash's best friend Pikachu tries to fend off Entei's attack with Thunderbolt. But it builds a massive Shadow Ball that sends Ash and Pikachu flying out of the crystal mansion. Just when it looks like there is no one to turn to, hope swoops in—or rather, Charizard. It catches its old pals in midair.

"I can't believe it!" Ash says, glad to see his Fire-type friend.

Charizard flies them back into the crystal mansion to help them face Entei. Ash lets Entei know that he and his Pokémon pals are like a family: if you mess with one, you mess with them all. But when Charizard is on the losing side of a headbutt, Entei nearly knocks Ash out of the crystal castle again. This time, Misty, Brock, and even Team Rocket's Jessie, James, and Meowth rush to pull him back in.

"We won't let you fall," Brock promises.

"We're like family too," Misty adds.

Although Ash is happy for the help, he's wondering what made Team Rocket turn into good guys.

"If anything ever happened to you, we'd be out of show business!" Meowth says, admitting their selfish motivation.

Ash is safe for now, but the battle has really just begun. Ash hops on Charizard's back. Entei strikes again with a serious Hyper Beam. Charizard dodges it by soaring up high, then sends a fierce Flamethrower down to Entei. It dodges the blaze but sends back a Flamethrower blast of its own. Then, Entei flashes another Hyper Beam, and Charizard fires Flamethower at the same time, causing a huge explosion. Entei sends a glowing Shadow Ball, but Charizard dodges it, and it blows clean through the side of the crystal mansion.

Entei jumps out through the hole, landing on a crystal tower. It climbs the side of the mansion, all the while being chased by Charizard's fiery Flamethrower. Molly is so worried about the Legendary Pokémon she calls Papa that crystal spikes begin to appear like steps to help it chase Charizard into the sky.

"Don't hold back, give it everything you've got!" Ash says, encouraging Charizard.

Charizard uses Fire Spin to wrap Entei in a whirlwind of flames. It escapes but continues the fight. So, Ash tries to reason with the powerful Legendary Pokémon.

"If you really care about Molly, you'll let her come with us!" Ash pleads. "It's not right for her to stay here with you."

"Whether it is right or wrong, I do as she wishes," Entei replies, sending over another Shadow Ball blast.

Charizard quickly responds with Flamethrower to stop Entei's attack. Since they're both so strong, their attacks again explode in midair. Delia covers Molly to protect her from the blast. Molly is starting to see that Delia and Ash really care about her; she's not imagining their friendship.

The battle continues, with crystal spikes popping out of thin air in time to aid Entei as it chases after flying Charizard. However, one gets ahead and smacks Charizard clear across its face. Confused, Entei seizes the opportunity to strike Charizard in close range with another strong Shadow Ball. Charizard plummets to the ground. Entei places a paw right on Charizard's neck.

"Entei, don't!" Ash cries out to protect his brave pal, which no longer looks able to battle.

"This will end it!" Entei swears, building another Shadow Ball.

But before Entei can fire it, one strong little girl stands to protect Charizard.

"Stop," Molly begs. "No more fighting. Please, Papa!"

She runs up to her Legendary Pokémon papa and buries her face in its leg, tears running down her face. Entei obeys her wishes.

Brock and Misty tell Molly she already has the makings of a great Pokémon Trainer because she cares for Pokémon and knows when to stop battling.

"We always battle hard, but we always stay friends because we all love Pokémon," Ash adds. "Come with us, Molly."

"On the outside, the battles might be hard," Misty says.

"But the friends are real," Brock promises.

"It's just what your papa would want," Delia vows.

Moved by their pleas, Molly walks over to Delia and holds her hand.

"I want things real again," Molly replies, her eyes filled with tears.

And just like that, the crystal begins melting away. Entei retreats, explaining that its job was to be the father that made her happy in the crystal world, but now, she will be happier in the real one. However, before it can leave, crystal spikes shoot up from the floor, trapping everyone right where they are.

Entei thinks fast and uses Hyper Beam to blast a path through the crystal points. Ash asks Charizard to carry Molly out. Then, the rest of the crew follows on foot. Ash calls Professor Oak on his PokéGear to warn him that they have Molly, but the crystal is still on the attack. Outside the window, Schuyler sees the crystal climbing even farther through town and up to the Pokémon Center. Professor Oak thinks the Unown have so much Psychic energy that they're out of control. They have to flee the area as fast as they can.

Now in the heart of the great hall, Ash, Misty, Brock, Pikachu, Team Rocket, Delia, Molly, and Charizard come face-to-face with the swirling sphere of Unown. Ash tries to run in and break up their rhythm, but he bounces right off the Unown ball. Next, Charizard tries to break through it with Flamethrower, but the Unown just return to their round formation. Now, Pikachu wants to give the Unown a shock.

"Pikachuuuuuuuuuu!" it shouts, giving Thunderbolt its all.

Charizard tries to add Flamethrower, but the Unown are still too strong. Suddenly, spiky crystals pop up out of the floor. They worry they're trapped for good, but then they hear a loud roar. Entei has returned!

Entei tells Molly that if she believes in it, there's nothing it can't do—including putting an end to the Unown's power over her home. With that, it begins to attack the Unown. It fires a big Shadow Ball blast. Then, Entei charges at the Unown sphere, but it gets caught.

"Molly, help me!" Entei calls out. "Believe in me."

"You can do it, Entei!" Molly cries, giving it her all.

> ## "IF YOU BELIEVE IN ME, THERE IS NOTHING I CANNOT DO."
> —ENTEI

A white glow breaks through the sphere of the Unown. Charizard uses Flamethrower and Pikachu adds Thunderbolt to help Entei. Then, it fires a gleaming blue beam across the great hall. An amazingly bright light breaks through and swallows the Unown. Then, Entei is also lifted into the light. The giant Legendary Pokémon disappears before their eyes.

The light closes, and the tiles, marked with the Unown, rain down on the great hall. A portal opens in the ceiling, and the Unown are transported out of the real world. As quickly as it had come, the crystal evaporates in a wave. The mansion is returned to its true glory. All of the lush gardens of Greenfield are restored. Everyone celebrates that the area is back to its normal beauty, but there's still one very important piece of the puzzle to fall back into place.

The portal places the Unown back in the ancient chamber and releases the most precious captive of all: Molly's father, Professor Spencer Hale. There is nothing more important or real than the love Molly shares with her real papa. And now, she can't believe she has also made so many caring new friends! It seems the little girl's lonely days are over.

LOCATIONS

GREENFIELD

A town that is no misnomer, Greenfield is a lush valley with rolling hills covered in fresh green grass and fields featuring a rainbow of wildflowers. Rivers run under little stone footbridges. Tall trees sway in the gentle breeze. Everywhere you look is the perfect place for a picnic. It's no wonder with views like that why Misty couldn't wait to visit this beautiful town!

THE HALE MANSION ON THE HILL

On top of a grassy hill in the center of the town of Greenfield sits a beautiful mansion. In front, there are perfectly manicured patches of grass trimmed in yellow and pink flowers. There are beautiful sculptures on pedestals around the garden. The long driveway is lined with green trees. In the middle is a big round fountain that splashes sparkling blue water.

The mansion itself is made of pale gray brick with an orange roof. It has two wings marked with tall, pointed spires. Inside, the mansion has high ceilings and lots of sunlight from all of the windows. There is a great hall that has an elegant staircase. It was so appealing and vast, the Unown stayed right there.

ANOTHER DIMENSION

When Professor Spencer Hale is surrounded by Unown inside the ancient chamber, he is transported through a portal into another dimension.

MOLLY'S BEDROOM

Upstairs, Molly's bedroom is pink and purple. The carpet has a golden design. Her bedding is pink, surrounded by fuchsia and lavender curtains and a decorative canopy. Gold gilded columns support arches that frame her room. She has a Teddiursa toy, a Ponyta rocking Fire Horse, and a Donphan-shaped slide. Even with all of those beautiful accoutrements, the most treasured things in her room are a book featuring Entei and Unown that her father gave her and two framed photos on her desk. One is of her father and mother, and the other is from her trip to Pallet Town to visit Delia, Ash, and Professor Oak.

MOLLY'S CRYSTAL DREAMLAND

With the help of Unown, Molly's imagination becomes a virtual reality. Inspired by her favorite book (the one her father gave her), waves of crystal turn her home and the surrounding area into all kinds of amazing and terrifying playgrounds for Molly's mind.

THE CRYSTAL MANSION

With the help of Unown, the Hale mansion transforms into Molly's fantasy world. The entire home, gardens, and even the surrounding city get covered in crystal. From the outside, the mansion begins to look like a giant, strange flower. On the inside, Molly's imagination even redecorates.

MOLLY'S CRYSTAL BEDROOM

The room glows with rainbow light. Her bed has turned lavender, with a blue crystal headboard. The canopy has become a tall cascade of lilac ruffles, twisting and turning up so high, they seem to have no end. The columns have turned into purple tree trunks with magenta knobs and a ruffled skirt. Her carpet has also turned into thin three-layered crystal circles that spill out like waves on the shore. From the giant window in her room, Molly can see the whole world created from her imagination.

THE CRYSTAL BEACH

The sandy beach of Molly's dream world is right next to a patch of red tropical flowers. It looks exactly like a page in her favorite book, and it has beautiful blue water that washes in and out, just like the regular tide. However, this is no ordinary ocean! When Misty suggests that they have a Water-type battle, Molly sends a huge wave to have the match underwater. At first, Misty and even Ash are worried they'll drown, but since it's imaginary water, they're totally fine. And so, Misty calls on Goldeen and Staryu to battle Molly's Kingdra and Mantine.

THE CHAMBER OF THE UNOWN

Deep in the desert lies an ancient city where Schuyler discovered a previously unopened chamber. Professor Spencer Hale rushes over to see the amazing find. Inside, the stone walls are covered with carvings that look like a mysterious Pokémon that Professor Hale has been studying—the Unown.

On the back wall, there is a decorative mantel. At the bottom rests a box filled with tiles that have markings that look like the Unown. It is at this mantel that their portal appears, disappears, and reappears.

GREENFIELD POKÉMON CENTER

In Greenfield, the local Pokémon Center is right up a dirt road, nestled into nature. The front doors are made of glass, and cobblestones lead up to the entrance.

Here, in a special office, Professor Oak and Schuyler continue their research and advise Ash. Luckily, they're not the only ones working hard to help the town. The emergency response team also sets up at Nurse Joy's Pokémon Center.

THE CRYSTAL GREAT HALL

Waves of blue crystal seal the windows and doors. They crawl up the stairs and turn the great hall of the Hale mansion into layers of dark, sparkling ruffles.

CRYSTALIZED GREENFIELD

The grassy knolls, wildflowers, and even windmills that Greenfield is known for all get swallowed by the crystal sprawl. Even the local Pokémon Center isn't safe!

THE CRYSTAL FIELD

Inside the mansion, Ash, Misty, Brock, and Pikachu find themselves on steps that lead to a land that looks just like old Greenfield, with grass, trees, and wildflowers as far as the eye can see—only, the sky is perfectly pink. And when Brock challenges grown-up Molly to a battle, a battlefield suddenly appears right before them.

THE PARK

Just outside of Greenfield, there's a little park where Ash, Pikachu, Misty, Togepi, and Brock first met Lisa and Aipom. It has a jungle gym with a slide, some swings, and a picnic table. If you ask Ash and Lisa, though, it's the perfect park for a Pokémon Battle!

CHARICIFIC VALLEY

Carved into a mountainside as orange as the Fire-type Pokémon is an area that pays homage to Charizard. It is a total paradise with beautiful mountain views and a fountain that turns into a waterfall! There are both statues of Charizard and the real Pokémon, along with a Charizard enthusiast named Liza, and they all call Charicific Valley home. In fact, Ash's Pokémon pal Charizard is staying there when the news breaks that Entei has captured Delia.

CHARACTERS

ASH

Our hero loves to battle, but this time, he's in a fight for his mother, Delia. Nothing, not a crystal wasteland or even Entei, can stop him. However, he'll have to step into the shoes, errr, mind of a lonely five-year-old girl to solve the puzzle and save his mom! Luckily, he has some good old friends who pitch in to help him.

PIKACHU

Pikachu's Thunderbolt is one of the final blows that broke through the Unown's globe.

CHARIZARD

After hearing that Delia was captured on the news, Charizard knew that Ash needed its help. And did the Fire-type arrive from Charicific Valley just in time! As Ash and Pikachu were falling from the crystal mansion, Charizard swooped in and surprised them by catching them both in its arms. Then, it bravely battled Entei to help Ash rescue Delia.

CYNDAQUIL

BULBASAUR

NOCTOWL

CHIKORITA

TOTODILE

DELIA

Delia isn't just Ash's mom in this movie; she also steps in to be, as Molly calls her, "Mama." At first, Delia is frightened when she is captured by Entei and taken to the crystal

mansion, but she soon comes to understand the scared little orphan girl who just wishes for a family.

Delia actually knows Molly's real family because she met her father, Professor Spencer Hale, back in his school days in Pallet Town. In fact, Molly and her real mother and father had come to visit Delia and Ash a few years back. Although Molly and Ash might have been too young to remember the trip, a photo of them all together in Pallet Town sits in a picture frame in Molly's room and on Delia's refrigerator.

When Delia catches wind of the crystal wasteland from the TV news, she races over to Professor Oak's lab to volunteer to help. Little did she know she'd wind up in the heart of the trouble, inside the crystal mansion. Once there, Delia is happy to comfort Molly, but she won't lie to her. When it comes time for Molly to face the truth and bring an end to the crystal wasteland, Delia steps up to reason with her out of love. Molly knows she can trust Delia because she can tell Delia really cares for her. Their bond helps see the frightened, lonely girl through a very difficult trial. They say friends are the family you choose, and in this movie, that certainly rings true.

BROCK

Caring Brock definitely feels a sense of responsibility for his pal Ash and is always there for him. At first, Brock stopped Ash from chasing Entei into the crystal wasteland because he was concerned for his safety. Brock was just trying to protect Ash, but he can't blame his friend for being willing to risk it all to save his mom. So, later that night, when Ash tries to sneak into the crystal mansion alone in search of Delia, Brock and Misty join him. He would never leave Ash hanging.

In fact, when grown-up Molly wants to battle, Brock steps up to challenge her. Brock selflessly tells Ash that he'll distract Molly so Ash can continue on the search for his mother. Ash can always count on Brock!

VULPIX

ZUBAT

ONIX

"HEY, I MADE YOU LAUGH. THAT'S MY FIRST VICTORY TODAY." —BROCK

MISTY

The Cerulean City Gym Leader, Misty and her Pokémon pals are right there when Ash needs their help! Together, they brave the crystal wasteland to rescue Delia and bring Molly back to reality.

TOGEPI

STARYU

PROFESSOR SPENCER HALE

The professor is a renowned Pokémon Researcher who studied with Professor Oak in Pallet Town. So, he's also an old friend of Delia, Ash's mom.

Since his school days, Professor Spencer Hale has made a name for himself as one of the most important authorities on Legendary Pokémon. His current obsession, however, is a mysterious species: the Symbol Pokémon, Unown.

Although he is a serious scientist, Professor Hale certainly has a soft side. He loves to play with his daughter, Molly. He has boundless energy for giving her piggy-back rides and reading to her. His work often has him traveling to special sites, but he loves nothing more than being home with her.

Strangely enough, Professor Hale's wife mysteriously disappeared two years ago. It was a high-profile case, but no one was able to solve it. So, their daughter, Molly, is his whole world.

MOLLY HALE

Professor Hale's five-year-old daughter is cute as a button and very curious. Brave and smart, she isn't afraid of anything—not even giant Pokémon. She loves to read books about Pokémon, just like her father. In fact, her favorite book is a special one he gave her all about Entei and Unown. It is the pages of that very book that fill her head and inspire the dream world the Unown create around her.

Living in a fabulous mansion, you would think Molly is a girl who has it all. But in fact, she has been sad since her mother went missing a couple of years ago. Her father is forced to travel a lot for work, which leaves her lonely in that big empty house. Her loneliness only grows when her father goes missing, too. So, it's no wonder that in her dream world, all this little girl wants is a mama and a papa. When Ash and his pals show up at her door, she's just excited to meet new friends! Her wishes are so innocent inside her dream world that it's a shame they cause such harm to the real world.

But once Ash and his friends are able to help Molly see that she is in control of Entei and the crystal world, she uses the power of her mind to save her home, Greenfield, and even her father! That's quite an achievement for such a young girl.

Throughout the movie, Molly splits into twins who do not stay so little. While Molly rests in her bedroom, a second Molly transforms her age and appearance to battle Ash's pals Brock and Misty.

GROWN-UP MOLLY

When Molly has the chance to meet real Pokémon Trainers Ash and Misty, she admits to Entei that she wishes she were old enough to be one. Entei promises Molly that she can be anything she puts her mind to, and in her dream world, that even means growing up in an instant. By the time she travels from her bedroom to the battlefield, she appears to be an adult. So, she then accepts Brock's challenge for a Pokémon Battle. However, even if she looks like a grown-up, she sure doesn't act like one. Playful and giggly, Molly still has the tastes of a child, even though she's in an adult's body.

SCHUYLER

Professor Hale's research assistant, Schuyler, is the first to alert him to the discovery of the ancient chamber with the unique markings that look like Unown. The young Pokémon scientist is thrilled to show the man he admires, Professor

Hale, his findings. He is the only one in the chamber when Hale disappears into thin air, and he is tasked with relaying the bad news. He is also at the mansion when it turns to crystal. But he won't give up. Schuyler devotes himself to helping Professor Oak and the rescue team with their investigation to find Professor Spencer Hale and solve the cause of the crystal wasteland.

DAVID

At the Hale mansion, David is the head of the staff. Schuyler meets with him to tell the story of Professor Hale's disappearance. He also delivers the ancient chest filled with the marked tiles to David.

TWEEN MOLLY

On her dream world beach, Misty tells grown-up Molly that she is the Cerulean City Gym Leader to tempt her into a battle. Grown-up Molly just can't believe that someone so young could be so important. Just like a little sister excited to look like her big sister, grown-up Molly transforms into a girl of Misty's age right before her eyes. As if that weren't surprising enough, tween Molly then covers them in a huge wave so they can have an underwater Water-type battle.

At first, Molly loves battles. But after an epic fight between Charizard and Entei to rescue Delia, Molly sees that she has to rejoin the real world.

TEAM ROCKET

As per usual, Jessie, James, and Meowth are hot on Ash's trail hoping to steal some strong Pokémon. So, when they see Ash trying to sneak into the crystal mansion, Team Rocket decides there must be some valuable Pokémon there that they can poach. However, their plans don't even get off the ground. In fact, when they take to the sky in their hot air balloon, Entei immediately shoots them down. When they crash-land

inside the crystal mansion, they can't believe their eyes. And Ash can't believe their behavior. For a second movie in a row, they could be called "good guys." It's perhaps one of the most bizarre things in this movie, and this movie has some strange happenings! Team Rocket actually helps save Ash when he nearly falls out of the crystal mansion.

Moved by what's happening, Team Rocket identifies with the troubled, complex heroes of the story. Jessie thinks she has a lot in common with Molly. She also feels she is "adorable, yet indomitable." James, on the other hand, identifies with Entei. He feels he is "powerful and inscrutable." But a true Pokémon fan knows their true nature, and Team Rocket will be back to their usual shenanigans soon enough.

WOBBUFFET

LISA

While passing through a park, Ash meets a Pokémon Trainer named Lisa and her pal Aipom. Lisa is training for the Johto League and wants to get all the practice she can. So, she asks if Ash wants to have a battle right then and there. The fun battle is waged all across the playground.

THE BATTLE BETWEEN LISA AND ASH

ROUND 1 LISA VS. ASH WINNER

ROUND 2 LISA VS. ASH WINNER

ROUND 3 LISA VS. ASH WINNER

ROUND 4 LISA VS. ASH WINNER

ROUND 5 LISA VS. ASH WINNER

ROUND 6 LISA VS. ASH **WINNER**
In the end, the fun battle ends in a draw when Ash's pal Pikachu jumps off the swing and lands head-to-head with Quagsire.

After the battle, Lisa and Aipom have lunch with Ash, Pikachu, Chikorita, Misty, Togepi, and Brock. Then, she offers to show them the way to the local Pokémon Center in Greenfield so they can rest.

Along the way, Lisa wants to give them a peek at the beautiful town, known for its lush landscape. But they're all surprised to see it crystalized.

Although she only just met Ash, she lends him her own PokéGear so he can communicate with Professor Oak back at the Pokémon Center while he travels to rescue his mom in the crystal mansion. Lisa knows someone's safety is more precious than any piece of technology.

OFFICER JENNY

Always on the case, Officer Jenny races to the Pokémon Center in Greenfield to help.

NURSE JOY

Nurse Joy opens up the Greenfield Pokémon Center to all those who need a place to stay during the strange events in Greenfield. The emergency response team, Professor Oak, Officer Jenny, and even the TV news crew all monitor the situation from her spot.

TV NEWS CREW

A reporter and cameraman are live at the scene as soon as Officer Jenny is. They take their job seriously! Their news stories are being broadcast  in real time through a live feed. So, not only is Ash's ally Charizard able to see the story unfold all the way in Charicific Valley, but also Molly, Delia, and Entei are streaming the video from inside the crystal mansion. The news crew is right up in the action, reporting every angle. They capture the scene at Pokémon Center, the bulldozer attempt, when Entei abducts Delia, and more! They are chasing the story, no matter the risk. Everyone tuning in is relying on the reporter to explain the events.

PROFESSOR OAK

Upon hearing that Spencer Hale, one of his star students, has gone missing, Professor Oak begins to dig through his research to help solve the  mystery. Luckily, before his disappearance, Professor Hale had sent Professor Oak his most recent findings. Hoping he can help, Professor Oak heads to Greenfield with Delia and sets up an office in the Pokémon Center to monitor the situation. Together with Schuyler, Professor Oak pieces together the mystery behind the Unown's involvement in the crystal wasteland. It is Professor Oak who first suggests that Unown tapped into Molly's imagination and created the alternate crystal world from her wildest dreams.

TRACEY SKETCHIT

Back at Professor Oak's lab, Tracey tries to help his teacher with the research.

LIZA AND CHARLA

Lover of all things Charizard, Liza makes a brief cameo at Charicific Valley as she and her Pokémon pal Charla are glued to the television news,  watching the story in Greenfield unfold.

FEATURED POKÉMON

When Molly and her father, Professor Hale, are reading her favorite book, she says that the Legendary Pokémon Entei reminds her of her father. However, the connection doesn't seem clear to Professor Hale or even Entei when it appears in her crystal world. Immediately after covering the mansion in crystal, Entei is the next thing that the Unown manifest for Molly. She calls Entei "Papa," and it takes on the task of protecting her and also delivering exactly what she wants, even if it's capturing Delia! In this movie, Entei is able to travel from the crystal world into the real one, as per Molly's will.

Even more amazingly, in Molly's crystal dream world, Entei can communicate with humans. So, Entei always reminds Molly that if she believes something, it will come true. She innocently uses her power to instantly be old enough to battle and also to stop intruders with spikes. No matter what she does, Entei has got her back. It is always by her side and vows that its only job is to make her happy.

Entei offers to be her father for as long as Molly wishes. Ultimately, with the help of Delia, Ash, Misty, and Brock, she chooses to let go of her fantasy realm and rejoin reality. But the Unown have grown so strong that they won't let her go, and Entei again steps up to save Molly. Entei asks for Molly to once again believe in it, and with the power of her heart, she helps Entei break the sphere of the Unown. The real world and Greenfield are restored, thanks to Entei!

Although Ash argues that Entei is just an illusion like everything else, Entei vows that it is, in fact, the real Legendary Pokémon.

Not much is known about Unown. They are a mysterious Pokémon that are the subject of Professor Hale's studies. Unown look like different letters of ancient script, and together, they can spell trouble.

When Professor Hale first encounters them in the desert chamber, they appear out of carvings on tiles that are stacked in a chest. They swirl around Professor Hale, and he is transported through a portal into a whole different dimension.

After his disappearance, his daughter curiously tries to discover his whereabouts. She too touches the marked tiles, igniting their power. Through a portal, they travel from the ancient chamber right into the great hall of the Hale mansion.

Then, the circle of Unown that surrounds her grows into a giant floating globe of Unown, churning and chanting in unison.

Unown have the ability to read others' thoughts and wishes. They can then create new realities around those desires. So, Professor Oak suspects that the crystal world is actually Molly Hale's wildest dreams come true. Oddly enough, the crystal world looks just like drawings in her favorite book. It seems that the Unown have in fact tapped into her mind.

At first, it seems that Molly is in complete control of the crystal world, transforming it and even herself into whatever she wishes. However, when Molly finally chooses to return to reality, the Unown have grown so tough with Psychic power that they take over. Luckily, with the help of Entei, Charizard, and Pikachu, the Unown are sent back to the ancient chamber through the portal they arrived in. When they're finally contained again, Professor Hale is returned to the real world and dropped back in the ancient chamber.

INTERESTING ITEMS
TH BOOK

Given to Molly by her father, this hardcover book about Pokémon like Entei and Unown is by far her favorite. It is the book he reads to her at bedtime before he leaves to investigate the ancient chamber. As Molly's crystal dream world unfolds, it seems that she is drawing inspiration from the pictures in this very book.

TH CHEST OF UNOWN TILES

Professor Spencer Hale first finds this chest under the mantel in the ancient chamber. Inside the chest are stacks of tiles with markings that resemble the Unown. It seems the chest is not just a container to hold the marked tiles; it seems to also contain the curious power of Unown.

THE MARKED TILES

Found inside the chest are tiles that appear to have markings that look like the Symbol Pokémon. When Professor Spencer Hale and his daughter Molly touch these special tiles, the markings light up with a strange blue glow. Then, the tiles seem to release real Unown. The power of the tiles seems as mysterious as the Pokémon themselves.

THE BULLDOZER

Greenfield's emergency response team tries to send in a bulldozer to tear through the crystal world. While a bulldozer usually clears a path, this time, the path clears the bulldozer. The crystal perimeter throws the bulldozer out. Luckily, no one was physically hurt. The only damage was to Molly's feelings. As she watches the TV news report live on the scene, she wonders why the bulldozer would try to attack her and her perfect dream world.

TOTALLY AWESOME TECHNOLOGY

PROFESSOR SPENCER HALE'S COMPUTER

This laptop was originally used by Professor Hale to log his research, take photos of his findings, and communicate with his colleagues like Schuyler and Professor Oak via email and video chat. However, after he disappears, his laptop is turned over to his daughter, Molly. She uses it to search through his studies to find clues to his disappearance.

MOLLY HALE'S COMPUTER

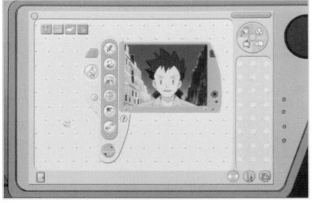

Molly's pink laptop is stationed right in her room. It's arguably the only item inside the mansion that remains the same when her home is transformed into her imaginative crystal mansion. Her background wallpaper is yellow, with white flowers lined up in neat rows. Her father often receives video calls from Schuyler on her laptop. Once she's living in her dream world, Molly uses her computer to watch her surroundings by streaming the live news coverage from Greenfield.

Molly also uses her laptop to send a video message to Professor Oak at his makeshift office at the Greenfield Pokémon Center. She warns the whole crew to leave her and her "mama and papa" alone. How she was able to send a message there is a mystery that probably only the Unown can answer!

PROFESSOR OAK'S LAB COMPUTER

Taking up nearly an entire wall of his Pallet Town lab, this sophisticated computer helps Professor Oak with his research. From the large monitor, he can sift through many windows of research materials and also video-chat with fellow Pokémon scientists.

LISA'S POKÉGEAR

Although Ash is a new friend, Lisa generously offers to lend him her PokéGear as he heads out to the crystal wasteland. She tells him he can use it to communicate directly with everyone back at the Pokémon Center. Because of the PokéGear, Professor Oak and Schuyler were able to guide Ash through the crystal world and give him the vital information he needed to save his mom and help its unwitting creator, Molly.

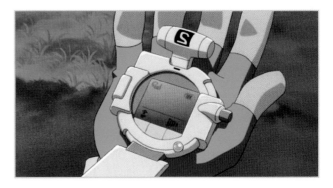

THE EPIC BATTLE

Ash, Delia, Brock, and Misty try to reason with Molly to get her to see she is living in a crystal dream world of her own imagination. They want to help her come back to reality, but Entei tries to protect its beloved Molly and her crystal paradise. Ash and Pikachu try their best to battle back Entei, but they're knocked out of the tower. Luckily, backup swoops in to save them—Ash's old Pokémon pal Charizard. But his Fire-type friend doesn't stop there: Charizard takes on the task of standing up to the Legendary Pokémon Entei. This is the epic battle that ensues.

The two attacks explode right in the middle of the room. Molly, Delia, and the whole crew try to cover themselves from the embers raining down..

Worried about Molly, Entei quickly aims a glowing purple Shadow Ball right at Charizard and Ash. They're able to dodge the attack, but it blasts a hole through the crystal tower. Entei leaps out of the wreckage and onto the side of the other crystal tower. Charizard and Ash chase after it, immediately firing another Flamethrower.

Nimble Entei dodges it by climbing up to the top of the tower. Ash instructs Charizard to try another fierce Flamethower. This time, the attack knocks Entei right off the top of the tower. As it falls, even Ash is worried that Entei might be injured. Molly, concerned for her "papa," quickly imagines some help. A giant crystal spike grows out of the side of the tower, giving Entei a safe place to land.

Entei and Charizard lunge at each other to begin the fight, literally butting heads. Charizard is knocked to the ground and slides across the floor, nearly knocking Ash out of the tower again. This time, his friends who are like family—Brock, Pikachu, Misty, and even Team Rocket—grab on to Ash.

Charizard stands back up with a roar. Entei responds with a shot of Hyper Beam that sends everyone running besides Charizard and Ash. Hopping on Charizard's back, the pair soars above the scene. Then, Charizard fires Flamethrower. Entei dodges it, then jumps up some crystals to try another Hyper Beam. It barely touches Charizard's tail.

Suddenly, more step-like spikes begin to pop out of the crystal mansion. Entei climbs them like a stairway that leads it all the way back up to battle airborne Charizard.

Standing on a high spike, Entei sends another strong purple Shadow Ball over to Charizard. It dodges it, but the crystal mansion takes the hit hard. A fireball bursts into the air from the impact.

Now, back at the top of the tower, Entei shoots a sharp Hyper Beam. Charizard responds with a fiery stream of Flamethrower. But they're both too quick to take a hit.

Charizard swoops around to face Entei, now standing back on the mansion floor. Charizard fires Flamethrower, while Entei shoots another Hyper Beam.

"DO YOU THINK WE'RE GOING TO GET A BIGGER PART IN THE NEXT MOVIE?" —MEOWTH

Entei leaps off the top of the tower, and again, crystal spikes pop out to offer steps for the Legendary Pokémon. As it climbs back up, Ash asks Charizard to give this next attack its all. So, Charizard surrounds Entei in swirling flames with Fire Spin. Entei yelps, feeling the burn.

Entei leaps out and onto the other tower, responding by unleashing a Hyper Beam blast. Charizard dodges it. Then, Ash takes over, using his strongest weapon—his words. Ash pleads with Entei to end the battle and let Molly go back to the real world with Ash and his friends.

Entei responds with a fierce no by way of two intense Hyper Beams. Then, it works up a big purple Shadow Ball. Ash thinks fast and has Charizard block the attack with Flamethrower. But the Shadow Ball grows bigger and stronger in midair. When it explodes, it sends fire and smoke everywhere. But Ash, Charizard, and Entei are completely unfazed. The battle rages on!

Entei lets out a roar so strong, spikes break out of the tower, creating a storm of crystal shards. Then, Entei jumps down its spiky steps and tackles Charizard.

Charizard tries to fire back Flamethrower to throw Entei off, but it chases Charizard up the tower again, leaping from one new crystal spike to another.

Charizard is swooping around to avoid the emerging spikes, but one smacks it right in the face. Woozy, it falls onto another spike. Then, Entei seizes the opportunity to fire a bright Shadow Ball in close range. It's so strong that it breaks the spike, and Ash and Charizard fall down to the floor of the crystal mansion.

Charizard is left unable to battle, but Entei puts its paw right on Charizard's neck, vowing to end it with another close-range Shadow Ball. But before Entei can fire its final attack, Molly rushes over and pleads with her "papa" to end the fighting. Watching her treasured Entei and Charizard battle so viciously has frightened her. Crying into Entei's furry leg, she begs Entei to stop the battle.

Brock and Misty are so proud of Molly for standing up for what she believes in and for Charizard that they tell her someday she'll make a great Trainer and possibly even become a Gym Leader. At the end of this epic battle, she finally sees that she belongs in the real world with her new friends Ash, Pikachu, Brock, Misty, and Delia.

PokÉMoN: LuCARIo AND THE MYSTERY OF MEW

STORY

Centuries ago, before even Poké Balls existed, two armies clashed in a valley, threatening to destroy the neighboring land of Cameran. Although it had no fight and took no side, Cameran was trapped in the middle of their war. If their battle raged on, one side might win, but Cameran had everything to lose. From her castle balcony, the reigning queen of Cameran, Lady Rin, put her faith in her bravest knight, Sir Aaron.

Lucario, Sir Aaron's best friend, calls to him through powerful crystals to warn him of the danger. Pidgeot arrives at the castle to carry Sir Aaron to the scene. As they make their way, they're attacked in midair by Skarmory soldiers. Pidgeot struggles to dodge them all and eventually gets whacked with Steel Wing. Pidgeot soars down to the ground to drop off Sir Aaron before it plunges into the brush.

Sensing the plight of his pal and the man he calls master, Lucario races across the valley to Sir Aaron. The Aura Pokémon is ready to help, but Sir Aaron has a different plan.

"I have abandoned the queen and the kingdom," Sir Aaron says. "I'll never return."

Shocked, Lucario chases after Sir Aaron. But Lucario is quickly silenced when the knight throws down a staff with a crystal orb. The Aura Pokémon is pulled into the crystal orb, cut off from the world for centuries.

"Why master, why?!" Lucario cries out as it disappears.

From the castle balcony, Lady Rin can hear the Tree of Beginning crying in the distance. Pidgeot returns, with Sir Aaron's crystal cane in its beak. Holding his prized possession, Lady Rin fears this means her knight will not return.

Inside the Tree of Beginning, the Pidgeot that carried Sir Aaron has transformed into the Legendary Ho-Oh. Then, it reveals itself to really be the Mythical Pokémon and master of disguise, Mew.

A sudden burst of light from the Tree of Beginning miraculously washes over the valley. Transformed by the glow, the armies stop their war. Peace is restored, and Lady Rin assumes this must have happened because of her brave knight, Sir Aaron.

Hundreds of years later, Lady Rin's descendent, Lady Ilene, rules over Cameran. The castle has a lively Annual Festival that pays tribute to Sir Aaron. People and Pokémon dress up in costumes, and the main event is a Pokémon Competition. So, of course, Ash Ketchum is there to enter. His friends Brock, May, and Max are there to cheer him on.

Pikachu wins the first round against Breloom, qualifying for the finals. There, Ash and Pikachu face off against a girl named Kidd and her Pokémon pal Weavile. With a Thunderbolt so strong it can be seen from miles away, Ash and Pikachu win the Pokémon Competition!

Later that night at the Festival Ball, Ash is dubbed "Aura Guardian," Sir Aaron's title, for the year. Then, Lady Ilene hands him the crystal cane. Ash is thrilled to hold a relic that belonged to a local legend. But when he looks into the crystal, he is the first person to hear from Lucario.

> ## "YOU WERE MORE TO ME THAN JUST MY STUDENT. YOU WERE MY CLOSEST FRIEND."
> ## —SIR AARON

"Why did you betray me?" Lucario cries out from its crystal cage.

But only Ash seems to have heard the voice. So, Ash shrugs it off, and the ball begins. Brock asks Kidd to dance, even though he doesn't seem to know how. May dances with another Trainer. Max chows down at the buffet. Pikachu dances with a playful Aipom. Ash's Pokémon pals Corphish, Phanpy, Swellow, and Grovyle are hanging out with May's friends Combusken, Munchlax, and Squirtle. Everyone is having so much fun, but Ash is stuck doing his new royal festival duties, sitting on a throne.

Ash is very familiar with three other guests at the ball: Jessie, James, and Meowth. But Ash and his pals can't tell it's Team Rocket because they're disguised in costumes. Meowth is munching on the smorgasbord, but not even free food can distract Jessie from dancing with a handsome stranger. On the other hand, May feels like she's met her dance partner, James, before but can't place where.

May and Ash's Pokémon pals slip out of the ball to play in the palace. Meowth tries to follow them but instead overhears a secret call made by Kidd to her partner, a man named Banks.

Apparently, Kidd is on a mission that is running over budget. She promises Banks that it will all be worth it and asks him to send her a map of the castle. Through a pair of specialized glasses, outfitted with a mic and an earpiece, Kidd can stream all the data Banks sends.

"There's a Mew hiding out here. And I'm planning on hunting it down," Kidd tells Banks.

Through her binoculars, Kidd can't believe what she's seeing. She's disappointed in her Weavile's bad behavior. She's not the only human surprised. Max, wondering where all the Pokémon went at the ball, happens upon the scene. He tries to get in and help, but the door is frozen.

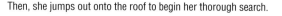

Then, she jumps out onto the roof to begin her thorough search.

"So what's she up to?" Meowth wonders.

Meowth tries to follow Kidd but crash-lands in a room where Pikachu, Corphish, Phanpy, Swellow, Grovyle, Combusken, and Squirtle are all playing with their new friend that looks like Aipom. The Pokémon rush to help poor Meowth.

Through her specialized binoculars, Kidd watches the scene unfold. Before all the Pokémon, Aipom instantly transforms into its true self—Mew. Kidd hands her Pokémon Weavile pals a special transmitter and asks them to plant it on the Mythical Pokémon so she can track it.

Weavile chase down Mew in the playroom and try to freeze it in Icy Wind. Although Mew is able to dodge their frosty attack, Weavile grabs it and holds it against the wall. Pikachu hits it with a jolt of Thundershock. Then, the other Weavile tries to send over Shadow Ball, but Pikachu stops it with a fierce Thunderbolt.

"YA GONNA ATTACK OR DO A BALLET?"
—MEOWTH

"Sir Aaron," Lucario demands answers as it approaches Ash with its eyes closed. "Why did you abandon the queen?"

Ash admits he doesn't understand the question. When Lucario opens its eyes, it sees it's talking to the wrong guy. Embarrassed and confused, Lucario runs out of the ball, through the castle garden.

Lucario returns to the spot where it first began its friendship with Sir Aaron. Memories flood its mind, but they are bittersweet since it feels its Trainer Sir Aaron abandoned it and his duty to the kingdom. When Lucario opens the door, it doesn't see its home. Instead, its old room is now a museum filled with treasures in glass cases.

Lady Ilene, Mime Jr., Nanny, Ash, May, and Brock find Lucario there. Lady Ilene hugs Lucario and tries to explain that it has reemerged far into the future.

"But I was in this room just a few days ago," Lucario says.

"Please believe me," Lady Ilene replies. "It may seem like days ago, but the reality is you haven't walked in this palace for centuries."

Lucario can't believe it. To Lucario, the war that nearly destroyed the area is still top of its mind. So, Lady Ilene takes the opportunity to get Lucario's eyewitness account of the events of their most famous local legend. She wants to know all about Sir Aaron's bravery, but Lucario intends to tell his side of the story.

Suddenly, Mew transforms into Meowth. In unison, Weavile prepare another Ice-type attack, but Pikachu blocks it with a big Thunderbolt. The attacks explode in midair, throwing Pikachu across the room and into the arms of an unlikely Pokémon—Team Rocket's Meowth. Before there can be any more fighting, Mew Teleports, taking Meowth and Pikachu along with it.

Mew again changes to Pidgeot, flying Meowth and Pikachu to the Tree of Beginning. Back at the Festival Ball, the staff speaks out.

"It's that voice again," Ash says, mystified.

Then, Lady Ilene asks Ash to assume the pose of the Guardian to signal the start of the Festival fireworks. But an even bigger lightshow happens inside the castle. The crystal cane begins to shake and beam brightly. Then, Lucario appears.

"Sir Aaron deserted the queen," Lucario says angrily. "He fled and trapped me inside the staff."

May, Ash, and Brock are all surprised to hear its testimony. Lady Ilene promises to help Lucario uncover the truth and the fiction in the legend.

"I will do what I can to help you," Lucario vows to Lady Ilene.

Lucario adds that it senses that Ash's Aura is just like Sir Aaron's.

Suddenly, Max comes running in to tell his friends that he spotted Mew! Shortly thereafter, Kidd arrives and tells the same story, explaining that Pikachu and Meowth disappeared with the Mythical Pokémon. Lady Ilene and Nanny explain that Mew loves to come to the castle to play with their toys, but it's never returned any it's taken.

"Does anyone know where Mew took them?" Ash asks. "I have to go rescue Pikachu!"

Lady Ilene leads them all out on her balcony. From there, they can see the ancient Tree of Beginning. She explains that although it looks like greenery, it is actually a rock formation that Mew calls home. Then, Lady Ilene warns them that Mew can change its form and rarely appears as itself. So, they'll need to depend on Lucario.

"The legend says Lucario could lead the Guardian to anyone because it had learned the power to see the Aura inside all things," Nanny explains.

But that's not the only special talent along for their difficult journey. Now that she's out of her costume, Brock recognizes Kidd to be Kidd Summers, the famous athlete and adventurer he has seen on TV. In fact, she holds more world records than anyone.

"I came here to explore the Tree of Beginning and solve the mystery of what it really is," Kidd admits. "Yet another first for me."

Ash thanks Lucario for helping him find his friend. Hurt after Sir Aaron abandoned it, Lucario doesn't feel it has any friends, and it doesn't want any, either. But it has agreed to go because Lady Ilene asked it to.

So, the super group of Ash, Misty, Brock, Lucario, and Kidd head out on the road to the Tree of Beginning. While the crew rides in Kidd's vehicle, Jessie and James have snuck in the trunk to find their friend, Meowth. Lucario leads the way through a thick fog, guided by Aura.

"Long ago, there were humans who could sense Aura and control its power, like Sir Aaron, for instance. Apparently he passed his skills on to Lucario," Kidd explains.

According to Lucario, Ash also possesses this Aura power.

"BUT NO MATTER HOW HOT IT GETS, WE ALWAYS KEEP OUR COOL." —JAMES

Meanwhile, inside the Tree of Beginning, Pikachu wakes up in a pile of leaves to find itself in Mew's home. It is so green and lush. There are rock ledges covered in grass, with pockets of glistening crystals and colorful flowers. Throughout the area are beautiful blue creeks and even a few waterfalls. Plus, Mew has a very impressive collection of toys.

On the road, Ash and his crew come across some active geysers. So, they are forced to wait until the path is clear. They pass the time swimming in some hot springs. Well, everyone except Lucario. He is remembering the last time he was at these springs. It was with Sir Aaron, who encouraged him to dip his toes in. Lucario enjoyed it back then, but when Ash suggests that Lucario join them now, it walks away in a huff.

From the water, May spots an iridescent flower bud on a rocky ledge. Ash climbs up to get a closer look. When he slips, he accidentally rips the flower out, but luckily, May catches it.

Later that night, Ash goes to replant this special blossom. When the Time Flower is in his hands, it projects the past when Ash ripped it out of the ground as he went falling from the ledge.

"What's going on?" May says, surprised by the vision.

Kidd explains Ash is holding is Time Flower, a special blossom that, through Aura, can help someone see things that happened in the past.

But Lucario doesn't need to touch the Time Flower to be reminded of the past. It is haunted by what now seem like painful memories of Sir Aaron, the friend whom Lucario feels betrayed by.

"You humans can't be trusted!" Lucario says.

Then, Lucario adds that it would bet that Ash would abandon Pikachu one day. Hurt by its cruel words, Ash lashes out, telling Lucario he bets that it deserted the cause and the queen, not Sir Aaron. Lucario then suggests that Pikachu ran away from Ash to be free of him.

"Take that back!" Ash shouts, tackling Lucario to the ground.

The two grapple as they roll down a hill and into a river. May and Brock shout from the sidelines, trying to get them to stop, but they won't. So, when Lucario throws Ash across the water, May jumps in to hold him back.

"That's enough, Ash!" May says.

Lucario walks off, but the tension is still there.

Ash is upset by the things Lucario said. May reminds Ash that he also said some awful stuff.

Max goes to talk to Lucario, and he brings a big chocolate bar. Lucario has never had the delicious treat before. It tastes good, and Max's kindness makes it feel better.

The next morning, Lucario continues to lead the crew to the Tree of Beginning. On the way, Lucario realizes it is at the place where it was trapped in the crystal staff. It kneels on the ground, accidentally triggering a Time Flower.

Now, Ash and the crew see that fateful day. They watch Sir Aaron fly off on Pidgeot, seemingly abandoning both Lucario and the fight as the army charges into the area. With all its might, Lucario tries to fight the army in the Time Flower vision. But suddenly, just as quickly as the army of the past arrived, it disappears into thin air as the Time Flower closes back up. However, the case of the legend has been reopened. After seeing Lucario's painful memory with their own eyes, all of the crew now believes Lucario's story, including Ash. He walks over to the Aura Pokémon.

"I'm sorry I said all the stuff last night. It wasn't right," Ash says, apologizing to Lucario with tears in his eyes.

Now that everyone knows it was telling the truth, Lucario feels a sense of relief and closure. Ash then promises Lucario that he will never abandon Pikachu. It

seems that the two have come to respect each other, but the real trouble has just begun.

"Regirock!" the giant Pokémon shouts, surprising the crew.

Then, it lifts Kidd's vehicle into the air and tosses it like it's a ball. Lucario holds it off while the crew runs for it. The Aura Pokémon leads them straight into the Tree of Beginning. They are all in awe of the spectacular, ancient Pokémon habitat. Cradily, Lileep, Omanyte, and Omastar bathe in the clear blue creek. Aerodactyl, Altaria, and Ledyba fly above. Armaldo snacks on berries. Nidorina and Nidorino walk through the grass. It's amazing to see all these happy Pokémon, but Ash has another one on his mind—his best buddy Pikachu.

Yesterday, they may have been an unlikely pair. But today, Ash and his new friend Lucario run off together to find Pikachu.

Kidd also snaps into action, sending out a chain of survey robots to explore the area and collect data. At his supercomputer, Banks is busy analyzing all the information from these rock formations. He can't believe the scientific breakthrough the survey robots are reporting. It seems the Tree of Beginning is a living thing. It gets its energy from sunlight and is part of the local ecosystem.

Suddenly, an alert beams across Banks' computer. Something is wrong. Some of the crystals have turned red hot.

On the other side of the Tree of Beginning, Pikachu can sense Ash is in the area. It runs to the edge of a rock ledge and shouts for its pal.

"Pikachu!" Ash hollers back, happy to hear he's close to his best friend.

Then, a third call rings through the air: Regice. It blocks Ash with Ice-type attacks. Ash tries to explain that he's just here to find his friend, but that doesn't stop the giant Legendary Pokémon. So, Lucario and Ash race to find another path to Pikachu.

Along the way, they're reunited with May, Max, Brock, and Kidd. Regice is now chasing after the whole crew. Then, they run into Team Rocket, who are being chased by Registeel and Regirock.

"You know we're desperate if we're coming to you," Jessie admits.

Lucario tells them to run. Then, it tries to hold off the Legendary Pokémon with a powerful Focus Blast.

Jessie, James, Ash, Brock, Max, May, Kidd, and Lucario run over a rock bridge. When they're safely across, Lucario fires another Focus Blast to break up the bridge. Regirock and Registeel are trapped on the other side.

But inside another rock tunnel, they're hardly safe. A strange bright red blob is swallowing Jessie and James whole.

While the crew keeps running, Kidd sends images of the red blobs from her specialized glasses over to Banks to analyze.

"Banks, what is that thing?" Kidd asks.

"I guess the best equivalent would be white blood cells," Banks explains, reading the data.

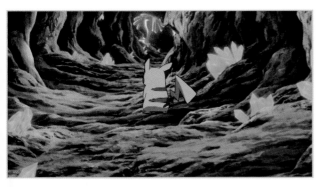

It seems the Tree of Beginning produces these red blobs like antibodies to protect the habitat and destroy foreign objects. But they only swallow people, not Pokémon. While the crew keeps running to escape the red blobs, Ash decides to stay to find Pikachu and act as a decoy for his friends. Ash is very surprised when Lucario stays back with him.

"I won't leave you until you find Pikachu. I know you'd do the same for me," Lucario vows.

Ash smiles, happy for his new true-blue pal. Then, he calls on two more friends for backup, Corphish and Grovyle.

Unfortunately, deep in the Tree of Beginning, May, Max, and Brock don't get very far before the red blobs catch up with them. Before they're swallowed, they take out all their Pokémon. They are so sad to see their Trainers disappear into the red blobs. Luckily, Kidd is able to escape.

Meanwhile, Ash has caught up with Pikachu in a rock crevice with a network of crystal roots. He can hear that his pal is close. So, Ash boldly jumps from root to root to make his way to his pal. But when Pikachu gets blown off a root by a strong gust of wind, Ash bravely risks it all to catch his best friend in midair. They're happy to finally be reunited, but they're also in free fall.

Kidd arrives, and not a moment too soon. She springs into action using a special grappling hook and rope to swing and rescue her buddies Ash and Pikachu. After they land safely on a rock ledge, Ash thanks the real-life action hero Kidd.

"Pika pika Pikachu!" it cheers, happy to be reunited with Ash.

"I WON'T LEAVE YOU UNTIL YOU FIND PIKACHU. I KNOW YOU'D DO THE SAME FOR ME." —LUCARIO

Then, Ash introduces his best friend to his new friend, Lucario. And Pikachu introduces Ash to its new Mythical Pokémon pal, Mew. But their meet and greet is disrupted by Regice.

Kidd, Ash, Pikachu, Lucario, Meowth, Mew, Corphish, and Grovyle run through a tunnel to escape the attack. But inside, they're faced with red blobs and Registeel. Kidd and Ash get swallowed, and Registeel grabs Lucario.

"Pikachu, you can't save me. Just take care of yourself. I love you, pal! You're my best friend; remember that!" Ash says, wrapped in a red blob.

Pikachu refuses to give up and tries to pull Ash out, but it's no use. The red blob shrinks until it disappears.

"Ash!" Lucario cries out.

Mew places its paws on a crystal. It begins to glow green. And soon, every crystal in the Tree of Beginning has the same glow. Mew uses its power to return all of the missing Trainers. Their Pokémon rejoice.

But before Ash can thank Mew, it sinks to the ground. It's clear the Mythical Pokémon needs help. Kidd scoops it up in her arms.

The crystals that once glowed with power are being reduced to dust by a red-hot heat. Banks calls Kidd to alert her to the emergency. The ecosystem is breaking down. Mew and the Tree of Beginning create a delicate balance, and that balance has been disturbed. The Tree of Beginning is headed for a catastrophic collapse. If it doesn't survive, neither will Mew.

With its last bit of strength, Mew points Kidd, Ash, and Lucario deep into the heart of the Tree of Beginning. Inside the round room, crystal roots grow from a giant crystal formation on the ceiling. An identical crystal formation is directly beneath it, and a stream of energy flows between them.

At the edge of the crystal formation, Lucario thinks it spots Sir Aaron's gloves. It uses Aura to confirm that they are actually his. It becomes clear that after sealing Lucario in the crystal staff, Sir Aaron came here.

Ash finds a Time Flower nearby, and the unwritten part of the Legend of the Champion unfolds before their eyes.

When Sir Aaron arrived hundreds of years ago, he came to the heart of the Tree of Beginning to sacrifice his Aura to save the local people of Cameran. He called out to Mew to make his selfless offer.

"The power of Aura will prevail," Sir Aaron said, covering Mew in its glow.

Sir Aaron cried out with all his might as Aura exploded with strength.

Then, the Time Flower ends the vision, sealing Sir Aaron's heroic deed. Lucario kneels down before the crystal and bows its head.

"Forgive me for doubting you, Master," Lucario says.

Then, Mew explains to Lucario that it must use Aura to save the Tree of Beginning. Kidd tries to stop it, warning Lucario that it will meet the same fate at Sir Aaron. But that is a sacrifice Lucario is also willing to make for the greater good.

"The Aura is with me!" Lucario cries out.

But Lucario isn't strong enough alone to make an impact. Ash steps up and slips on Sir Aaron's gloves.

"You said that my Aura was like Sir Aaron's," Ash says. "It's time to test if it's really true."

Ash refuses to let the Tree of Beginning and all the Pokémon in it suffer when he knows he can help. Together with Lucario, they use the power of Aura to surround Mew in a glow. At the last second, Lucario pushes Ash away to protect him.

"Leave the rest to me, Ash," Lucario tells him.

Lucario focuses all of its might, and Mew ascends to the top of the heart. The green glow that surrounds it grows so strong that it nurtures the entire Tree of Beginning back to health instantly.

The crystals across the area, even over in Cameran, shoot a green light skyward, signaling the restoration.

Across the valley, Lady Ilene and Nanny rejoice at the sight! Banks calls Kidd to congratulate her on the monumental victory. He plans to call the press immediately, but Kidd stops him. She doesn't want her world record to destroy the glory of the hidden treasure that is the Tree of Beginning.

Lucario sits down to rest next to the crystal where Sir Aaron is suspended in time. There, the Aura Pokémon triggers a vision from another Time Flower. This part of the past is just after Sir Aaron gave his all to save Cameran. In his final moment, Sir Aaron feels guilty for sealing Lucario in the crystal staff without an explanation, but he did it to protect his best friend. Sir Aaron clings to a wish that someday, Lucario will be released into a peaceful time.

Lucario's eyes fill with tears as it learns the whole truth. Now Lucario is not only in a time of peace, but its heart is also at peace. Jolts of Aura pulse across its body. Ash is worried his new friend is slipping away.

"I have to go, Ash," Lucario says. "Aaron is waiting for me."

And with that, Lucario disappears, taking the form of a green glow. Another green glow rises from the crystal, and the two glows become one big ball of light that rises into the giant crystal in the ceiling.

Then, Ash and Kidd also reunite with Ash's friends May, Max, and Brock. They're happy to see each other but sad to lose their friend Lucario.

"No, Lucario isn't gone," Ash promises. "Its Aura is with me."

LOCATIONS
CAMERAN

A brick bridge leads travelers to the beautiful city of Cameran. Famous for an Annual Festival that honors their local hero, Sir Aaron, many people and Pokémon flock to the area for the Pokémon Competition and celebrations.

THE CASTLE

The jewel in the crown of Cameran is the spectacular castle. A huge white brick building, it is more than just a home; its many rooms are filled with different activities during the Annual Festival. Crystals connected to the Tree of Beginning are scattered across the castle. There's a clock at the top of its tallest spire.

BALL ROOM

During the Annual Festival, Lady Ilene hosts a ball for all the travelers. Before the dancing begins, she congratulates Ash on his Pokémon Competition win and awards him a crystal staff that once belonged to Sir Aaron. At the time, Ash and Lady Ilene have no idea that what's inside that crystal will change the course of history.

COSTUME ROOM

Inside the castle is a room dedicated to costume options for the Annual Festival. All the outfits are designed just like the clothing the citizens of Cameran wore in Sir Aaron's time. Attendees can go in and pick the perfect one out. It's there that Ash, May, Max, Brock, and even Pikachu find awesome new outfits.

TOY ROOM

Arguably, the toy room is Mythical Pokémon Mew's favorite part of the castle. The room has fun toys and plenty of places to play. This is one amazing space where you're free to bounce a ball inside.

During the Annual Festival Ball, Mew shows Pikachu, Corphish, Phanpy, Swellow, Grovyle, Squirtle, Munchlax, and Combusken the toy room. Although it starts as fun and games, when Kidd sends in Weavile to put a tracking device on Mew, their playtime turns into battle time.

"NO, LUCARIO ISN'T GONE. ITS AURA IS WITH ME." —ASH

THE BALCONY

Perched on the side of the castle, this balcony provides the best view of the Tree of Beginning. Lady Ilene leads Ash and his crew onto this balcony to discuss their mission. She also watches their journey with Mime Jr. and Nanny from this treasured spot.

GREAT HALL

From her throne in the Great Hall, Lady Ilene hears Lucario's account of what happened on the fateful day when Sir Aaron disappeared. Next to her throne is an incredible mural of the champion.

LUCARIO'S ROOM/MUSEUM

When Lucario is released from the crystal staff, he discovers his former room in the castle has been converted into a museum filled with artifacts from Sir Aaron and Lady Rin.

THE TERRACE

From the castle terrace, Lady Rin watched over the valley and the Tree of Beginning.

THE VALLEY

An expansive valley connects the Tree of Beginning and the kingdom of Cameran.

Centuries ago, two armies clashed in the rocky valley. Lucario and Sir Aaron journeyed to this area to try to stop the violence and protect Cameran.

Then, hundreds of years later, Lucario leads Ash and his crew across the valley to the Tree of Beginning.

THE HOT SPRINGS

When some active geysers that are shooting water like a fountain into the street block the road, Ash and his crew decide to take a swim in the nearby hot springs. From the water, May spots the first Time Flower.

LUCARIO'S LAST SPOT

Along the road to the Tree of Beginning, Lucario senses the rocky spot where its most painful memory happened. At the top of a cliff, Sir Aaron sealed it in the crystal staff and left on the back of Pidgeot.

TREE OF BEGINNING

Across the valley from the castle is the ancient Tree of Beginning. However, its name is misleading. It might look like a tree, but it's actually a giant rock formation.

There are many tunnels, cliffs, and crevices that make up the Tree of Beginning. The rocky terrain is covered with grass, patches of wildflowers, fruit trees, and crystal formations. Through it runs a beautiful blue creek and a few waterfalls.

Many wild Pokémon (like Cradily, Lileep, Omanyte, Omastar, Aerodactyl, Altaria, Ledyba, Armaldo, Nidorina, Nidorino, and even Mew) call the Tree of Beginning home.

According to Banks, the Tree of Beginning is part of the local ecosystem. It might be mostly rock, but it's a living thing that gets its energy from sunlight.

THE HEART

Deep in the center of the Tree of Beginning is a mystical part called the heart. There are crystal roots that act like columns. In the middle of the round room, there is a stunning crystal formation on the ceiling, and twin formations on the floor directly beneath it. Between the twins runs a surging energy.

The heart is the place of the Tree of Beginning where you can get to the heart of a problem. There, Aura can heal tremendous troubles like the ancient war and also strengthen Mew.

When Mew leads Ash, Lucario, Pikachu, and Kidd to the heart, they find Sir Aaron's gloves there. Then, two Time Flowers fill in the blanks in the legend's story, proving to Lucario that Sir Aaron was a true friend and champion.

MEW'S HOME

Marked by a tall pile of toys it's collected from the castle, Mew welcomes Pikachu and Meowth to its lush little home inside the Tree of Beginning.

BANKS' COMMAND CENTER

Sitting high up in a skyscraper, Banks' command center is full of amazing resources. One wall is completely covered in screens, another in books. Right in the center are a keyboard, buttons, a comfy chair, a treadmill, and even more screens. It's an impressive setup for an even more impressive guy, Banks. Kidd really relies on the data he analyzes from the command center.

CHARACTERS

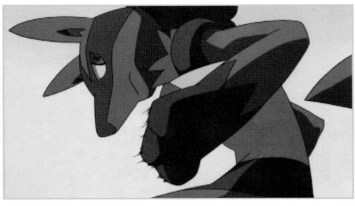

ASH

In Cameran, Ash not only wins an honor bestowed on Sir Aaron, but he also discovers he has the same Aura as the legendary champion. He takes this power seriously, and when the time comes, Ash is brave enough to use it—no matter what the cost to his personal safety might be.

THE AURA GUARDIAN

With his best buddy, Pikachu, Ash wins the Annual Festival Pokémon Competition. His prize is a two-part honor. Firstly, he will be called the Aura Guardian for a year. Secondly, he is the temporary caretaker of Sir Aaron's crystal staff. But little did Ash know he's the only one with the special Aura power to release Lucario from said staff.

WHEN COSPLAY IS REAL

In the costume room at the castle, Ash picks out an outfit that looks just like Sir Aaron's uniform. Little does he know at the time that they share so much more than style! When Lucario returns, it has to do a double take to make sure that Ash isn't the original Aura Guardian himself.

PIKACHU

In one day, Pikachu wins two battles. Along with its Trainer, Ash, it wins the Annual Festival Pokémon Competition. Then, during the ball that evening, it defends Mew from a pair of Weavile. Exhausted, Pikachu then passes out. So, Mew takes it back to its home in the Tree of Beginning. Although it's in a magical place, Pikachu misses its best friend. But fear not, Pikachu, Ash is on his way!

CORPHISH

PHANPY

SWELLOW

GROVYLE

MAY

Ash's travel companion, May, is a helpful friend with a good eye. She's the one who spots the first Time Flower. She also steps in to stop Ash when his argument with Lucario goes too far.

COMBUSKEN

MUNCHLAX

SQUIRTLE

MAX

Max seems to always be in the right place at the right time. At the castle, May's little brother sees Mew Teleport right before his eyes. So, when Pikachu and Meowth are missing, Max runs to tell his friend Ash and then helps him on his mission.

Then, after Lucario and Ash's big blow-out fight, Max comforts the Aura Pokémon by offering it its first taste of chocolate.

BROCK

At first, Brock thinks the Pokémon Competition runner-up is cute. But when he sees her out of her costume, he realizes she's the famous adventurer Kidd Summers, and he falls head over heels for her. He's a big fan!

At the ball, Brock does get the chance to dance with his heroine, Kidd. But he's so nervous that he forgets how to move to the beat.

MUDKIP

FORRETRESS

TEAM ROCKET: JESSIE, JAMES, AND MEOWTH

Always one step behind Ash and his crew, Jessie, James, and Meowth make it to Cameran for the Annual Festival. However, this time, everyone is wearing a costume. So, the trio's inclination toward wearing disguises matches the dress code. They fit right in!

DANCING IN THE DARK

At the Festival Ball, James accidentally winds up partnering with May. As they dance, May gets the feeling she knows her partner, but James insists they've never met.

TURNING OVER A NEW LEAF

When Pikachu passes out from protecting Mew from Weavile, Meowth finally gets its paws on the prized Pokémon. But it doesn't even try to catch it. Strangely enough, after overhearing a conversation Kidd has, Meowth thinks she's up to no good. And Meowth, well, it actually wants to do good and keep tabs on her. When Meowth winds up mixed up in Pikachu's battle with the Weavile, Mew even thinks it's a good guy and brings Meowth back to its home in the Tree of Beginning. Meowth's Festival costume is a knight in shining armor, and it seems to be living up to its outfit.

MEOWTH OR BUST

When Jessie and James catch wind of Meowth's disappearance, they sneak in Kidd's trunk to hitch a ride to the Tree of Beginning. They might not have the best track record with Pokémon, but they sure do love their buddy Meowth.

CACNEA

WOBBUFFET

CHIMECHO

SIR AARON

The hero of the famous Legend of the Champion is Sir Aaron. He lived in a time hundreds of years ago, before there were even Poké Balls. Back then, Sir Aaron was the protector of Cameran. He possessed the unique power of Aura, and he trained his best friend, Lucario, to harness its power of Aura.

At the time, he was Lady Rin's closest advisor. He took his job very seriously and would do anything for his queen.

BRAVERY KNOWS NO BOUNDS

When Cameran faced its biggest threat yet, Sir Aaron was ready to make the greatest sacrifice. But in order to stop the war and protect his best friend, he lied to Lucario. He pretended to abandon the Aura Pokémon and the queen. Then he trapped Lucario in a crystal staff before flying away on Pidgeot.

But that was no ordinary Pidgeot—it was actually Mew that carried him to the heart of the Tree of Beginning. However, it would take Lucario a long time and a Time Flower to discover that Sir Aaron saved the day and did everything he did out of love for his friends and his homeland.

TRIBUTE TO SIR AARON

To celebrate the champion, Sir Aaron, Cameran holds a festival every year. People and Pokémon from all over come to celebrate his memory. All over the castle in Cameran, there are murals of his brave deeds that protected the kingdom.

As part of the Annual Festival, there is a Pokémon Competition. The winner is dubbed with the same title that Sir Aaron was known by—the Guardian of Aura.

AURA TWIN

It's rare that someone possesses the same Aura. But Lucario is freed because the crystal staff is finally in the hands of someone with the same Aura as Sir Aaron: our hero, Ash Ketchum.

LADY RIN

Back in Sir Aaron's time, Lady Rin ruled Cameran as its queen. When the war began, he begged her to flee the city. But like a true leader, Lady Rin refused to leave her citizens.

LADY ILENE

The direct descendent of Lady Rin, the reigning queen of Cameran looks like her twin. Lady Ilene knows the Legend of the Champion by heart and presides over the Annual Festival. It is Lady Ilene who awards Ash his prize for winning the Pokémon Competition: the crystal staff that belonged to Sir Aaron and the title of Guardian of Aura.

When Lucario returns, she welcomes it into its castle home with open arms. She feels for it and gives it a big hug. A sympathetic leader, Lady Ilene understands how hard it must be for Lucario to land hundreds of years into the future. She listens to Lucario's side of the legend story and vows to help it find out the truth.

Lady Ilene's Pokémon pal loves to impersonate other people.

MIME JR.

NANNY

Nanny is always by Lady Ilene's side. She knows all about the castle and the Legend of the Champion. Nanny also keeps Ash in line at the Festival Ball, ensuring that he adheres to the traditions and is dignified.

KIDD

Little did Ash know that his opponent in the final round of the Annual Festival Pokémon Competition was none other than the famous Kidd Summers! She's not just a Trainer—she's a woman who holds so many world records that she holds the world record for world records. Part athlete, part adventurer, Kidd has soared higher, dived deeper, and space-traveled farther than anyone else. And her biggest fan is Brock!

She's in Cameran to locate the Mythical Pokémon Mew, another challenge for the record books. But when she finds Mew in the Tree of Beginning, she cancels her mission. She has too much heart to turn the natural wonder into a tourist attraction.

Along the way, Kidd generously volunteers her resources, her research data, her vehicle, and her skills to help Ash find Pikachu. In fact, she even rescues them both when they're free-falling through crystal roots. Ash and his crew certainly lucked into meeting this real-life superhero.

WEAVILE

Kidd asks her Pokémon pals Weavile to put a tracking device on Mew, but their attempt descends into a battle that forces Mew to flee with weakened Pikachu and Meowth.

BANKS

Kidd's right-hand man, Banks, is there to scan all the data she collects. From a command center, he communicates with Kidd. He puts together information and makes important connections that help her on her missions. It was Banks who figured out that the Tree of Beginning is a living thing. He's someone Kidd has really come to count on when she's out in the field.

LEGENDARY AND MYTHICAL POKÉMON

MEW:
THE NEW SPECIES POKÉMON

Height	1'04"
Weight	8.8 lbs
Type	Psychic

Mew calls the Tree of Beginning across the valley from Cameran home. But it's more than just a place it lives: the two give each other life. If one is hurting, so is the other one. The Tree of Beginning and Mew are connected. They depend on each other for survival.

There is only one thing that can restore the Tree of Beginning and Mew's strength: the power of Aura. Back hundreds of years ago, Mew took the form of Pidgeot to carry Sir Aaron to the heart of the Tree of Beginning so he could harness his power to end the war. His best friend, Lucario, and Ash followed in his footsteps more than a thousand years later to restore that delicate balance.

TOY COLLECTOR EXTRAORDINAIRE

Playful Mew loves nothing more than games and toys. It has quite an impressive stash, or rather a mountain, of toys it has taken from the castle in Cameran. Mew tries to cheer Pikachu up with a Hitmontop top and a Shuckle-shaped whistle.

SIR AARON'S SECRET HELPER

Centuries ago, Mew, disguised as Pidgeot, teamed up with Sir Aaron to save Cameran by carrying him to the Tree of Beginning. They had a special bond that saved the day! Then, as Pidgeot, it delivered the crystal staff to Lady Rin for safekeeping. However, until Ash and Lucario uncovered the truth, no one knew that Mew had a hand in the legend.

MASTER OF DISGUISE

Rarely seen as Mew, the ancient Mythical Pokémon is known for its ability to quickly transform itself into other Pokémon.

ALL OF MEW'S POKÉMON TRANSFORMATIONS IN THE MOVIE

PIDGEOT   HO-OH   TAILOW   PICHU   TREECKO

MIME JR.   AIPOM   PIKACHU   MEOWTH

LEGENDARY POKÉMON THAT GUARD THE TREE OF BEGINNING

REGIROCK:
THE ROCK PEAK POKÉMON

Height	5'07"
Weight	507.1 lbs
Type	Rock

REGISTEEL:
THE IRON POKÉMON

Height	6'03"
Weight	451.9 lbs
Type	Steel

REGICE:
THE ICEBERG POKÉMON

Height	5'11"
Weight	385.8 lbs
Type	Ice

FEATURED POKÉMON

LUCARIO

When Lucario is finally released from the crystal staff, it tells a very different story than the legend that has been passed down through the years. Even though it seems like ancient history that happened hundreds of years ago, Lucario wants to find the truth behind what really happened that fateful day, and it won't give up until it has the answer.

AURA OR AREN'T YOU?

According to the legend, Lucario could find anyone because it had learned the power to see the Aura inside everything. In other words, it could recognize someone by their Aura.

Lucario initially mistook Ash for Sir Aaron, only to find out, strangely enough, they had the exact same Aura.

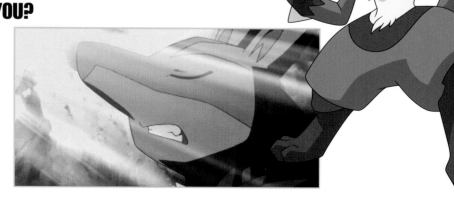

THE CANDY MAN CAN

Lucario is sincere, righteous, powerful, and intelligent. But it doesn't seem to have a funny bone. If Lucario wore a suit, it would never loosen the tie. It's just not a laid-back kind of guy. However, when Max tries to cheer Lucario up after its fight with Ash, he does get a smile. All it took was a bite of Max's candy, which was actually Lucario's first taste of chocolate. Lucario finally saw how delicious life in the future could be!

TWO WRONGS EVENTUALLY MADE A RIGHT

At first, Lucario was only going to the Tree of Beginning out of a sense of duty to the queen. Lucario did not trust Ash; the two were like oil and water. Ash didn't like Lucario's aloof attitude. Lucario felt like it had been abandoned by Sir Aaron and didn't trust any humans, especially Ash. Eventually, their anger erupted in petty name-calling that led to a physical fight where they both ended all washed up—in the banks of a river, that is. Both Ash and Lucario were in the wrong. But eventually, in this one case, Ash and Lucario proved the old adage incorrect: two wrongs made a right!

They stuck together through the journey as teammates, not friends. Through his devotion to finding Pikachu, Ash was able to prove to Lucario that he had heart. Then, when Ash opened a Time Flower right where Lucario was sealed in the crystal staff, he saw with his own eyes that Sir Aaron had abandoned Lucario. Both Ash and Lucario had told the truth, and now, they shared a bond of trust strong enough to turn them into an unstoppable duo. Together, Ash and Lucario joined their power of Aura to save Mew and the Tree of Beginning.

ALL'S WELL THAT ENDS WELL

Lucario might have accompanied Ash on his journey to find Pikachu only because Lady Ilene asked it to. But along the way, Lucario found exactly what it was looking for: answers. Why had his best friend, Sir Aaron, abandoned him? What happened to Sir Aaron? And how did the epic war end?

One Time Flower revealed that Sir Aaron had sealed Lucario in the staff, pretending to abandon it. But more Time Flowers, found in the heart of the Tree of Beginning, revealed Sir Aaron's final moments. It became clear that he had put on an act to protect Lucario. Sir Aaron knew he would drain his power of Aura to stop the war and save Cameran, but he knew he couldn't stop Lucario from the same sacrifice. So, to save his best friend, Sir Aaron sealed Lucario in the crystal staff, hoping it would be freed in more peaceful times.

Seeing Sir Aaron's bravery and the full story, Lucario realized that Sir Aaron was the amazing man he had known, a true hero.

HOUNDOOM
THE DARK POKÉMON

During the great war that threatened Cameran, Houndoom from the red army attacked Lucario.

Height: 4'07"
Weight: 77.2 lbs

DARK	FIRE

BONSLY
THE BONSAI POKÉMON

Along the road, the crew met a ravenous Bonsly that tried to eat Kidd's lunch. Who can resist Brock's cooking? Luckily, no one went hungry when Lucario caught it and gave it a berry instead. Bonsly then followed its new pals through their journey to the Tree of Beginning.

Height: 1'08"
Weight: 33.1 lbs

ROCK

POKÉMON THAT LIVE AT THE TREE OF BEGINNING

POKÉMON SPOTTED IN THE ANNUAL FESTIVAL POKÉMON COMPETITION

THE LEGEND OF THE CHAMPION

Hundreds of years ago, two armies consisting of thousands of angry people and Pokémon clashed in the valley between Cameran and the Tree of Beginning. Lady Rin, the reigning queen, knew that no matter which army was victorious, her kingdom was caught in the middle and would be destroyed. She and her people were peaceful and wanted no part in the war.

To protect the kingdom, Lady Rin's champion, Sir Aaron, bravely stepped up to put an end to the war. He had the unique power of Aura, and because of this, he was known as the Guardian of Aura. The wise and courageous knight knew that there was only one hope for the kingdom: he had to journey to the Tree of Beginning, the home of Mew. He flew on a Pidgeot into the heart of the incredible, ancient landmark.

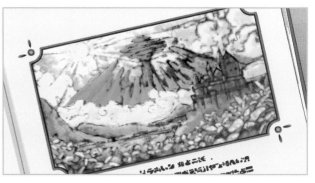

Once inside, a green glow burst from the Tree of Beginning and the local crystals. The terrible armies that threatened Cameran were instantly changed. Anger and hatred were replaced with understanding and hope. Peace was restored.

For hundreds of years, no one knew exactly how he had done it, but Sir Aaron never returned, and neither did his best friend, Lucario. Pidgeot returned all that remained of the Guardian of Aura—his crystal staff. And that is why Sir Aaron will forever be celebrated as a true hero who saved Cameran.

INTERESTING ITEMS

CRYSTAL COMMUNICATION

Hundreds of years ago, there were no cell phones. Lucario called Sir Aaron using the power of Aura to communicate through the local crystals. It placed its hand on one, and the sound would travel through to Sir Aaron. This technique is how Lucario, while in the valley, was able to warn Sir Aaron and Lady Rin about the war between the two armies.

THE WAR THAT ALMOST DESTROYED THE KINGDOM

During the time of Lady Rin and Sir Aaron, two armies clashed in the valley. One was dressed in red armor, the other in green armor. There were thousands of soldiers, both people and Pokémon. However, they were not fighting in their own kingdoms: their battle raged near Cameran. So although Cameran had no stake in the quarrel, it would suffer. The champion of Cameran, Sir Aaron, stepped up with his best friend, Lucario, to stop the war. Centuries later, the legend says the kingdom was saved by Sir Aaron's bravery, but no one was exactly sure how until Ash Ketchum was on the case.

THE CRYSTAL STAFF

The Legend of the Champion takes place in a time before there were Poké Balls. So, to protect Lucario from the same fate Sir Aaron knew awaited him, he sealed Lucario in a crystal staff. Then, Mew, disguised as Pidgeot, delivered the crystal staff to Lady Rin. For more than a thousand years, no one in Cameran knew Lucario was sealed inside that very crystal staff.

It became tradition that the crystal staff was passed onto the winner of the Pokémon Competition at the Annual Festival. It wasn't until Ash Ketchum won that Lucario was released! Strangely enough, Lucario initially thought that Ash was actually Sir Aaron because, amazingly, they have the same Aura.

THE ANNUAL FESTIVAL

To celebrate Sir Aaron, the champion who saved Cameran hundreds of years ago, the kingdom throws a big celebration every year. The castle opens its doors to hordes of partygoers. Everyone dresses in period costumes so they look as though they are living in Sir Aaron and Lady Rin's time. There is a fun Pokémon Competition and a ball with fireworks in the evening.

The year Ash attended, he entered the Pokémon Competition and won it with his best buddy Pikachu. As his prize, Ash was given the Guardian of Aura title by Lady Ilene. Then, he was also awarded a relic from Sir Aaron: the crystal staff. However, the year Ash won was even more action-packed than usual because he released Sir Aaron's best friend, Lucario, from the crystal staff.

THE FESTIVAL COSTUMES

Festivalgoers are invited into the costume room at the castle to pick out some fancy duds for the big event.

Ash picks a costume without realizing he's dressed up in Sir Aaron's uniform.

Pikachu gets a court jester costume, complete with a pointy hat.

Brock goes for a skullcap and cape.

May picks a beautiful gown.

Max chooses ye olde shorts and a jaunty hat.

TOTALLY AWESOME TECH

MEW'S TOYS

Mew has a mountain of toys at the Tree of Beginning. Taken from the castle, the playful Pokémon just can't get enough. When Pikachu is sad because it misses Ash, Mew tries to cheer it up with a Hitmontop-shaped top and a Shuckle-shaped whistle.

TIME FLOWER

This iridescent bud can show past events through the power of Aura. It catches clips and can replay them if triggered by the right Aura. Legend has it that Sir Aaron could look into the past with this special Time Flower. So, Ash, his seeming Aura twin, was also able to open their stories.

May first spots a Time Flower up on a rocky ledge while the crew is swimming in some hot springs. Ash climbs to get a closer look and accidentally picks it. When he touches the Time Flower again, it replays his fall.

There is a Time Flower in the exact spot where Sir Aaron sealed Lucario in the crystal staff, proving its side of the story. But that story didn't end there…

When they discover Time Flowers in the heart of the Tree of Beginning, all the blanks are filled in the Legend of the Champion. Those Time Flowers show Sir Aaron's sacrifice and prove he is the true hero the legend paints him to be. Through the Time Flowers, Lucario sees first-hand that he did everything to protect Cameran and his best friend. He didn't betray Lucario

after all; he saved it. In the last chapter of Sir Aaron's story, Lucario not only finds peace, but also the strength to use the power of Aura it learned from Sir Aaron to save Mew and the Tree of Beginning.

SIR AARON'S GLOVES

When Lucario, Kidd, Ash, Pikachu, and Mew arrive in the heart of the Tree of Beginning, they find one artifact that proves Sir Aaron was there: his gloves. Hundreds of years later, they are still lying there on a crystal formation.

As they see in a Time Flower flashback, Sir Aaron strengthens Mew with the power of Aura through his special gloves. So, when Ash steps up to help Lucario again give Mew strength from the power of Aura, he uses Sir Aaron's old gloves.

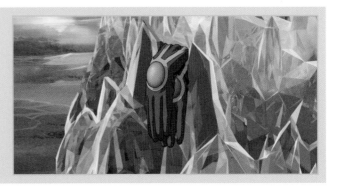

KIDD'S KIT

This world record breaker comes prepared for her mission with super-advanced tools and tech. She's a state-of-the-art kind of superhero! Here are some of the impressive pieces she traveled with to Cameran.

ALL-TERRAIN VEHICLE

Kidd's ride is no ordinary car. Her ATV is outfitted with a satellite dish on the roof, can come to a halt instantly, and is meant for all kinds of conditions. It can fit Ash and his crew inside, and Team Rocket snuck in the trunk.

HEADSET

Through the orange-tinted glasses, Kidd can see data that her partner Banks sends to her, and she can also send data back. It's like a mini computer screen, with a microphone attached so they can also chat. Plus, the sporty glasses are an awesome accessory to her already super-cool outfit.

BINOCULARS

Through these sophisticated lenses, Kidd's binoculars can help her see over a hundred feet away. So, she can keep her distance but still collect important info for her mission. They allowed her to see Mew hanging out in the toy room.

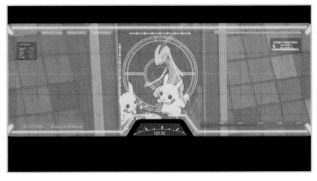

TRANSMITTER

To track her next world record-making mission, Mew, Kidd gives her Pokémon pals Weavile a transmitter to tag on the Mythical Pokémon. Although the Weavile fail to pin one on Mew and cause quite a commotion, Kidd eventually does get to meet the New Species Pokémon.

SURVEY ROBOTS

When Kidd first sets foot in the Tree of Beginning, she can't believe her eyes. She wants to learn everything she can about this place and send the data back to her partner, Banks. So, she pulls out a string of survey robots. The data they collect eventually gives them the knowledge to save Mew and the Tree of Beginning.

POKÉMON RANGER AND THE TEMPLE OF THE SEA

STORY

Deep in the sea, floating by all kinds of Water-type Pokémon unassumingly is a rare Pokémon Egg. It passes by a chain of Corsola and a curious Qwilfish, bounces between Luvdisc, and even rides on Mantyke.

Then, suddenly, a bright white spotlight singles out the egg. Three black helicopters piloted by goons who work for the evil pirate Phantom are hovering above the precious egg. They light the way for Phantom's dark submarine to sneak up to the exact spot and snatch the egg with a metal arm.

Inside the submarine, the egg is carefully placed on a pedestal to be presented to Phantom. Six of his goons line the room. They jump to attention as Phantom walks in. He's a big, tough guy with a red coat and hat. His snarl peeks out from a long beard that is strapped with two belts. Atop his cane sits a Chatot named Casey.

"This is sure to give me what I desire," Phantom says with a cackle. "Wait for me, my Sea Crown."

But before Phantom can get his grubby hands on the delicate egg, a brave Pokémon Ranger named Jackie Walker grabs it. He dodges the other goons, running up onto the wall and right out of the room. Jackie races through the ship, cleverly slipping through the grasp of the Phantom's goons.

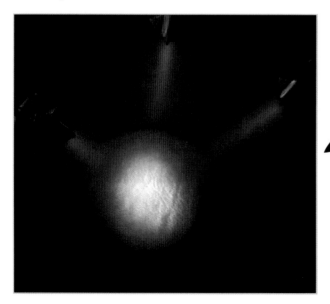

Atop the submarine, Jackie meets Phantom again face-to-face. Phantom surrounds Jackie with his goons, Pinsir, and Parasect. But Jackie uses his Capture Styler, a special piece of technology that only Pokémon Rangers possess, to signal a Mantine passing by that he needs a ride, pronto. A lasso of light circles Mantine, and then it jumps up in the air so Jackie can hop on and make his escape.

Pinsir is so angry that it fires Focus Blast into the sea below. So, Mantine replies with a cunning Confuse Ray to make sure none of Phantom's Pokémon goons can try to stop them as they swim away under the cover of the ocean.

Meanwhile, Ash, Brock, May, and Max are on the road, looking for the next town, when they see giant water bubbles in the distance. They rush over to get a closer look and see a girl directing Water-type Pokémon to do tricks in the bubbles. Brock recognizes her instantly as Lizabeth, a star in the Marina Underwater Pokémon Show.

Lizabeth introduces her new friends to her family: her grandfather, Shep; her father, Kyle; and her mother, Meredith. They invite Ash and his crew to ride to the next city in their traveling trailer. There, they meet Buizel, which shows them a very precious item: the egg! But before they can ask about it, it's show time!

In a town center, they set up a gigantic bubble. From high platforms, Meredith and Kyle, dressed in cool costumes, dive in. Then, their Pokémon pals  Meditite and Medicham use Psychic to help them levitate next to the bubble. There is also a clown dressed in a Sharpedo costume making the crowd laugh. The star of the show, Lizabeth, rides Seel and flies between bubbles. For the big finale, Politoed brings Pikachu, Ash, Brock, May, and Max all into bubbles. What a show!

After the show, things get even more interesting. Buizel tries to hand May the precious egg. The clown steps in, takes it from her, and then gives it back to Lizabeth. However, that was just enough time for greedy Team Rocket to see it and decide to tip off Phantom on its location to collect a reward.

That night, while May is sleeping, the egg bathes the room in a red glow, and it sends May a dream. In it, she is swimming in the ocean, surrounded by Water-type Pokémon. In the distance, she sees a beautiful, swirling temple that looks like a shell. Then, the Mythical Pokémon Manaphy greets her.

The next day, while they're eating a picnic lunch, May tells everyone about her dream, but they don't think it's just a dream at all. Lizabeth tells May that she's actually had the same dream. Shep, Meredith, Kyle, and Lizabeth are all descendants of the People of the Water, the people who built that structure she saw: the sacred Sea Temple.

Meanwhile, tricky Team Rocket sneaks into their trailer to steal the egg. When they get their hands on it, they're all covered in a red glow with a unique charge running between them. When it disappears, they've changed bodies. James is Jessie, Jessie is Meowth, and Meowth is James. They try to make their escape on a pedal-powered blimp, but the clown and Ash are right behind them.

The clown uses his Capture Styler to capture a nearby Fearow. Pikachu hops on Fearow's back, and the two fly up to Team Rocket. Pikachu grabs the egg, and then Fearow bursts their blimp. The egg is safe for now, thanks to the clown, who reveals his true identity to be Jackie Walker, Pokémon Ranger. He also reveals the true identity of the egg: it is the rare Mythical Pokémon that travels the oceans, Manaphy. Jackie is on a mission to safely deliver Manaphy to the Sea Temple, Samaya. May can't believe Jackie's mission is exactly what she dreamed of!

But their celebration doesn't last very long. As they pack up the campsite, Phantom shows up with his black helicopters. Two Beedrill begin the attack by firing Pin Missile.

"Remember, there are only two types of people on this planet: those who are chased, and those who do the chasing," the Phantom says, leaping from his helicopter. "I go for the role of chaser every time."

Ash and Jackie make a break for it with the precious egg. Jackie uses his clown training to trick Phantom into thinking the egg is under a handkerchief. Instead, it's two balls. Jackie throws one at the Phantom. He quickly swats it away, but the ball bounces right back, slapping the pirate across the face.

Galen, Phantom's favorite goon, and his Pokémon pal Beedrill have caught up with Ash and the egg. Beedrill tries another Pin Missile, but Pikachu destroys it in midair with Thunderbolt. But when Beedrill adds a Sludge Bomb blast, the egg goes flying out of Ash's arms. May races to catch it. Ash tells her to run back to the trailer to get it to safety while he and Pikachu hold off Galen and Beedrill.

May and Max run as fast as they can to protect the egg, but Phantom catches up.

"Now, that belongs to me!" Phantom insists, closing in on May and Max.

"No, Manaphy doesn't belong to anyone!" May bravely talks back.

Phantom tries to rip the egg out of her hands, so Max jumps on his back and starts pulling at his beard. All Phantom can get a grip on is the lid of the egg container, which pops off, sending the egg flying. May slides across the ground to catch it. Once in her hands, it begins to glow red. Then, white light takes shape, and from that, Manaphy is born right in May's arms.

"Mana," Manaphy says before it starts to cry.

Manaphy might be a Mythical Pokémon, but it's a baby. May rocks it in her arms. Jackie thinks fast and pushes the Phantom into Galen so they can all escape to the trailer. Once inside, they speed off. But the Phantom's helicopters aren't far behind.

Manaphy finally stops crying—well, unless someone else tries to hold it. It only wants to be with May.

"I'm getting the feeling that Manaphy thinks you're its mother!" Lizabeth says.

Clink! Clank! Phantom's two grappling arms poke through the roof of the trailer. Grandpa Shep tells everyone to hurry forward into the first car. During the high-speed chase, the crew carefully steps over the narrow latch to get to the front. Once they're all in, Shep unlatches the back trailer. It flies off the road and down the hill, dragging one of Phantom's helicopters with it.

Kyle pulls the car up to ruins left by the People of the Water. But Team Rocket is already there, and the Phantom is still hot on their trail.

The crew hurries down some stone steps that dead-end at a wall—or so it seems. Kyle lifts his wrist with a turquoise bead bracelet up to a red dot on the wall. A dial with a tribal pattern lights up in the stone. Kyle carefully turns the dial so that the wall becomes a door.

Shep, Kyle, Meredith, and Lizabeth lead Ash and his crew through a narrow waterway. They're all paired up with Water-type Pokémon to make the passage: Shep with Goldeen, Kyle with Seel, Meredith with Poliwhirl, Max with Buizel, Ash and Pikachu with Corphish, Lizabeth with Gorebyss, Brock with Marshtomp, and May with Squirtle and Manaphy by her side.

At the end of the waterway is a round shrine that is painted with colorful pictures of Samaya, the Sea Temple.

"It's exactly like I saw it in my dream!" May says.

Shep, Meredith, and Kyle explain the legendary Sea Temple. Inside, there is a treasure called the Sea Crown. Many thieves have tried and failed to steal it, as the People of the Water set a couple of traps to protect it. Firstly, the Sea Temple is invisible to mortals. Samaya can only be seen at the time of a total eclipse of the moon, when the People of the Water were said to have held a festival honoring Water-type Pokémon. Secondly, Samaya has no set location; it just goes with the flow of the tide. Only Manaphy can locate the Sea Temple at any time.

"So that's why all those men were all after Manaphy!" May says.

Meanwhile, Team Rocket finally meets the man they tipped off about the egg—Phantom, the pirate. Jessie, James, and Meowth beg to join him. He gives them a job as custodians to clean his helicopter. They happily accept, but only because they intend to trick him and steal the treasure once he finds it.

To avoid tipping off the pirate about their whereabouts, Ash and his friends canoe out of the ruins through a grotto. Then, Jackie, Lizabeth, Kyle, Meredith, and Manaphy board Shep's big boat, the *Blue Lagoon*. There at the shore, they say goodbye to their new friends Ash, Pikachu, May, Max, and Brock so they can finish their mission.

Ash and his pals are sad they're not going along to the Sea Temple, but no one is sadder than Manaphy. It bursts out crying because it misses May. So, Manaphy uses Heart Swap to switch Ash and Jackie. Ash now finds himself in Jackie's body aboard the *Blue Lagoon*. Jackie finds himself stuck on the shore with Pikachu on his shoulder. Shep quickly runs to turn the ship around to get the whole team back together.

Aboard the boat, Manaphy gives May a big hug. She tells the Mythical Pokémon how happy she is to see it.

"Happy! Happy!" Manaphy replies.

May can't believe her ears. Manaphy is talking! Jackie, on the other hand, is starting to worry than Manaphy is too attached to May and won't want to leave her to fulfill its destiny at the Sea Temple.

The time has come to release Manaphy into the ocean so it can make its way through the seas and find its way home to Samaya.

The *Blue Lagoon* stays close behind to keep an eye on Manaphy and make sure it doesn't get into trouble. Jackie parasails up in the sky behind the boat to keep watch. Shep leads Ash, Pikachu, Brock, May, Max, and Lizabeth to a special glass observation deck at the bottom of the boat. There, they can see Manaphy swimming, along with so many different Water-type Pokémon.

That night, lonely Manaphy sits atop a rock and sings. Water Pokémon and everyone on the *Blue Lagoon* boat gather to hear its beautiful voice. May is still hiding. For her commitment to helping Manaphy, Lizabeth gives May her turquoise bead bracelet, the Mark of the People of the Water.

The next day, Grandpa Shep and Kyle can't contain their excitement as they look at their navigation.

"Tonight's the night," Shep says. "The total lunar eclipse!"

"I hope we're on time," Kyle says, checking the route.

Their only chance to see the Sea Temple is if they arrive during the eclipse. While Shep and Kyle plan their route, Manaphy jumps up on the back deck, looking for May. Max, Ash, and Ash's Pokémon pals Corphish, Donphan, Pikachu, and Aipom entertain Manaphy to distract it.

The next day, May and Ash go for a swim with Manaphy and Pikachu. They're all enjoying life on the open sea. As Manaphy continues on its journey, May worries that Manaphy will get lost, but the Mythical Pokémon keeps swimming by to say hi. May's brother, Max, teases her that she is acting like a worried mom.

Jackie asks May to give Manaphy some space. He is concerned that if they get too close, Manaphy won't want to fulfill its destiny and stay at the Sea Temple. May is sad, but she wants to do the right thing for her friend Manaphy. Just then, Manaphy swims up to wave hello to May.

"I'm sorry," May says as she runs out crying.

Manaphy looks confused. It swims next to the ship, shouting "happy" with each stroke to get May's attention. But May is sitting below the railing so Manaphy can't see her crying. When Lizabeth sees May like this, she goes over to comfort her.

"I know it's hard," Lizabeth says.

"I DON'T KNOW THE MEANING OF THE WORD 'FAILURE'!" —JACKIE WALKER

May steps out on the deck, and her bandana blows off. Manaphy sees it sink into the ocean and goes after it. But a Sharpedo's fin gets to it first and carries it farther into the ocean.

"Mana," it wonders where the bandana could be.

Just as Manaphy spots it on Sharpedo, the bandana lands on Remoraid and gets carried even farther.

Back on the *Blue Lagoon* boat, Ash, Lizabeth, Max, Brock, and May are getting worried because they can't seem to find Manaphy. So, Lizabeth decides to take her friends out in her family's yellow submarine to go looking for the Mythical Pokémon. Inside, May is very worried about Manaphy and worries it's her fault that it disappeared.

But soon, Manaphy finds her bandana on Cloyster and swims up to their yellow submarine.

"Happy, happy!" Manaphy says to May. "Love you."

"And I love you, too!" May cheers.

The submarine and the *Blue Lagoon* continue on their journey. Just as planned, they arrive during the eclipse of the moon. They see the stunning Sea Temple before them.

Ash opens the hatch to the submarine and can't believe his eyes. Before him lies the spiraling, gleaming, towering underwater palace he'd only heard about in the legend, and it's real! But May has one thing on her mind.

"Manaphy! Manaphy!" May cries out.

Manaphy hears her voice and jumps out of the water, right into her arms. Then, the friends follow the purple path past fountains and columns. Manaphy begins to sing a melody. A chorus of voices responds.

"That's got to be the People of the Water for sure!" Lizabeth says as her turquoise bead necklace begins to glow.

Just then, another submarine pulls up to the Sea Temple. It's Phantom! He cackles as he races up the stairs to find the treasure he's been plotting to rob, the Sea Crown. But he's not the only villain who made it. Team Rocket stowed away on his submarine, and they're right behind him. But luckily, someone is right behind all of them! Using a special breathing device, Jackie the Pokémon Ranger swims toward them, riding on Mantine.

Meanwhile, Ash and his friends have made it to a tablet with ancient writing, but they can't read the instructions.

"Would you like me to tell you what it says then, kids?" Phantom says, surprising them. "It's the least I can do to thank you for guiding me here."

"Phantom!" Ash yells.

"You know you have no power here! This temple belongs to the People of the Water!" Lizabeth shouts at Phantom.

Phantom just laughs in her face and reads the stone tablet: "Beyond this door, which may only be opened with the People of the Water's Mark, lies the crown, and whosoever shall wear this crown shall be known as the King of the Sea."

Then, he takes out a stolen turquoise bead bracelet, the Mark of the People of the Water. The crown carved into the stone glows, and the tablet sinks into the floor. The glow runs up the wall and forms a dial with a red center. The Phantom turns the dial like a handle, and it opens up to a passageway. Ash and his friends chase after the Phantom.

Before them lies a tower covered in crystal spikes—the Sea Crown. A column of water surrounds it. Manaphy jumps out of May's arms and into the column. Manaphy tries to fight off Phantom as he grabs a giant crystal, but it's no match for the strong pirate.

Suddenly, the column of water drops to the ground, and water starts pouring out into the Sea Temple. It's beginning to flood. But the Phantom doesn't care; he keeps grabbing crystals. Lizabeth is angry, but she knows that if they want to survive, they have to return to their submarine for safety.

As they race down the steps, they run into Jackie. They tell him about Phantom's evil plan, and he springs into action. He finds Phantom with a sack full of the stolen Sea Crown crystals.

"Not bad for an old man, but this belongs to the People of the Water and the Water Pokémon. You seem to have forgotten that!" Jackie says.

Then, he sneaks up behind the pirate and grabs a couple of crystals, quickly placing them back in the Sea Crown. Phantom chases after him. Jackie is able to put most of the crystals back before Phantom corners him. Jackie is trapped between a crystal rock and a hard place.

"Well, Pokémon Ranger," Phantom sneers. "Your time is up!"

A wave of water pours down from above, knocking them both off of the platform where the Sea Crown sits. The tide slams Phantom into a lamppost, and he loses his grip on a crystal. It falls into the water.

Ash, Pikachu, and May are ready to board the submarine, when Manaphy instead swims back to the Sea Crown. May, Ash, and Pikachu chase after it. Manaphy grabs the abandoned crystals left in Phantom's sack and tries to lift them. They help it replace the missing pieces, but they are still short one, and the Sea Temple is still sinking.

Phantom flees to his submarine, but Jackie beats him to it. He offers Casey the Chatot a ride and then seals the door, leaving Phantom outside his own submarine. But Phantom grabs ahold of a spare engine and zooms off.

Meanwhile, inside the Sea Temple, the water level is rising as it sinks deeper and deeper into the ocean. But Ash, Pikachu, May, and Manaphy won't give up. They run up stairs, down stairs, and through every hall, looking for the missing crystal.

"Pikachuuu!" it cries out, pointing at a crystal poking out of a fountain.

Ash grabs it. There is no time to waste. For safety, he puts Manaphy, May, and Pikachu inside a capsule that fell off of Phantom's submarine. Then, our hero races back to the Sea Crown. The water is so high that Ash has to swim most of the way.

The crystal accidentally slips out of his hands and falls deep down below the platform, which is also covered in water. The crystal gets lodged in a stone carving. Ash swims down and tries to grab it, but he runs out of air and floats back to the top of the water, exhausted.

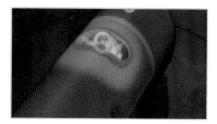

Manaphy can sense that Ash and the Sea Temple are in real danger. So, with a glowing red Heart Swap, it shows Ash that his friends are rooting for him. They appear to him in a vision.

"Ash, be strong. I know you can do it!" May says, appearing in a vision.

"Pika pi,"
Pikachu agrees.

Knowing they're counting on him, Ash regains his strength. He takes a deep breath and tries again. In one dive, he grabs the crystal. Then, he places it back into the Sea Crown.

The Sea Crown instantly lights up, and streams of yellow lights swirl through the Sea Temple, restoring it. Water Pokémon, including the Legendary Kyogre, flock to the Sea Temple.

While May marvels at the sight, Phantom sneaks up and steals Manaphy.

"As long as you're by my side, I can always find the temple," Phantom says, speeding off. "Then, I can take what truly belongs to me!"

But a stream of light carrying Ash rises up out of the water and stays right on Phantom's tail.

Shep, May, and all of Ash's friends can't believe his unique power.

"Whosoever shall wear this crown shall be known as King of the Sea," Shep explains, reciting the legend. "And it's true!"

The golden light dives in and out of the sea. Water-type Pokémon begin to surround Phantom. Before the evil pirate knows it, Kyogre is tossing him out of the ocean. Up in midair, Ash seizes the opportunity to grab Mythical Manaphy.

But the fight isn't over yet. Phantom's submarine comes to rescue him, and he and his goons set their course for Manaphy and Ash. So, the Water-type Pokémon step in. Wailord pummel the submarine next to dozens of Luvdisc, Mantine, Goldeen, Mantyke, and more.

"Manaphy!" it cheers.

Together with their Water-type friends, Ash, Brock, May, Max, Shep, Kyle, Lizabeth, Meredith, Pikachu, and Buizel head to the Sea Temple to celebrate.

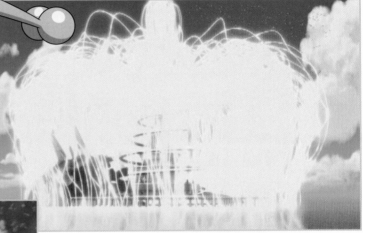

"Mission complete," Jackie relays the message back to Pokémon Ranger Headquarters.

But there is one thing left to do.

"Mana!" Manaphy says, swimming up to the *Blue Lagoon*.

The Mythical Pokémon jumps up into May's arms.

"I'm so proud of you and all that you've done," May tells Manaphy. "You won't forget me?"

"Love you, May," Manaphy says.

With one last hug, Manaphy says goodbye and returns home. The Sea Temple sinks back into the sea, returning to its secret hiding spot. It is safe again thanks to Ash, May, their friends, and of course, the Mythical Seafaring Pokémon.

Phantom's goon Galen uses Supersonic. All of the nearby Pokémon become upset and confused. They cry out. But selfish Phantom doesn't care—he wants to defeat Ash and become King of the Sea.

Once again, Manaphy begins to sing. The sound of its voice breaks through the sting of Supersonic, and the Water-type Pokémon are soothed. They are all able to focus on fighting Phantom.

Mantine strike with Bubble Beam. Chinchou sneak inside the submarine and unleash Spark. Phantom's submarine completely loses power. Then, Manaphy rides in on Kyogre, which fires a fierce Hyper Beam. An explosion surges through the submarine, and Phantom is finally crushed.

LOCATIONS

PHANTOM'S SUBMARINE

The evil pirate Phantom gets around on this dark giant that can sneak through the sea. On the outside, it has sharp, spiky wheels. But inside, it has something even more powerful: a highly sophisticated computer complete with a tracking and navigation system.

However, in the end, it all goes up in smoke. To save Manaphy and put an end to Phantom's evil plans, Water-type Pokémon unite to destroy it. Wailord pummel it. Chinchou fry the electrical wiring with Spark. Kyogre fires Hyper Beam to blast it to pieces.

COMMAND CENTER

Deep in the belly of the ship, Phantom gives his orders from the command center. He sits in a chair hung from the ceiling, watching the monitor and listening to his goon Galen's reports. Here, he plots his attacks and barks his demands to his crew.

HELICOPTER TRIO

Three black helicopters are housed on the deck of Phantom's submarine. Outfitted with sophisticated computers, they can even help locate the tiny Egg of the Prince underwater. These helicopters make seafaring Phantom a force to be reckoned with both in the air and on land.

KITCHEN

Kitchens are known for keeping eggs, but on this submarine, Jackie isn't about to leave one behind. As he races to make his escape with the Egg of the Prince, Jackie spills potatoes across the kitchen floor to stop Phantom's goons.

DECK

Atop the submarine is a deck. From here, Jackie makes his escape and Phantom follows Manaphy.

GLASS ARM

Out of a special door, a tiny glass globe attached to a metal arm can be maneuvered. This delicate machine is how Phantom was able to capture the Egg of the Prince.

MINI SUB

Phantom's submarine also caries a smaller scaled-back version, but don't underestimate this sub because of its

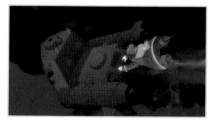

size. It's still amazingly outfitted with a sidecar, an extra engine, and all the bells and whistles.

In this mini sub, Phantom follows Lizabeth's yellow submarine all the way to Samaya. However, Jackie jumps in and drives it away, carrying Casey the Chatot with him. But Phantom comes prepared, as he quickly jumps on an extra engine and rides it like a Jet Ski to follow Manaphy.

The mini sub also has a little sidecar that Team Rocket stows away in. Later, May, Pikachu, and Manaphy find it and hop in to stay safe and dry when the Sea Temple starts to sink.

POKÉMON RANGER HEADQUARTERS

When Jackie checks in with Judy, he calls her at her desk in this incredible control room. The walls of the round space are covered in colorful screens. In the center of the room is a glowing globe. From this HQ, Judy and her coworkers monitor the delicate balance of the world and its Pokémon inhabitants.

THE TOWN CENTER

Right in the middle of the city, Lizabeth and her family put on their big show. A crowd gathers to watch them and their Pokémon friends jump from water bubble to water bubble. It's an amazing sight to see!

THE MARINA GROUP'S TRAVELING SHOW TRAILERS

Lizabeth lives with her grandfather Shep and parents Kyle and Meredith in two trailers. They travel from city to city to put on their famous Marina Underwater Pokémon Show.

The front trailer has wood paneling with gold ornaments. On the side is a beautiful mural of the sea filled with Water-type Pokémon. The front trailer also has the motor and steering that pull along the second trailer.

Attached by a metal clamp, the second trailer is where their kitchen and living quarters are. The sleek, silver sleeper trailer has bunk beds where their friend Buizel loves to hang out. It's here that they also hide the Egg of the Prince.

THE SEA TEMPLE, SAMAYA

The majestic Sea Temple Samaya is absolutely stunning, but it's also invisible. It can only be seen at the time of the total eclipse of the moon, when the People of the Water were said to have held their festival. Shep, Kyle, Meredith, and Lizabeth are all descendants of the People of the Water. They are thrilled to see their legend come to life when they arrive at the exact moment of the eclipse. They see the same Sea Temple that both May and Lizabeth have seen in their dreams.

The shell-like spiraling tower has many waterways, columns, fountains, and lights. The entire Sea Temple is surrounded in an air bubble, so a human lucky enough to find it can breathe inside. It glistens even beneath the sea. It houses a precious artifact: the Sea Crown. Many thieves have tried to steal the valuable Sea Crown and the power it bestows. So, to protect it, the People of the Water built Samaya and set it adrift on the tide. Even though it moves freely and invisibly through the ocean, Manaphy have been born with the ability to locate it.

THE STONE TABLET

To get to the Sea Crown, one first must be able to read the ancient stone tablet and follow its instructions: "Beyond this door, which may only be opened with the People of the Water's Mark, lies the crown, and whosoever shall wear this crown shall be known as the King of the Sea." When the stone senses the Mark of the People of the Water, the carving of the Sea Crown lights up, and the tablet sinks into the floor. A dial is revealed on the wall that leads to the passageway to the Sea Crown.

THE SEA CROWN

On a high stage lies a tower of crystal known as the Sea Crown. This precious piece is on a pedestal surrounded in a column of water. It glistens and glows, and its remarkable power keeps the delicate balance of Samaya. If even one crystal is removed, the Sea Temple will flood and sink to the bottom of the ocean. And that's precisely why Ash and his friends have to stop Phantom!

THE BLUE LAGOON

Shep's ship ferries his family, Jackie, Ash, Pikachu, May, Max, and Brock to the Sea Temple. From the *Blue Lagoon*, they follow Manaphy on its very important journey to ensure its safety.

OBSERVATION DECK

At the bottom of the boat is an amazing section lined in glass. From this observation deck, you can spot many Water-type Pokémon. Everyone aboard the *Blue Lagoon* has their eyes on one Pokémon friend: Manaphy.

YELLOW SUBMARINE

The *Blue Lagoon* carries a small vessel for special operations: a yellow submarine. Lizabeth borrows it to take Ash, Pikachu, Brock, Max, and May to find Manaphy when it chases after May's bandana. Then, they continue on in the sub to Samaya.

THE RUINS

Tucked away near the ocean lie the ruins of a once great stone structure built by the People of the Water. A blue and red star design in a tile marks the entrance. It might look run-down, but inside is a vibrant, cultural treasure—murals that tell the legend of the Sea Temple. But it's not easy to find.

Down the ancient steps and stone corridor, there is a secret door that can only be accessed by someone who bears the Mark of the People of the Water. Then, a glowing, round dial with a red center will appear. Shep unlocks this door to reveal a narrow waterway that leads to a sacred site. Everyone pairs up with a Water-type Pokémon to make the journey: Shep with Goldeen, Kyle with Seel, Meredith with Poliwhirl, Max with Buizel, Ash and Pikachu with Corphish, Lizabeth with Gorebyss, Brock with Marshtomp, and May with Squirtle and Manaphy by her side.

The waterway leads to a round hand-painted shrine with murals that tell the story of Samaya and the Sea Crown. The floor is a mosaic with star designs. There is a special column that acts as a light switch for those in the know, like Kyle.

To leave undetected by an enemy like Phantom, there is another entrance or exit. It's a cavernous grotto that connects directly to the ocean.

CHARACTERS

ASH

Our brave hero is always up for a challenge, and they typically take place on the battlefield. But in this film, his greatest test will be seeing how long he can hold his breath underwater.

When greedy Phantom tries to steal the Sea Crown, it's up to Ash and his swimming skills to replace the final jewel. Despite the odds and the depths, he restores the ancient treasure. And now, because of his amazing effort, you can also call Ash King of the Sea.

PIKACHU

Ash's best friend has good eyes. Pikachu spots the final crystal missing from the Sea Crown.

It also rides on Fearow to stop Team Rocket from escaping with the egg.

BROCK

When the crew finally finds water and Water-types along the road, it is Brock who instantly recognizes the generous girl sharing her supply. He even has clippings of Lizabeth, a star of the Marina Underwater Pokémon Show.

He might hope to get to know Lizabeth better, but Brock winds up spending more one-on-one time with her grandfather, Shep. In the kitchen, Shep teaches him to make pizza.

MARSHTOMP

Marshtomp swims Brock through the narrow passageway at the ancient ruins.

CORPHISH

Ash and Pikachu hitch a ride with Corphish to head down the waterway at the ancient ruins.

SWELLOW

SCEPTILE   **AIPOM**   **DONPHAN**

BONSLY   **FORRETRESS**

MAY

It's a special thing when you can call any Pokémon a friend, but it's even rarer when that friend is a Mythical Pokémon. May shares a deep bond with Manaphy. In fact, it doesn't just think of her as a buddy—it calls her "mama."

TOO CLOSE FOR COMFORT

When Jackie worries that Manaphy won't want to leave May and stay at the Sea Temple, he asks her to back off. It breaks May's heart to hear the Mythical Pokémon crying out for her, but she wants to do what's best for Manaphy. It's hard to let go, but nothing will ever come between the friendship they share. Even though it ultimately has to say goodbye to fulfill its duty at Samaya, Manaphy and May will never forget each other. They will always carry with them the sweet memories of the time they shared.

BANDANA-RAMA

When May loses her bandana in the breeze, she has no idea that Manaphy follows it deep into the ocean. May and her pals all worry it's in danger. So, they hop in the yellow submarine to find it. Along the way, all May can do is blame herself that Manaphy has gone missing. She worries that giving it space was a bad idea. But when they're reunited and she sees Manaphy was just after her bandana, she realizes how independent and brave her Mythical Pokémon pal has become.

SQUIRTLE

Squirtle swims May down the narrow passageway at the ancient ruins.

COMBUSKEN

MUNCHLAX

EEVEE

MOTHER, MAY I?

After May slides in the dirt to save it, the Egg of the Prince hatches right in her arms. So, the first thing baby Manaphy sees is her smiling face. From then on, the pair is inseparable. The Mythical Pokémon only wants to be held by May and even learns its first few words from her: "happy," "love you," "May," and of course, "mama."

MAX

May's little brother can't believe his eyes as he watches his sister turn into the "mom" of a Mythical Pokémon. He teases her for worrying, being cautious, and showering her "baby" with affection. But, hey, that's what any good mom would do! And Max has certainly benefitted from the love of his big sister, too. Maybe he's just jealous that, for once, he's not the baby.

However, Max certainly proves himself to be a fearless and smart member of the crew. He isn't afraid to speak up, and he knows all about Pokémon like Manaphy.

But he's not all talk, either. When Phantom tries to rip the Egg of the Prince out of May's arms, Max jumps on his back and pulls on his beard to stop him. Max has got brains and bravery!

THE MARINA GROUP

The Marina Group puts on the famous traveling Marina Underwater Pokémon Show. The stars are a family: Grandpa Shep, Kyle, Meredith, Lizabeth, and their Water-type and Psychic-type Pokémon pals. The family members are all descendants of the People of the Water and proudly wear turquoise bead jewelry like their ancestors.

SHEP

The elder of the group, Shep knows the legend of Samaya by heart. He sees it as his duty to protect the Sea Temple and pass on his heritage. Shep also has a delicious pizza recipe he shares with Brock. With age comes wisdom (and occasionally, dough).

Shep is also the proud owner of an incredible boat—the *Blue Lagoon*. On this boat, he sails his family, new friends, and Jackie to the Sea Temple.

KYLE

Lizabeth's father, Kyle, is dedicated to helping Manaphy find the Sea Temple. He also dreams of seeing the amazing Samaya during the total eclipse of the moon. And in this case, dreams do come true!

MEREDITH

Lizabeth's mom has beautiful jewelry, but it's not just for show. It's the Mark of the People of the Water.

LIZABETH

Max rudely begs Lizabeth for water when they first meet, but she is happy to share. She has plenty of water and Water-types!

Along with her family, Lizabeth travels in a trailer from city to city, putting on quite a show. But it's not all an act: Lizabeth is truly a caring friend. She comforts May when she is worried about and separated from Manaphy. To cheer her up and show her appreciation for her help, Lizabeth gifts May her turquoise bracelet.

Lizabeth is also dedicated to the Manaphy mission. She steps up to steer the yellow submarine. A bright, daring, and compassionate leader, it's no wonder people are drawn to watch Lizabeth in action, whether it's in a play or in real life.

BUIZEL

Buizel travels around with the Marina Group. It lives in the trailer with them and loves to make new friends. So, when Ash and his crew arrive, Buizel welcomes them and even shows them the secret egg.

POKÉMON STARS OF THE MARINA UNDERWATER POKÉMON SHOW

JACK WALKER

Better know as Jackie the Pokémon Ranger, this hero is on a mission to save Manaphy. He'll do whatever it takes to help the Mythical Pokémon fulfill its destiny and find its way to the Sea Temple.

A BLESSING IN DISGUISE

At first, Jackie disguises himself as one of Phantom's goons. He scrubs the floors of his submarine for a month, waiting for the moment when he can save Manaphy. So, he doesn't waste a moment when the precious egg arrives on the ship. Phantom doesn't lay a finger on it before Jackie snags it and makes a great escape.

Then, Jackie goes undercover again with the Marina Group. He pretends to be a clown in their show to help carry Manaphy. And he's quite entertaining! Jackie is a natural jokester.

WARM AND FUZZY

Jackie has always enjoyed adventure. Back when he was a kid, he went hiking up a mountain and got caught in an unexpected blizzard. He found a cave to hide in, but he was freezing. Luckily, some wild Swablu, Altaria, Sentret, and Furret saw him and decided to help. They surrounded him like a big blanket and warmed him up. Ever since, he knew he wanted to devote his life to helping Pokémon, which is why he became a Pokémon Ranger.

JUDY

Jackie's contact back at Pokémon Ranger HQ, Judy has a no-nonsense personality. She keeps Jackie on track and monitors his mission.

> "WE MUST ALSO PROTECT MANAPHY AT ALL COSTS! ESPECIALLY FROM THE CRUSTY OLD CODGER WITH THE BEARD." —JACKIE WALKER

ZABU, DABU, AND GABU

These three are Shep's old friends. He trusts them with his beloved boat, the *Blue Lagoon*, and counts on them to sail it over to him when it's time to carry Manaphy to Samaya. Although the trio wants to continue on the journey, Shep tells them this is one adventure where he has to leave his friends behind.

PHANTOM

This evil pirate thinks he knows it all, but he also wants it all. He'll stop at nothing to steal Manaphy and the Sea Crown.

Although he has a lot of goons to do his bidding, he isn't afraid to get his hands dirty. Impressively strong and tough, Phantom is always on the front lines, fighting to get the Mythical Pokémon and talking a lot of smack along the way.

HIS TWO CENTS

Phantom likes to divide mankind into two types, and of course, he always pumps himself up with compliments. Here are some of his classic lines:

- "Remember, there are two types of men in this world of ours: those who look good with rare jewels, and those who do not. For my money, the Sea Crown and I are a match made in the heavens above!"

- "Remember, there are two types of men in this world: those who have unlimited desires, and those who do not!"

- "Remember, there are only two types of people on this planet: those who are chased, and those who do the chasing."

- "There are two types of men in this world: those who are completely crushed, and those who do the crushing."

DO YOU MIND?

Phantom has had his eyes on stealing the incredible Sea Crown, spending a lot of time and resources on his evil plan. He somehow obtained a turquoise bracelet, the Mark of the People of the Water. Phantom is also able to read the ancient script on the stone tablet that leads to the Sea Crown. Phantom knows the legend very well. He's studied hard, but unfortunately, for all of the wrong reasons. Perhaps if he had put his mind to doing good, he could have been an important historian instead of a self-serving pirate.

CROWN JEWELS

Phantom thought the tower of crystal known as the Sea Crown would not only give him wealth, but it would also give him the power to be the King of the Sea. However, a true leader would know that theft does not give one status or respect. His greed almost ruins the very prize he's after. Luckily, Jackie, Lizabeth, Ash, and their pals are on the case!

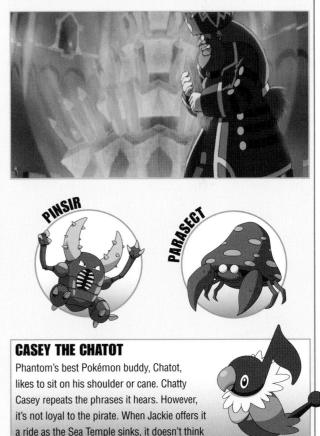

CASEY THE CHATOT

Phantom's best Pokémon buddy, Chatot, likes to sit on his shoulder or cane. Chatty Casey repeats the phrases it hears. However, it's not loyal to the pirate. When Jackie offers it a ride as the Sea Temple sinks, it doesn't think twice and leaves Phantom to fend for himself.

TEAM ROCKET

Up to their usual tricks, Jessie, James, and Meowth have their eyes set on treasure. Although they are initially following Ash, Pikachu, and their crew, they soon turn their attention to the precious Egg of the Prince.

But when they get their greedy paws on the egg, it uses Heart Swap to switch them up. They all change bodies: Meowth is Jessie, James is Meowth, and Jessie is James. It's a crazy mix-up that teaches them what it's like to be in their friends' shoes—literally. Luckily, it wears off, but their appetite for treasure doesn't.

They tip off Phantom on the location of the Egg of the Prince, hoping for a reward. But when that doesn't work, they volunteer to become Phantom's goons. He assigns them to cleaning duty, and they bide their time scrubbing as they plot to steal the Sea Crown out from under the Phantom. But the trio and their plans wind up washed up when the Sea Temple begins to flood.

WOBBUFFET

MIME JR.

GALEN

BEEDRILL

As Phantom's most trusted goon, Galen mans the controls inside the submarine and is by his side when he battles for the precious Egg of the Prince. He is always one step ahead, suggesting various courses of action. There is nothing too evil for Galen to think of or do. It is Galen who suggests using Supersonic to confuse all the Water-type Pokémon that have come to protect the Sea Temple.

JESSIE: "THIS ISN'T WORKING…"

JAMES: "WHO CARES?! WITH THIS BABY, WE'LL NEVER HAVE TO WORK AGAIN!"

"AND IT'S LIFTOFF FROM LOSERLAND!" —TEAM ROCKET

MYTHICAL AND LEGENDARY POKÉMON

MANAPHY:
THE SEAFARING POKÉMON

Height	1'00"
Weight	3.1 lbs
Type	Water

When Ash, Pikachu, May, Max, and Brock first meet the Mythical Pokémon, it's still a Pokémon Egg—the Egg of the Prince, to be exact. Pokémon Ranger Jackie and the Marina Group are on a secret mission to protect the precious Pokémon Egg and deliver it to its proper habitat, the Sea Temple. So, of course, Ash, Pikachu, May, Max, and Brock volunteer to help Manaphy make its way to Samaya.

A GOOD EGG

While still an egg, Manaphy is very powerful. It sends May a dream about itself and Samaya. It also uses Heart Swap to protect itself from Team Rocket and cleverly uses its power when necessary. Manaphy might not have a lot of experience, but it has good instincts. It knows its place is at the Sea Temple, and even though it's a baby, it wisely won't let anyone or anything get in its way. Manaphy knows the responsibility that comes with being Prince of the Sea.

BURST INTO SONG

Manaphy has a beautiful voice that can captivate both people and Pokémon. But it's as powerful as it is pretty. When it lifts its voice in song, it is so strong it breaks right through the Supersonic Galen sent, saving the Water-type Pokémon in the area.

HATCHING A PLAN

Just as Phantom and Galen are fighting for the Egg of the Prince, it flies through the sky. May dives to save it, and in an instant, Manaphy is born right in her arms. From then on, Manaphy treats May like she's its mother. It likes to be held in her arms. And even when it's swimming across the sea on its journey, it always checks to make sure she's watching it. In fact, when the *Blue Lagoon* pulls out of the port to help Manaphy make it to Samaya, the Mythical Pokémon is upset that May isn't with them. It uses Heart Swap on Jackie and Ash so Shep will have to turn the boat around and let May and its new friends board. Manaphy knows strength is really in numbers, especially when one is your "mama."

KYOGRE:
THE SEA BASIN POKÉMON

Height	14'09"
Weight	776.0 lbs
Type	Water

The Legendary Sea Basin Pokémon is at the scene at Samaya to lend a hand (or rather, fin). Manaphy rides on Kyogre's head. And it is Kyogre that delivers the final blow of Hyper Beam, causing an explosion so strong that Phantom's submarine is reduced to scraps.

FEATURED POKÉMON

Jackie uses his Capture Styler to capture Mantine and make his escape from Phantom's submarine with the Egg of the Prince. Then, Mantine uses Confuse Ray to stop Phantom's Pokémon pals from attacking them as they swim off.

WAILORD
Height: 47'07"

WILD POKÉMON THAT HELPED YOUNG JACKIE

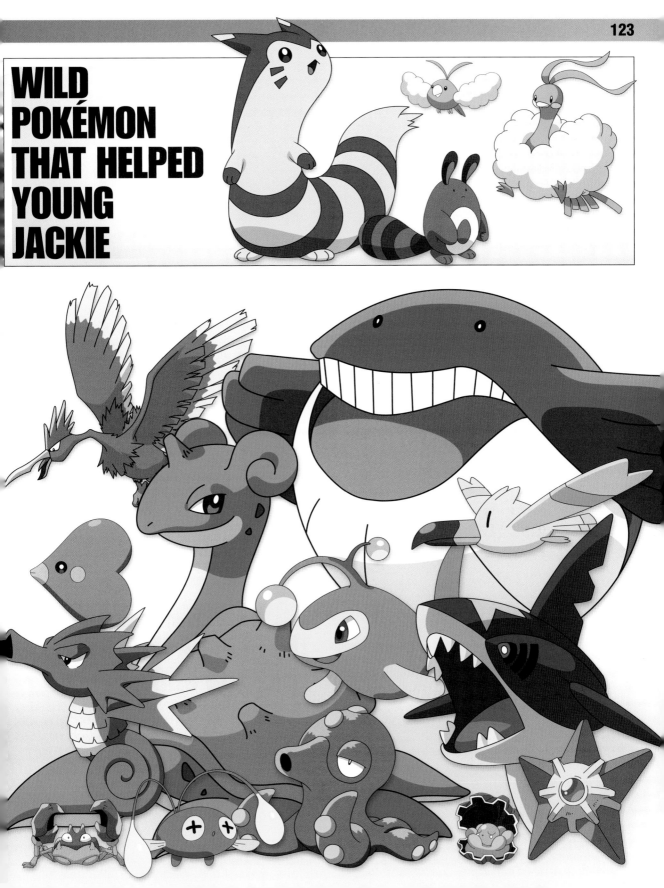

INTERESTING ITEMS

POKÉMON RANGERS

People like Jackie Walker dedicate themselves to protecting Pokémon and nature. This group of well-trained and dedicated professionals call themselves Pokémon Rangers.

CAPTURE STYLER

Pokémon Rangers don't catch and train Pokémon, but they do team up with them. To solicit their help, Pokémon Rangers use a special yellow, green, and black wand. It sends out a lasso of light that temporarily links the Pokémon to the Pokémon Ranger. Once the Pokémon is captured, the Pokémon Ranger can get the support they need from their new friend to save the day.

For example, Jackie captures Mantine to make a quick escape from Phantom's submarine. He also uses his Capture Styler to get a nearby Fearow to give Pikachu a ride up to Team Rocket's flying contraption so it can grab the Egg of the Prince. A Capture Styler sure can come in handy for a Pokémon Ranger on a mission!

EGG OF THE PRINCE

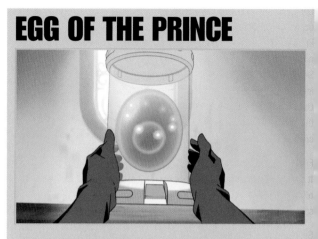

This is code for Manaphy's egg since it is the Prince of the Sea. Contained in a special glass jar, it is transported by Jackie and the Marina Group. But although its shape is contained, the egg's power cannot be. It uses Heart Swap to surprise Team Rocket and give them a true out-of-body experience. It also sends May a vision of Samaya while she dreams.

MAY'S VISION

When Buizel turns the switch on the Egg of the Prince's container, Manaphy sends May a vision—a peek at the legendary Sea Temple. A red light beams over her face as she sleeps, and she is transported under the sea. The pink ocean is filled with Water-type Pokémon surrounding an incredible swirling underwater structure that she later realizes is the Sea Temple, Samaya. She also sees Manaphy in her dream for the first time.

THE MARK OF THE PEOPLE OF THE WATER

It might look like stylish jewelry, but the turquoise bead bracelets and necklaces that the Marina Group wears are actually the Mark of the People

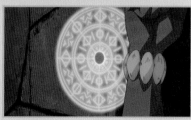

of the Water. With these accessories, they can unlock secret doors at the ruins and the Sea Temple. Somehow, the evil pirate Phantom got ahold of a piece.

THE INCREDIBLE BUBBLES AT THE MARINA UNDERWATER POKÉMON SHOW

This traveling show goes from town to town entertaining crowds of people and Pokémon. The Marina Group performers Shep, Lizabeth, Kyle, and Meredith and their Water-type Pokémon friends swim in and out of giant bubbles thanks to the help of their Pokémon pals Poliwag, Poliwhirl, Medicham, and Meditite. It's quite a sight to see!

THE LEGEND

Long ago, the People of the Water traveled the oceans and lived alongside the ocean Pokémon in peace and harmony. To honor their Pokémon neighbors, they built a magnificent underwater Sea Temple called Samaya. Inside lies an incredible crystal treasure, the Sea Crown. Over the years, many thieves have tried to steal the sacred jewels, so the People of the Water created clever ways to protect it.

Firstly, the Sea Temple blends in with the water. It can only be seen at the time of a total eclipse of the moon, when the People of the Water were said to hold their Annual Festival.

Secondly, although the Sea Temple was built where Manaphy lived, it is not stationary. It has no set location; it is constantly adrift and flows with the tides. Born with a special homing instinct, only Manaphy can find it deep in the ocean. This is precisely the reason Phantom is obsessed with catching Manaphy and also why Jackie is on a mission to safeguard the Mythical Pokémon as it makes its way through the ocean to Samaya. The Pokémon Ranger and his pals won't rest until it's home at the Sea Temple. Then, and only then, will Manaphy and Samaya be safe.

Supposedly, People of the Water dream about the Sea Temple. After May recounts her dream about it, Lizabeth says she has also had the same vision.

The entire legend is painted in beautiful, colorful murals and mosaics at the ruins of the People of the Water.

TOTALLY AWESOME TECHNOLOGY

BREATHING DEVICE

What looks like a little white straw coming out of Jackie's mouth is actually a complete technological marvel. Using this small breathing device, Jackie can travel and stay under the sea just like a Water-type Pokémon.

TEAM ROCKET'S RICKETY FLYING CONTRAPTION

Team Rocket thinks this bike-bottomed blimp is the perfect escape vehicle when they steal the Egg of the Prince. But it's easily busted when Fearow pokes its beak through it, blasting Jessie, James, and Meowth off again.

POKÉMON: THE RISE OF DARKRAI

THE STORY

Tonio, a scientist in Alamos Town, is reading from the diary of his grandfather, the famous architect Godey. The entry is about Dialga and Palkia, two Mythical Pokémon that tangle in an epic battle in another dimension.

Suddenly, his computer starts reporting some kind of abnormal activity. Dialga, the deity of time, and Palkia, the deity of space, are locked in an epic battle just like the one described in the diary.

The next day, Ash, Pikachu, Dawn, and Brock hop in Alice's hot air balloon, powered by her Pokémon pal Chimchar, to travel across the lake to Alamos Town.

Alice plays a special song on her Leaf Whistle. Then, Pidgey and Pelipper arrive to show her which way the wind is blowing.

Team Rocket is right behind Ash and his crew in a Carnivine-shaped balloon. But when the trio tries to catch Drifloon with a net, the airborne Pokémon send them blasting off again with Gust.

On the way, they see the super-tall Space-Time Towers and garden designed by Godey 100 years ago. Alice offers to give them a tour of her hometown and the towers.

On the way around Alamos Town, Ash and his pals can't resist a battle challenge from some local Trainers. The match-ups find Ash and Pikachu battling Maury and Torterra, Dawn and Piplup versus Kai and Empoleon, and Brock and Croagunk against Allegra and Infernape.

Alice then takes them to her favorite place in town, the garden Godey designed behind the Space-Time Towers. It has many fountains, colorful mosaics, and wild Pokémon like Yanma, Azumarill, and Shinx.

Ash, Dawn, and Brock take out their Pokémon so they can play in the beautiful garden. But when Shinx and Piplup fight over a berry, Alice again plays her Leaf Whistle, and a calm comes over all the Pokémon.

Suddenly, Gallade comes to get Alice and show her a part of the garden where stone columns have been strangely toppled. At the scene, Baron Alberto blames the Mythical Pokémon Darkrai.

Baron Alberto hears something rustling in the bushes and assumes it's Darkrai. So, he calls on his Pokémon pal Lickilicky to use Hyper Beam. But when the figure emerges, it turns out to be one toasted Tonio.

Tonio tells Alice and the crew that he is busy investigating a Space-Time abnormality his tracking device picked up.

Alberto tries to distract Alice from helping Tonio by offering to have her over for dinner, but she is repulsed by the arrogant baron.

Just then, another Space-Time abnormality ripples across the garden. Darkrai rises out of the ground and says, "Do not come here."

Baron sics Lickilicky on it, and the two begin to battle. Ash gets caught in the crossfire and finds out first-hand why Darkrai is known to give its foes nightmares. He finds himself in the same garden, but it's completely empty. Then, a purple shadow with red eyes emerges from a dark fog. When it disappears, Darkrai and Pikachu appear. But they all get swallowed into some strange quicksand.

Ash feels a jolt of electricity and opens his eyes to see he and Pikachu are at the Pokémon Center. It was all a dream, or rather a nightmare caused by Darkrai, Nurse Joy informs him.

Anxious to study the data, Tonio returns to his lab. While reading through Godey's diary, he finds a picture of Alicia, Alice's grandmother. Although angry Darkrai had battled many of the wild Pokémon in the garden, Alicia went out of her way to make it feel welcome. She then played the Leaf Whistle to bring them all together.

Tonio also reads a secret plan Godey left for the future, something he called "Oracion."

Back at Baron Alberto's castle, Team Rocket has disguised themselves as reporters interested in doing a documentary on the royal. Vain Alberto can't wait to be on camera.

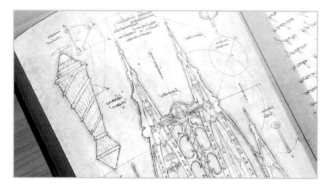

Meanwhile, Alice gives Ash, Pikachu, Dawn, and Brock a tour of the Space-Time Towers. She takes them to the stadium with stained-glass windows, both spires, the lobby, and Tonio's basement lab.

Tonio shows Alice the picture of her grandmother Alicia with his grandfather, Godey. Alice notices that there's a song written on the back of the picture with no title, but a swirly little symbol.

Laid out on a table, Piplup, Pikachu, and Chimchar discover some decorated round discs. Tonio tells them that they are to be played in the Bell Tower, right between the Space and Time Towers.

While Ash races up the spiral staircase on foot, Alice takes the rest of the crew up in her hot air balloon.

The Bell Tower has stained-glass windows and a gorgeous gold organ. Tonio and Alice show them how to place the disc they picked out. The song rings out across Alamos Town, and the locals dance in the street.

Afterward, Allegra, Maury, and Kai challenge Ash, Dawn, and Brock to another round. The crew happily accepts, but they're interrupted by an even bigger battle—the epic one between Palkia and Dialga.

Tonio can't believe the data coming in from the different dimension as a bright light engulfs Alamos Town.

Darkrai appears and cries out to the sky, "Go away!" Baron Alberto arrives and instructs Lickilicky to battle back Darkrai. Unfortunately, there's collateral damage from their battle, and

many of the Pokémon in the city square are caught in nightmares.

Ash asks Pikachu to try Volt Tackle, but when Darkrai uses Double Team, it doesn't know where to strike.

Baron Alberto tells Ash to step aside and has Lickilicky use Hyper Beam. But when Darkrai blasts back, he sends the Licking Pokémon into a nightmarish sleep. Then, Alberto, lined with a purple light, transforms into Lickilicky. The vain baron is more upset about his looks than the outcome of the battle.

Back at the Pokémon Center, Nurse Joy has her hands full with all the sleeping Pokémon and an even stranger Pokémon phenomenon: Pokémon ghosts, lined in a purple light, flying around.

Just then, Ash runs into the Pokémon Center, followed by Lickilicky-looking Alberto. Tonio explains that his data shows the city is experiencing a special force that's causing a Space-Time abnormality. Inside Alamos Town, the real world is merging with the dream world, and what they're seeing is the sleeping Pokémon's dreams. So, Lickilicky is dreaming it's the baron!

Allegra, Maury, and Kai arrive at the Pokémon Center to deliver some startling news—Alamos Town has been sealed off. Everyone heads to the bridge to find it covered in fog. Ash tries to race across, but he finds himself right back where he started.

Tonio isn't sure what is causing the bizarre problem just yet, but Baron Alberto is sure it's the work of Darkrai. He rallies the local Trainers to hunt it down.

Tonio is worried about Darkrai. He recalls a time when Alice slipped off a cliff in the garden and Darkrai saved her. He knows the Mythical Pokémon's nature is good, but he's the only one who knows the story.

Tonio heads back to the lab to examine all the data. He freeze-frames the screen

and sees that the deity of space, the Legendary Pokémon Palkia, sent the bright light that sealed the city off.

Meanwhile, the baron has led an army of local Trainers and their Pokémon into battle against Darkrai. It's not exactly a fair fight, but Darkrai is holding his own against almost a dozen other Pokémon and puts them all to sleep.

Baron Alberto, who still looks like Lickilicky, steps in to fight, but its tongue gets tied up in Wrap. The attack is soon turned against it as Darkrai swings him out of sight!

Back at the Pokémon Center, Tonio shares his findings with his friends Alice, Ash, Pikachu, Brock, Dawn, and Piplup. They deduce that Darkrai is the only one that saw Palkia and has been trying to protect the city.

Tonio, Alice, Ash, Pikachu, Brock, Dawn, and Piplup race to the Space-Time Tower and find Darkrai locked in battle with Palkia.

But then, another Legendary Pokémon arrives: Dialga, the deity of time. Strangely enough, the Pokémon back at the Center wake up, the baron becomes human again, and all of the ghost Pokémon disappear. The sky swirls with black clouds, and Tonio's data shows that the whole town is floating in another dimension.

The epic battle rages on as Dialga chases Palkia across Alamos Town. Tonio realizes the entry in Godey's diary predicted this very event.

Darkrai tries to stop them, but Dialga and Palkia focus their fire on the Mythical Pokémon. It falls to the ground in the garden. Alice, Ash, Pikachu, Brock, Dawn, Piplup, and Tonio find Darkrai and thank it for all that it's done to help Alamos Town. But Darkrai isn't going to give up!

As the epic battle continues, Tonio's tracking device shows that the city is being swallowed by the Space-Time rift and disappearing into another dimension. The fighting between Dialga and Palkia must be stopped before it's too late!

Tonio recalls a passage in Godey's diary talking about a song called "Oracion" with the power to soothe the fiercest rage. Alice helps them find the right disc, and then Ash and Dawn volunteer to deliver it to the bell chime.

It's a race against time, so Alice drops the pair off in her hot air balloon. Then, Darkrai swoops in to protect Alice from an intense stray Roar Of Time attack by Dialga. It's a valiant effort by Darkrai, but the attack is so powerful, she and Tonio still go flying from the impact. Luckily, Lickilicky and Tonio, with the help of Drifblim, were there to catch Alice.

Brock finds Darkrai floating in a fountain in the garden, and Alice rushes to its side. Darkrai has a flashback and remembers when Alicia, its first friend, made it feel welcome in the garden. The memory gives it the strength to soar up into the sky and try to again stop Dialga and Palkia by blocking their explosions of energy in a big bubble.

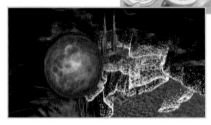

As Dawn, Piplup, Ash, Turtwig, and Pikachu carry the disc up the steps, they disappear right under their feet. When Ash slips off the side, Dawn grabs his arm. Then, Buizel thinks fast and uses Water Gun so they can surf the blast all the way up to the bell chime.

Dialga and Palkia overpower Darkrai, and it also disintegrates into the sky. Tonio's tracking device data warns that one more clash between the Legendary Pokémon will end Alamos Town for good.

Ash and Dawn drop the disc in the bell chime, but the tower has no power. So, Pachirisu uses Discharge and Pikachu uses Thunderbolt. Their Electric-type attacks are so strong, the song plays. Across the city, people and Pokémon are amazed by the beautiful sound. The Space-Time Tower is transformed, bathed in golden light. It's a beautiful sight!

Ash and Dawn plead with Palkia to restore Alamos Town and return to its dimension. The Legendary Pokémon listens to their prayer and disappears, leaving the city as if it had never experienced the terrible epic battle.

Back at Godey's garden, Alice, Ash, and all their friends tearfully thank the still-missing Darkrai for its sacrifice. Then, a giant shadow appears across the lake—it's Darkrai proudly standing watch atop the Space-Time Tower. Again, the great city Godey envisioned is a home where everyone is welcome.

LOCATIONS

ALAMOS TOWN

Atop a rocky island and surrounded by a lake, the only way to get to Alamos Town is by bridge or by a hot air balloon ride. But once inside the city, you'll find food vendors with sweet treats, quaint brownstone buildings and cobblestone streets, and the incredible Space-Time Tower and gardens designed by the famous architect Godey.

Ash and Brock headed to Alamos Town with Dawn so she could enter the local Pokémon Contest. Little did they know that their visit would also collide with an epic Legendary Pokémon Battle.

THE POKÉMON CENTER

In Alamos Town, Nurse Joy and Chansey offer a place to rest and recover for all who pay them a visit. But, boy, do they have their hands full when the local Pokémon pick a fight with Darkrai, the Pokémon known to give nightmares to its foes. Still, they have more than enough care to spare! They roll out blankets and get to work, helping both people and Pokémon recover. In fact, they're even there for Ash when he is also sent into a scary slumber.

THE SPACE-TIME TOWER

In the city center is a building made of two beautiful towers. The one on the left is for space, and the one on the right is for time (hence the name the Space-Time Tower). Designed and built by the renowned architect Godey 100 years ago, it is the jewel in the crown of Alamos Town.

THE GARDEN

Behind the tower is a sprawling park filled with lush greenery, colorful mosaic tiles, hanging gardens, water fountains, and lots of wild Pokémon. It even has a playground for Pokémon, complete with a seesaw, swings, and a slide! This big, beautiful garden is also home to the Mythical Pokémon Darkrai. Godey designed the unique grounds to reflect the harmony between people and Pokémon.

THE STADIUM

Attached to the Space-Time Tower is a giant arena specially designed to host Pokémon Contests. It is lined with stained-glass windows that flood the stadium with colored light.

TONIO'S LAB

Down in the basement of the Space-Time Tower is Tonio's specialized lab, filled with computer screens, machines, monitors, stacks of books, data reports, and discs that can be played in the bell chime. It's dark and isolated, leaving Tonio to his important work.

THE BELL TOWER

Between the Space Tower and the Time Tower lies the Bell Tower. It can be reached by climbing a tall spiral staircase, but as Ash discovered, it's much easier to simply take a hot air balloon all the way up. There is even a dock off the side to park your basket.

This decorative tower is connected to the two main towers, and on top is a round structure that holds a unique bell chime, also designed by Godey. This organ rings out across Alamos Town, playing a disc with a little ditty at the top of every hour. It is from this bell chime that Ash and Dawn play "Oracion," the song that saves the city.

The bell chime also makes the Space-Time Tower the biggest musical instrument in the world.

THE LOBBY

The ground floor of the Space-Time Tower has a decorative tile floor and a gorgeous mural of Alicia playing a Leaf Whistle in the garden surrounded by wild Pokémon. Beneath the mural is a ring of discs for the bell chime, one of which plays the sacred song "Oracion".

CHARACTERS

ASH

Ash thought he was visiting Alamos Town so Dawn could enter a Pokémon Contest, but he soon found himself in the center of the action as an epic Pokémon Battle between Legendary Pokémon unfolded.

THE DARK DREAM

Our hero was the first victim to fall prey to one of Darkrai's nightmares. However, Ash later realizes the nightmare wasn't a dream—it was real. The Mythical Pokémon was trying to warn him about Palkia's arrival.

In the vision, he is in the garden, but all alone. Inside a cloud of dark smoke, Ash sees a figure lined in purple light with red eyes. Could it be a peek at the Legendary Pokémon Palkia in another dimension? Then, Darkrai rises out of the ground. Ash tries to take out Turtwig, but his Poké Ball is just an empty shell. He can see Pikachu in the distance. But before he can reach him, Darkrai slides into the sand, creating a sinkhole that sucks in Ash and his best buddy.

Zap! Suddenly, Ash feels the jolt of an Electric-type attack. When he opens his eyes, he realizes Pikachu woke him up. He's so glad to see his pal! Ash can't believe he was rushed to the local Pokémon Center. His pals had been so worried about him! But Nurse Joy assures them that this isn't the first time she's seen someone who has been affected by Nightmare dealt by Darkrai.

DISC MAN

With his pal Dawn, Ash volunteers to climb up the Bell Tower to save the day and play the special disc with "Oracion." Along the way, Ash slips out of Alice's hot air balloon and slides down to the staircase. But no matter the danger, he never gives in! Luckily, with the help of his Pokémon pal Pikachu, they're able to power up the bell chime and play the sacred song.

PIKACHU

Along with its pal Pachirisu, the powerful Electric-type has enough juice to energize the bell chime to play "Oracion."

AIPOM

STARAVIA

TURTWIG

BROCK

Girl-crazy Brock instantly takes a shine to their tour guide, Alice. However, Croagunk keeps him in line.

But girls aren't the only thing on his mind. When the city starts to disappear, the brave Pokémon Breeder helps evacuate the locals to safety along with Nurse Joy.

When Darkrai falls from the sky into a pool in the garden, weak from trying to stop the epic battle between Dialga and Palia, Brock jumps into rescue it. He's just not the kind of guy who can turn his head when he sees suffering. Brock is always there to pitch in, no matter what the task or risk is!

CROAGUNK

SUDOWOODO

HAPPINY

DAWN

Although Dawn initially thought she was visiting Alamos Town to enter the local Pokémon Contest, what she ended up with was the kind of rewarding experience they don't give out ribbons for. Along with her friends, Dawn helped save Alamos Town by thinking on her feet and coming up with a clever solution. When the Bell Tower steps disappear, Dawn combines Buizel's Water Jet with Buneary's Ice Freeze to create new ones. When the bell chime needs power, she calls on Pachirisu to use Discharge, and then Ash and Pikachu add Thunderbolt to turn the organ on so it can play "Oracion" and end the epic battle. The only thing stronger than those Electric-type attacks is Dawn's brainpower!

PIPLUP

BUNEARY

PACHIRISU

BUIZEL

ALICE

Ash and his pals first meet Alice when she offers them a ride in her green hot air balloon. The Alamos Town native gives tours of the city from the sky. Her Pokémon pal Chimchar provides all the fiery fuel the balloon needs to stay up in the air.

She is also a music student. When she plays pretty tunes on the Leaf Whistle, Flying-type Pokémon show her which way the wind is blowing to help her steer her hot air balloon.

LOVE IS IN THE AIR

Alice isn't shy about telling Tonio she likes him. When the baron invites her over for dinner and says that he wants to marry her, Alice openly shuts down the arrogant Alberto because her heart belongs to Tonio. Alice has known Tonio since they were children and has always had a crush on him. She can read him like a book, but it seems all Tonio can focus on is his books.

A FRIENDSHIP THAT SPANS GENERATIONS

Deep down inside, Alice doesn't think Darkrai is responsible for the chaos caused by the Space-Time rift. It's lived peacefully in the garden for decades and was friends with her grandmother, Alicia. When Darkrai is hurt from trying to stop Dialga and Palkia, she rushes to its side. It is her caring and concern that reminds Darkrai of its bond with Alicia and motivates it to get back in the fight.

Not only is the Mythical Pokémon trying to protect its home, it's also trying to protect its pal Alice. When she bravely tries to beg Dialga and Palkia to end their epic battle, they turn their fire on her. But before the attacks can strike Alice, Darkrai jumps in front of her and takes the hits.

CHIMCHAR

ALICIA

Alice's grandmother is Alicia. She was a good friend to both Godey and Darkrai.

Alicia often played in the garden. One day, she found Darkrai hunched over under a tree. The other wild Pokémon didn't want it there, so it fought back and gave them nightmares. But Alicia saw through Darkrai's tough exterior and realized the Mythical Pokémon wanted to find friends and a place it could call home. She was the first one to welcome it to the garden. Alicia told Darkrai, "This is everyone's garden." With those words, Darkrai's anger disappeared, and it has lived there ever since.

Alicia also found a friend in the great architect Godey. She loved the magical garden he designed and played there often.

Alicia also played the Leaf Whistle. In fact, she taught Alice the sacred song "Oracion." In Alicia and Alice's case, the apple didn't fall far from the tree!

TONIO

Godey's grandson is a very smart scientist. From his lab tucked away in the basement of the Space-Time Tower, Tonio is able to focus on his research. He spends so much time in his lab

studying, Alice often finds him there asleep on the floor. He's constantly thinking about his findings and can get so distracted he doesn't see the wall in front of him and will walk right into it, just like he did at the Pokémon Center.

A GOOD READ

Tonio's mind is always on his work, but he loves what he does. In fact, if he didn't study so hard, Alamos Town might not have survived the Space-Time rift. After all, it was Tonio who used his computer and a tracking device to analyze the abnormal readings and describe the situation as it unfolded. He also put together that Darkrai was not the culprit of the chaos, but the protector of the city. Ultimately, Tonio figured out his grandfather, Godey, wasn't describing an event in the past in his diary but a problem he foresaw in the future—and that future was unfolding before their eyes. With that, Tonio was able to find the solution that would save Alamos Town and lead his friends to do it.

FALLING IN LOVE

One day, when they were playing in the garden, Alice slipped off of a cliff, and she thinks that Tonio saved her. Since he also likes her, Tonio never corrected her. He has carried the guilt that he never told her the truth; it was really Darkrai that rescued her from the fall. However, during the epic battle, he finally does get the chance to come to her aid. When Alice slides off of the bridge wall, Lickilicky grabs her by the tongue, and then Tonio is able to bring her back down on solid ground. Alice is so grateful to the man she adores, Tonio!

GODEY

A visionary architect, Godey dreamed up the plans for the Space-Time Towers and the surrounding gardens. Built 100 years ago, the landmark transformed the city skyline and stands as a testimony to the harmony between people and Pokémon.

But the incredible project wasn't the only thing he envisioned. Godey wrote in his journal about a battle between Dialga and Palkia in another dimension. He saw the future and felt their fight would cross over into Alamos Town and threaten the city. To safeguard his beloved hometown from such an event, he built a Bell Tower from which the sacred song "Oracion" could be played to soothe the rage of the Legendary Pokémon. Then, he left a diary with all the details about it. He truly was ahead of his time!

DRIFBLIM

Drifblim carried a device that collected data for his brainy buddy Tonio. It even helped him carry Alice when she nearly slipped off of the bridge.

DRIFLOON

> "IF WE DON'T ACT, EVERYTHING WILL DISAPPEAR INTO ANOTHER DIMENSION!"
> —TONIO

ALLEGRA, KAI, AND MAURY

These three Trainers couldn't wait to challenge the crew to a practice battle right in the city center, not once, but twice. They had so much fun!

In the first match-up, Ash and Pikachu faced Maury and Torterra, Dawn and Piplup battled Kai and Empoleon, and Brock and Croagunk went up against Allegra and Infernape.

The second time, they rotated battle opponents. Ash and Pikachu were ready to test their skills with Kai and Empoleon. Dawn called on Buizel, and Brock chose Sudowoodo. But they didn't really get the chance to battle. Before they had the chance, Palkia blasted a beam of light that sealed off the city. The crew knew they now had to focus on a real fight!

Maury, Allegra, and Kai were the first people in town to notice that it had been sealed off. Allegra asked Honchkrow to use Defog to demonstrate that the mist around the edge of the city was a border that couldn't be crossed.

The three Trainers and their Pokémon pals then pitched in to help in the efforts to save Alamos Town. They decided to follow Baron Alberto and unwittingly fought the Legendary Darkrai.

But Maury, Kai, and Allegra are courageous and helpful when their attention and powerful Pokémon are properly directed. Eventually, the three Trainers called on their Pokémon to use their attacks to fight back at the disintegration line.

EMPOLEON

HONCHKROW

INFERNAPE

TORTERRA

NURSE JOY

No matter how many patients come to the Pokémon Center, Nurse Joy is happy to help! Along with her pal Chansey, they care for dozens of dreaming Pokémon and Ash, who were all sent into slumber by Darkrai. She is no stranger to seeing that kind of injury since the Mythical Pokémon had lived locally for a long time. Nurse Joy has experience everyone can count on!

CHANSEY

BARON ALBERTO

This vain royal thinks he rules, but he's really just a self-serving nitwit. Baron Alberto is totally clueless when it comes to women and his worldview. He thinks everything revolves around him and what he wants. The baron wants to marry Alice, but she's far too smart to settle for a guy who only loves himself.

Baron Alberto is so arrogant, he will seize any opportunity to prove he's important. He doesn't realize that the reporters offering to interview him are tricky Team Rocket. Alberto just assumes he's so fascinating that the public deserves a documentary on him.

The baron also jumps to conclusions before having all the facts just because he wants to be the first one with an answer. He will proudly lead a charge, even if it's in the wrong direction—like that time he rallied local Trainers to fight the city's biggest ally, the Mythical Pokémon Darkrai. Alberto will take any chance to prove he's the best, and it makes him the worst.

LICKILICKY

When Lickilicky attempted to battle Darkrai, it was quickly sent to dreamland. With its eyes closed, it imagined that it was the baron. Strangely enough, in the strange new dimension, its wish transformed the baron into Lickilicky!

Being big and pink was a new look for Alberto, and it truly tested his patience, especially since people kept calling him Baron Lickilicky. However, the Team Rocket reporters suggested that the baron try to battle Darkrai since he was now a Pokémon. The baron imagined it would be awesome to get him saving the city on camera for all to see, so he stepped up and tried to battle Darkrai. He started with spinning Gyro Ball, but Darkrai easily dodged it. When the Baron Lickilicky followed up with Wrap, Darkrai used his tongue to swing him around and send him and Team Rocket blasting off across town.

TEAM ROCKET

Jessie, James, and Meowth followed Ash and his friends all the way to Alamos Town.

At first, the trio tried to fly in on a Carnivine-shaped hot air balloon. But when Jessie tried to catch Drifloon in a net, the Pokémon sent them blasting off.

Down on the ground in Alamos Town, the tricky trio decided their best position to steal Pokémon would be with Baron Alberto. They dressed up like TV reporters and flattered him with the idea that they were there to share his story with the world. Of course, the arrogant Alberto bought their line. Although Team Rocket never managed to capture any footage or Pokémon, they did manage to get blasted off again—this time, they were ejected by Darkrai, along with Baron Lickilicky.

WOBBUFFET

MYTHICAL AND LEGENDARY POKÉMON

DIALGA:
THE TEMPORAL POKÉMON

Height	17'09"
Weight	1505.8 lbs
Type	Steel/Dragon

The Legendary Pokémon is known as the deity of time because it is said that time began moving when Dialga was born.

PALKIA:
THE SPATIAL POKÉMON

Height	13'09"
Weight	740.8 lbs
Type	Water/Dragon

The Legendary Pokémon Palkia is known as the deity of space because it is said that it has the power to alter space.

DARKRAI:
THE PITCH BLACK POKÉMON

Height	4'11"
Weight	111.3 lbs
Type	Dark

The misunderstood Mythical Pokémon Darkrai has a bad reputation it doesn't deserve. It might lash out, but only when it needs to protect itself from prejudice, like the time Baron Alberto and the local Trainers ganged up on it because they thought it was causing the chaos. But loyal Darkrai was nobly trying to save the city they all loved!

Nevertheless, Darkrai has a strong sense of doing what's right. The Mythical Pokémon will do anything, including putting itself in harm's way between Dialga and Palkia, just to save its beloved hometown.

HOME SWEET GARDEN

Darkrai lives in Godey's gorgeous garden. It has called it home for decades ever since Alice's grandma, Alicia, first made it feel welcome. Since then, it has peacefully and happily hung out in the lush grounds.

WHEN THE NIGHTMARE IS REAL

If you tangle with Darkrai, it will put you into a scary sleep with Nightmare. The Mythical Pokémon has the power to give Pokémon and people terrifying dreams. However, when Darkrai attacked Ash, what seemed like Nightmare was actually a warning to our hero that Palkia was on its way to Alamos Town. And all those things it had said, like "Do not come here," and "Go away," were directed at Palkia, not Ash and his friends. Once they pieced together Darkrai's intent, it became clear that Darkrai wasn't afraid to look like the bad guy if it could do good.

FRIENDS

Alicia first made Darkrai feel at home in Alamos Town. Because of their friendship, Darkrai and Alice still feel a bond generations later. As a child, Alice slipped and fell off a cliff in the garden, and Darkrai raced to save her. As an adult, Darkrai put its own body before her hot air balloon to protect it from Dialga's intense Roar Of Time. In turn, Alice supported Darkrai and never believed the mean things she heard about it. She kept an open mind and helped her friends and hometown figure out the real problem, with Tonio's help, of course. And when Darkrai didn't think it could go on after falling from the sky when trying to stop Dialga and Palkia, it was Alice's kindness that restored its faith and strength. After all, love conquers all.

THE EPIC BATTLE

Known as the deity of time, Dialga lives in another dimension. But somehow, it crossed paths with its rival, Palkia, in the Space-Time rift and thus began an epic battle.

Dialga delivered a blow so strong it shattered one of the pink spheres on Palkia, the deity of space. To escape Dialga's fierce attacks, Palkia slipped into Alamos Town and sealed off the city. But Dialga followed it into Alamos Town to keep fighting. As their battle raged on through the streets, the entire area was lifted into another dimension and began to disintegrate. If they didn't act fast, Alamos Town would be lost to the other dimension forever!

Darkrai and its friends Ash, Brock, Dawn, Alice, and Tonio were committed to figuring out a way to save the day and the city. All the while, the Mythical Pokémon Darkrai challenged the two Legendary Pokémon but got caught up in its own fight against the misguided local Trainers who were attacking it under Baron Alberto's leadership.

After sending the local Pokémon into a dark slumber with Nightmare, Darkrai focused its attention on breaking up the battle between Dialga and Palkia. But instead of striking each other, they turned their attacks on Darkrai. It fell from the sky, landing in the garden. Alice, Ash, Dawn, Brock, and Tonio rushed to tell Darkrai how much they appreciated its help. They realized that Darkrai was trying to save the city, even though the other local Trainers had given it trouble.

Luckily, Tonio pieced together his data with Godey's diary entry. He figured out the way to put a stop to their epic battle. He knew that they had to play the song that means "prayer"—"Oracion."

Alice carried Ash and Dawn up to the Bell Tower to play the disc of "Oracion" in the bell chime. But in the meantime, Darkrai bravely put itself between Dialga and Palkia, absorbing their attacks. However, it wasn't able to hold it for long. As it fell back down from the sky and into the garden, Brock and Alice rushed to see if it was okay. Their concern reminded Darkrai of its old friend, Alicia. Remembering the bond they shared renewed Darkrai's strength, and it soared back up into the air.

But it was too late, and Darkrai disintegrated into the black sky. The other dimension was swallowing everything in sight. One more clash between Dialga and Palkia, and Alamos Town was done.

In the nick of time, Ash and Dawn, with the help of their Electric-type Pokémon pals Pikachu and Pachirisu, made the song "Oracion" ring out across the city. It soothed the rage of the Legendary Pokémon and even healed Palkia's injury. The Space-Time Towers began to transform as they glowed with a gold light. Then, the pair of Legendary Pokémon returned to their respective dimensions, restoring the delicate balance of Alamos Town.

FEATURED POKÉMON

When some columns in Godey's Garden have fallen over, Gallade goes to get Alice to show her the scene.

INTERESTING ITEMS

MUSIC DISCS

These patterned round discs play right in the Space-Time Tower's bell chime. All kinds of tunes are written on them, and one plays every hour on the hour from the Bell Tower. Tonio stores some in his basement lab, while others (like the one for "Oracion") are on display in the lobby.

GHOSTLY POKÉMON

When Alamos is sealed off and the real world merges with the dream world, Pokémon lined in purple light fly through the sky. These freaky Pokémon are see-through and can fly through walls. Bibarel spooks Ash, the baron, and Team Rocket in the street. But back at the Pokémon Center, there are a whole bunch: Bibarel, Buizel, Bronzor, Tropius, and Girafarig. However, the only thing worse than seeing these ghostly Pokémon is when they disappear because the city has nearly been swallowed by the other dimension.

GODEY'S DIARY

In his journal, Godey wrote about his life and even made predictions for the future. He foretold of a day that would come when a battle between Dialga and Palkia would threaten to destroy Alamos Town. Amazingly enough, he also figured out the antidote to stop their rage and send them back to their separate dimensions—the song "Oracion." Godey's private journal found itself in the very capable and wise hands of his studious grandson, Tonio. Although Tonio initially thought the entry was about an event in the past, his data helped him see it was unfolding in the present.

"ORACION"

Inside the nearly century-old journal, there was also an old black and white photo of Godey with Alicia. On the back of the photo was the musical composition of the sacred song "Oracion," as well as a hand-drawn symbol. These clues helped point Alice, Tonio, Ash, Brock, and Dawn in the direction of the right disc that would save the day!

Alicia also taught Alice to play the song that means "prayer" on the Leaf Whistle.

ALICE'S HOT AIR BALLOON

Green and yellow with red details, Alice's hot air balloon is a beautiful sight in the sky. Powered by Chimchar's Flamethrower, Alice typically uses the hot air balloon to give tours of her beloved Alamos Town. She offers Ash, Pikachu, Brock, and Dawn a special ride over to the city when she finds them on the edge of a cliff.

Alice also uses her hot air balloon to lift her pals up to the Bell Tower. At first, she just wants to show them the big bell chime. But in their second visit, it's a race against time to play "Oracion," and she bravely puts herself and her balloon at risk to help save the city. Although Darkrai boldly tries to protect Alice and the balloon from Dialga's stray attack, it gets so damaged in the battle, she and Dawn wind up falling out. Luckily, Dawn lands on her feet, and Tonio and Lickilicky are there to catch Alice.

TEAM ROCKET'S HOT AIR BALLOON

Team Rocket tries to ride into town in a Carnivine-shaped hot air balloon, but their flight is cut short. When Jessie tries to catch Drifloon in a net, it blasts them off with a windy Gust.

LEAF WHISTLE

Both Alice and her grandmother, Alicia, learned to play this special instrument. It has the power to calm Pokémon even when they're in the middle of a fight. When Shinx and Piplup fought over a berry in the playground, Alice knew just the tune to play to stop their battle and restore peace.

Alice also plays her Leaf Whistle to attract Flying-type Pokémon to visit her when she's up in her hot air balloon. After hearing her song, they show her which way the wind is blowing.

In Godey's garden, Alicia would play the sacred song "Oracion" on the Leaf Whistle for her granddaughter, Alice, when she was a little girl.

TOTALLY AWESOME TECHNOLOGY

TONIO'S DATA-COLLECTING DEVICE

Drifblim, Tonio's airborne Pokémon pal, wears a belt that carries a tracking device. The valuable information transmitted from this Pokémon's perspective feeds Tonio the information he needs to save Alamos Town.

TONIO'S PORTABLE TRACKING DEVICE

When he is out of his lab, Tonio brings a portable tracking device to read the data that Drifblim is collecting with him. From the screen, he can see the epic battle's impact on Alamos Town. Tonio can also chart Dialga and Palkia's vital signs, as well as get a sense of the strength of the other dimension.

POKÉMON: ARCEUS AND THE JEWEL OF LIFE

THE STORY

Ash, Pikachu, Dawn, Piplup, and Brock arrive in Michina Town on a warm, sunny day. They decide to go for a swim in a local lake where they meet two other Pokémon Trainers, Kato and Kiko. The pair challenge Ash and Dawn to a tag battle and offer their watermelons as a prize. Pikachu and Piplup win the round against Heracross and Beautifly. While they're all sharing the delicious snack, Kiko and Kato tell the crew they have to visit the incredible temple ruins while they're in town.

As they arrive at the foot of the temple ruins, another dimension opens in the sky. The whirlpool sucks up a tornado of water from the lake. Pikachu is able to break it with a Thunderbolt blast. However, it's enough to scare the wild forest Pokémon, which start fleeing the area. The Guardians of the Ruins, Sheena and Kevin, come running over.

Another bigger waterspout rises into the sky. The strong gust of wind sweeps up Pikachu and Piplup. Sheena summons Dialga, the Legendary Pokémon of Time, to save them.

Then, Dialga fires a terrific Roar of Time into the whirlpool. The sky seals back up, and the water returns to the river. But now, an even more epic fight begins as Giratina rises from the river and into the sky to battle Dialga.

Sheena clasps her hands together and prays, "Now transcend the confines of time and space!" Suddenly, she is transported into another dimension, where it is just she and Giratina. She speaks to the Legendary Pokémon, begging it to stop its attacks. But the Renegade Pokémon is too full of rage to listen to her.

So, Ash bravely runs into the river, right up to Giratina. The Legendary Pokémon recognizes its old buddy Ash and smiles. It agrees to stop fighting at Ash's request.

But soon, an even stronger waterspout appears and surrounds Dialga. To everyone's surprise, the Legendary Pokémon that rules space, Palkia, appears to stop it and save its old foe. Then, they return to their respective dimensions. Thanks to the Legendary Pokémon, there's peace on the river…for now.

Kevin and Sheena then give Ash, Pikachu, Dawn, Piplup, and Brock a private tour of the ancient temple ruins. They show them the Time-Space Axis, which indicates any disruption like the epic battle between Dialga and Palkia at Alamos Town. It has signaled that Arceus is about to wake up from its long slumber. Those waterspouts were signs of the whirlpools of energy swirling in its dimension. These whirlpools have also brought other dimensions together, ones that were supposed to remain eternally separate. They caused Dialga and Palkia's paths to cross and also brought Giratina into the conflict. But Kevin and Sheena are most concerned about when Arceus will reappear because it holds a grudge against humanity and will be out for revenge.

Sheena then tells Ash, Pikachu, Dawn, Piplup, and Brock about the unfortunate historic event that happened right there at the temple ruins. After Arceus saved the world from a giant meteor, it was left weak, and its 16 Life Plates were scattered across the wasteland that was Michina Town. A local man named Damos rushed to its aid to help it recover them. As thanks, Arceus lent Damos the Jewel of Life, an orb that held five of its Life Plates: Water, Grass, Ground, Electricity, and Dragon.

The gift transformed Michina Town into the fertile, thriving city it is today. The legend says that at the time of the solar eclipse, when Damos was supposed to give the orb back, he instead tricked the Mythical Pokémon by luring it into an arena full of Pokémon that attacked it. Betrayed, Arceus fled to recover from its injuries, vowing to return and settle the score. After thousands of years of sleep, it seems Arceus is ready to finally get justice.

Then, Sheena picks up what looks like a stone flower bud atop a fountain. When it opens, it reveals a glowing green orb inside—the Jewel of Life. Above it, there is a stone tablet with a carving begging the future generations to return the precious orb to its rightful owner, Arceus. Damos refused to return the Jewel of Life at the time because he thought Michina Town would go back to being a wasteland again, but the ancient people realized their mistake. As a descendant of Damos, Sheena felt it was her duty to right that wrong and soothe Arceus' anger before it was too late.

Suddenly, the Time-Space Axis chimes. This can only mean one thing—Arceus is back! And the Mythical Pokémon wastes no time, immediately starting with its strike on Michina Town.

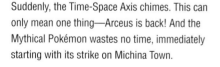

"WE HAVE COME HERE FROM THE FUTURE!" —SHEENA

Sheena races to present Arceus with the Jewel of Life and an apology for the way it was treated all those centuries ago. Arceus approaches, takes one look at the green orb, and smashes it in a single blow. The orb is a fake. Arceus is even angrier now because it thinks the people of Michina Town have tried to trick it again. Sheena clasps her hands together and speaks to it in its dimension, desperate to show Arceus that she truly thought it was real. But the Mythical Pokémon is so filled with rage that she can't reach it.

Dialga and Palkia arrive to try to protect Sheena and Michina Town. Arceus can't believe they'd side with humans. But their attacks are useless because Arceus is using its Life Plates to defend against their attacks. So, Ash cleverly has Pikachu use Thunderbolt. And it works! Without the Life Plate of Electricity, the Mythical Pokémon can't protect itself against Electric-type attacks.

Then, Giratina arrives to help save the city (and the world) from Arceus' angry attack. An epic battle has begun!

While Palkia distorts space to block Arceus' attacks, Dialga sends Sheena, Ash, Pikachu, Dawn, Piplup, and Brock back in time to stop this problem before it even happens. The crew is very surprised to find themselves transported through another dimension to ancient Michina Town.

They've arrived at the time of the solar eclipse, the fateful day Damos broke his promise. Before their very eyes, they watch Damos betray and attack Arceus. Damos stands next to a man with a red robe and a gold medallion on his forehead, taunting the Mythical Pokémon and vowing to never return the Jewel of Life. Sheena clasps her hands together and asks Dialga to send them further back in time.

In the present, the epic battles rages on. Dialga knows Sheena, Ash, Dawn, and Brock are their only hope. So, with all of its strength, it transports them to the morning of the fateful day. They're immediately surrounded by temple guards, who bring them to the man in the red robe, Marcus. Sheena tells Marcus that they came from the future and begs him to return the Jewel of Life. Intrigued, Marcus invites Sheena inside to chat. However, he has Bronzong hypnotize the rest of his guests. Then, his guards throw Ash, Brock, and Dawn in one jail cell and Piplup and Pikachu in another.

Ash, Dawn, and Brock are locked up with none other than Damos! He tells them Marcus threw him in jail because he had every intention of returning the Jewel of Life to Arceus. Ash puts all the clues together and figures out that Marcus had his Pokémon slave Bronzong use Hypnotize on Damos to get him to do his bidding and trick the Mythical Pokémon against his will. Damos can't believe he would ever do such a thing and that history remembers him as a selfish jerk.

Damos shares the same ability as Sheena to communicate heart to heart with Pokémon. Damos recounts the story of how he watched Arceus save the world from a meteor and subsequently used his special power to help Arceus when it lost its Life Plates. Then, Arceus trusted Damos with the Jewel of Life to turn the wasteland of Michina Town into a lush paradise. They truly saved each other, and Damon would never betray his friend Arceus. In fact, it was Damos who built the temple to honor Arceus.

At an elaborate table filled with food, Sheena is spilling her guts to Marcus. She warns him about Damos' plan to trick Arceus and how that affects the future. Marcus pretends to care, but he really just wants all the details so he can secretly perfect his evil plans. Marcus then tells Sheena that she can take Damos' place and return the Jewel of Life to Arceus. Sheena is thrilled that Marcus is giving her an opportunity to change history! But should she trust this scheming stranger?

A wild Pichu that watched Sheena's friends all get locked up decides to help free the captives. It crawls into the jail cell and leads Piplup and Pikachu out through a small secret tunnel. Together, they scamper through the kitchen to find the cell keys.

The solar eclipse has begun, and Arceus has arrived at the arena. Sheena greets the Mythical Pokémon with the staff, but to her complete surprise, it's empty. Then, Marcus signals all the Pokémon in the balcony to attack Arceus. Sheena can't believe she's been tricked. Worse yet, Marcus is dumping silver water on Arceus, trapping it in metal. He thinks if Arceus is destroyed, Michina Town will never have to lose the Jewel of Life.

Damos, Ash, Dawn, and Brock arrive in the nick of time to save Sheena, but now they have to find a way to free Arceus. As the silver water continues to pour down, Ash, Pikachu, Dawn, and Piplup run up to stop Marcus. But first, they'll have to battle Heatran and Bronzong.

Damos thinks fast and has Sheena hold his hand. Then, they say the passage that allows them to speak heart to heart with Pokémon. Together, Damos and Sheena ask the Pokémon in the arena to stop fighting and remind them that Arceus saved the world and brought so much to Michina Town. The Pokémon hear their words and cease firing.

Meanwhile in the present day, Team Rocket is exploring the temple ruins and winds up in the old kitchen. There, they find a staff containing the real Jewel of Life. But before they can take another step, a stray attack blasts them into the river.

Back in the past, Pichu, Pikachu, and Piplup deliver the keys to Damos. He opens the jail cell and wants to do one thing with his freedom: save his friend Arceus. But he's going to have to hurry!

Ash seizes the opportunity to wrestle Marcus now that he is defenseless without the help of Heatran and Bronzong. The Jewel of Life flies out of Marcus' hand. Ash chases it off the side of the platform. He's hanging on for dear life, but the Jewel of Life is caught between his feet. Pikachu catches it, and then the pair races to the bottom of the arena to return it to Arceus.

But Arceus is so angry, it doesn't hear Ash. More silver water rains down. Arceus is almost completely covered. Ash, Pikachu, Dawn, Piplup, Sheena, and Brock all begin to disappear. If this is to be Arceus' fate, if Arceus doesn't exist in the future, history has changed, and there is no need for Ash and his friends to be there.

Damos won't give up. He uses all of his strength to reach out to Arceus in its dimension. He finally gets close enough to place his hand on Arceus' head. A bright light bursts, breaking its anger. Damos shows Arceus that Ash has the Jewel of Life and asks the Mythical Pokémon to take it back.

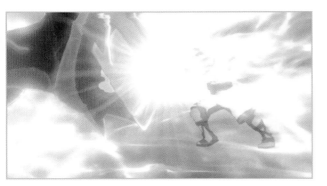

The Jewel of Life glows as it is returned to its rightful owner. Ash, Pikachu, Dawn, Piplup, Brock, and Sheena are restored. With a beam of golden light, Arceus is freed from its metal coffin. The Mythical Pokémon thanks Ash and Pikachu for their help, but Ash tells Arceus that all of his friends worked together with Damos.

Suddenly, the entire arena begins to collapse under the weight of the silver water. Arceus uses its might to save all the people and Pokémon inside. Then, it removes all the armor on the Pokémon, freeing them from Marcus' control. Arceus bids his friends farewell as it returns to its dimension to rest.

Sheena, Ash, Pikachu, Dawn, Piplup, and Brock say goodbye to their new friend Damos. Dialga summons them back to the present. There, they find the epic battle is still raging on. Ash calls out to Arceus to stop. When the Mythical Pokémon sees its old pal Ash, Arceus ends the battle and restores the entirety of Michina Town. Like the area, history has been improved.

As they look across the fertile fields of Michina Town, Brock can't help but wonder why Michina Town isn't a wasteland if they gave back the Jewel of Life. Arceus admits it can't take the credit there: the people and Pokémon of Michina Town have worked hard to make the city what it is today. Everyone played an important part, including our heroes who helped make history!

As they walk through the temple, they notice a message from their friend Damos. The stone tablet that was once a warning has been replaced with a picture of all of them and a message of thanks.

LOCATIONS
MICHINA TOWN

Nestled between rock formations, Michina
Town is a fertile paradise dotted with farms and
orchards all along the riverbanks. Looking at
all the plenty, it's hard to believe it was once an
empty wasteland covered in unforgiving rocky
terrain where the locals struggled to survive.

THE TEMPLE RUINS

To honor Arceus, the Mythical Pokémon that
helped transform the land, Damos led the
ancient people to build a terrific temple. Atop
the tallest rock in Michina Town, the temple is
incredible to look up at from the city grounds,
but it offers the best views of the valley from its
promenade. Down its rock face, waterfalls flow into a large lake.

When Ash, Pikachu, Dawn, Piplup, and Brock arrive, they're in awe of the landmark. The Guardians of the Ruins, Kevin and Sheena, offer to give them
a private tour. However, it's not just a history lesson, as our heroes become involved in a struggle that began thousands of years ago.

THE ALTAR

Deep within the temple is a special shrine that holds the sacred
Time-Space Axis, the tracking device that logs activity in the other
dimensions where Dialga, Palkia, Giratina, and Arceus live.

The floor has portraits of the Legendary Pokémon Dialga (the deity of
time) and Palkia (the deity of space) made in mosaic tile.

In one corner, a small fountain with a stone flower bud at the top holds
what Sheena believes to be the Jewel of Life.

On the opposite wall of the Time-Space Axis, sheets of water are used
as screens to play projections of the history of Michina Town and the
unfortunate fate of Arceus and its misunderstood hero, Damos.

THE KITCHEN

At one time, this kitchen was staffed by Pokémon. Chikorita did the
chopping, and Cyndaquil kept the fire going. But now, it's nothing but a
dusty old room with a few scattered relics. When Team Rocket happens
upon the forgotten room, James finds a helmet, while Meowth and Jessie
find dirty old crowns. While they are all focused on headgear, the real
treasure is hiding inside the scepter Jessie is holding. When the flower
bud at the top opens up, it reveals the lost Jewel of Life. Team Rocket
immediately recognizes it, but before they can sell it to the highest bidder,
Ash and his pals are back in time, solving the high crime.

THE TEMPLE IN ANCIENT TIMES

When Dialga transports Sheena, Ash, Pikachu, Dawn, Piplup, and Brock back in time, they arrive at the temple and see it in its original glory for the first time. The newly built building glistens in the light, and not a brick is out of place. After all, it hasn't been through thousands of years of wear and tear.

THE ARENA

This round room has a high ceiling and many spectator balconies. Unfortunately, it also became the stage for the betrayal of Arceus. It was here that the Mythical Pokémon was tricked and attacked by the very people and Pokémon it had helped.

However, Dialga sent Sheena, Ash, Pikachu, and their pals traveling to that day to rewrite history and save the Alpha Pokémon from the cruel deceit. It was there in the arena that they protected Arceus and the future.

THE POKÉMON HOLDING CELL

Marcus, the evil mastermind behind the betrayal of Arceus, doesn't respect the rights of any magical creatures (or Pokémon, as we call them). He keeps them in a holding cell down in the depths of the temple like slaves, only there to serve him. Without even a peep, Piplup and Pikachu get thrown in a cell. Luckily, a local Pichu that watched their arrival at the temple unfold snuck in to show them a secret tunnel out.

THE JAIL CELL

While Sheena is meeting with Marcus, Ash, Dawn, and Brock are separated from Piplup and Pikachu and thrown into a jail cell. But they're not alone: inside, they meet their only cellmate, Damos. At first, they think they're face-to-face with the man who betrayed Arceus, as the legend said. But once they get to talking, they realize he has been held captive by the true evil mastermind, Marcus. Because Damos wanted to return the Jewel of Life to his pal Arceus, Marcus threw him in that very jail cell.

MEETING ROOM

Sheena and Marcus sat across from each other at a long table, covered in bowls of fruit and serving pieces. The tiled room isn't your typical office, but Marcus conducted his business there. Sheena thought she was saving the day. But Marcus was only after all the information the woman from the future could give so he could fool-proof his wicked plan.

CHARACTERS

ASH

Always up for an adventure, Ash sure finds it in Michina Town, both in the present and in the past. When Dialga sends Ash and his pals back in time, Ash bravely saves the day. And in turn, he makes a new friend: the Mythical Pokémon Arceus.

FACE OFF

Our hero flies in the face of danger! But it's his face that saves the day, not once, but twice.

When Giratina stepped in to battle Dialga, Ash ran out into the river to ask it to stop. When Giratina saw the face of its old friend Ash, it smiled and (amazingly enough) did exactly as he asked. Giratina returned to its dimension, as did Dialga. But unfortunately, the peace Ash brokered didn't last very long.

The second time Ash's friendly face stops a battle, it's between Arceus, Giratina, Dialga, and Palkia. But more importantly, it's because Arceus had been wronged and Ash went back in time to make it right. On the night of the solar eclipse, Ash wrestled Marcus himself to get the Jewel of Life.

When it slipped down the arena wall, Ash jumped and caught it with his feet, barely hanging on by a peg. His best Pokémon buddy Pikachu followed him to catch the ball with its talented tail. Then, Ash hand-delivered it to Arceus, which was trapped in a pool of silver down at the very bottom of the arena. The Jewel of Life saved Arceus from a terrible fate, and it thanked Ash.

When Ash returned to the present, Arceus was still trying to destroy Michina Town and battling the Legendary Pokémon. Ash again went up to the Alpha Pokémon, and this time, he asked for a ceasefire. Arceus recognized his old pal Ash and did as he asked. Now, they had saved each other.

PIKACHU

Pikachu is always up for a battle, even when his opponent is the Alpha Pokémon. Pikachu's Electric-type attacks have quite an effect on Arceus since it's missing that Life Plate.

STARAPTOR

GLISCOR

MONFERNO

GROTLE

DAWN

What started as another stop on their journey turned into an exciting adventure back in time for Dawn. She and Piplup were right there to battle Marcus and do what they could to rewrite history.

MAMOSWINE

PIPLUP

BUIZEL

BUNEARY

PACHIRISU

BROCK

Ash's good buddy Brock has followed him through a lot of different places, but now, they've also traveled through time.

No matter where he is, Brock has one thing on his mind—girls. He tries to woo Damos' descendant Sheena, but his Pokémon pal Croagunk is there to keep him focused on the reason they're there, the temple ruins.

HAPPINY

SUDOWOODO

CROAGUNK

KIKO AND KATO

When Ash, Brock, and Dawn find watermelons floating in the lake, Kiko and Kato aren't far behind. Apparently, the delicious fruit found its way into the water from their farm. They offer to give them to Ash and his pals, but only if they beat Kiko and Kato in a tag battle.

Dawn and Ash can't resist a battle challenge, especially when the prize is so sweet. So, Kiko with Beautifly and Kato with Heracross battle Ash with Pikachu and Dawn with Piplup. It's a fun fight that ends with a big win for everyone. Even though Ash and Dawn are victorious, they share their watermelon with their new friends and all of their Pokémon. Then, Kiko and Kato share a travel tip with them that will change the course of history. The pair suggests no visit to Michina Town is complete without a trip to see the incredible temple ruins.

SHEENA

A Guardian of the Ruins, Sheena has made the temple her life's work. She not only knows the legend inside and out, but she is also hoping for the chance to rewrite it. Sheena is a descendant of Damos, the man who supposedly betrayed Arceus. Her family has protected the Jewel of Life for centuries, waiting for Arceus to return so they can do what's right and give it to the Alpha Pokémon.

Sheena anxiously watches the Time-Space Axis, waiting for the signal that Arceus has awoken from its long slumber. Then, she plans finally do right by the Mythical Pokémon on behalf of her people.

TRICKED BY THE TRICKSTER

Although Sheena knew the legend inside and out, the record failed to mention a key player in the story: a mysterious man named Marcus. When Sheena, Ash, Pikachu, Dawn, Piplup, and Brock first arrive in ancient times, it is Marcus who greets them at the temple. While he places all of Sheena's friends in jail, he invites Sheena to meet with him.

She is so trusting that she spills her story to Marcus in the hopes he'll help her stop Damos from tricking Arceus. But Marcus is truly the mastermind behind the betrayal. Sheena accidentally helps Marcus with his plans instead of stopping them. Then, Marcus asks her to return the Jewel of Life to Arceus and replace Damos. Sheena thinks this is the opportunity of a lifetime, but instead, she is given a fake.

By the time she realizes she is part of Marcus' evil plan, it's too late to take it all back. But Sheena isn't the kind of woman who gives up that easily! With the help of her ancestor Damos and her new friends, they are able to completely change the legend for good.

FROM THE HEART

Sheena possesses a unique gift: she can have heart-to-heart communication with Pokémon. She clasps her hands together and says, "Transcend the confines of space and time!" Then, she is immediately transported to another dimension where she comes face-to-face with the Pokémon she needs to speak to, whether it's Absol or Arceus, the Alpha Pokémon. The Pokémon can see her heart and its intentions clearly, so they can trust her. But, if a Pokémon is too full of rage, she can't reach it.

Using her unique gift, Sheena asks Dialga to send her back in time to help Arceus. Then, in the temple arena, she meets her ancestor Damos, who possesses the same gift and same strength of character. They link hands to speak to all the Pokémon and ask them to stop firing at Arceus. Together, they end the senseless attacks on the Alpha Pokémon.

KEVIN

A Guardian of the Ruins, Kevin arrives on the scene of the battle between Giratina, Dialga, and Palkia with his partner, Sheena. He also shows Ash, Pikachu, Dawn, Piplup, and Brock around the temple with her. However, he is left behind in the present when Dialga transports the crew back in time. Kevin keeps an eye on the battle, hoping Sheena and her new friends are successful.

DAMOS

THE BEGINNING OF A BEAUTIFUL FRIENDSHIP

Damos saw Arceus in action as it nearly sacrificed itself to save the world it created from a meteor shower that would have destroyed it. In the impact, Arceus lost its Life Plates and fell to the ground. While wild Pokémon gathered around Arceus to keep it warm, Damos helped hunt down the Life Plates to restore Arceus' strength. Deeply grateful to Damos, Arceus lent him the Jewel of Life so he could transform the barren wasteland that was Michina Town into the lush land it is now.

THE REAL BETRAYAL

Although the history books portrayed Damos as greedy, they got it all wrong. The legend said that Damos was the one who betrayed Arceus because he didn't want to return the Jewel of Life and watch the land become barren again, but actually, Damos himself had been betrayed.

Damos had every intention of returning the Jewel of Life, but not everyone in Michina Town agreed with him. Marcus, his former underling, did not want Damos to give it back to Arceus, so he staged a coup and threw his boss in jail.

Then, Marcus supposedly asked Bronzong to hypnotize Damos into luring the Alpha Pokémon in with false promises. The evil mastermind behind the whole horrible event in the arena was Marcus. Ash, Dawn, and Brock came to discover that Damos was wrongfully accused of the crime against Arceus. And they were there to set the record straight!

OPEN HEART

Just like his descendant, Sheena, Damos can communicate directly to Pokémon with his heart by clasping his hands together and saying their familial phrase. To connect with all the Pokémon in the arena, Damos and Sheena hold hands and speak to all of them together.

But when it comes time to talk to Arceus, Damos uses all of his heart to break through the Mythical Pokémon's anger and put his hand on its head. Then and only then can Arceus, trapped in silver water and nearly knocked out, see that there are honest humans there to help it.

Because of the strength of his character, the fearlessness of his determination, and the power of their incredible friendship, Damos is able to reach the Alpha Pokémon and return the Jewel of Life to it. Although it rewrote his story in history, Damos wasn't concerned about his image. He did it all because he wanted to help his friend Arceus and save future generations. Damos is a true hero.

PICHU: THE TINY MOUSE POKÉMON

Tiny Pichu knows its way around the temple. It can sneak through secret tunnels and knows just how to slip past the guards. So, when Damos is locked up, his "magical creature" pal Pichu snags the keys to help him escape. Along the way, Pichu also saves several other notables: Ash, Pikachu, Dawn, Piplup, and Brock.

TAPP

In charge of watching the jail cells is a misguided guard named Tapp. Like Marcus, he worries that if the Jewel of Life is returned to Arceus, the area will again be a wasteland. But he also knows that Damos speaks the truth and is a good man. He vouches for Damos, informing Ash, Dawn, and Brock that he is telling the truth about Marcus and his own intentions. And when Pichu, Piplup, and Pikachu come with the cell's stolen keys to bust their pals out, Tapp just looks the other way and pretends not to see it happening. Although he works for Marcus, he uses his own moral compass when push comes to shove.

MARCUS

History books have pegged Damos as the evildoer, but he was just manipulated by the real mastermind, Marcus. This power-hungry person used to work for Damos but sneakily staged a coup to take control of the temple and the Jewel of Life. He will stop at nothing to hoard the riches of Michina Town. Marcus sees his cruelty as a means to an end.

He pretends that his plot to destroy Arceus is really for the benefit of the whole town, but if it's so good for everyone, why does he keep it a secret? No one wants the area to return to a barren wasteland, but a true leader would find a way to work together for the common good.

A ROYAL PAIN

Instead of having a loyal team, Marcus enslaves Pokémon to do his bidding. He's no Trainer—he's a taskmaster. Marcus sees Pokémon as his personal servants. He even makes them wear special suits of armor to keep them captive.

He forces Bronzong to hypnotize Ash, Pikachu, Dawn, Piplup, and Brock the minute they arrive so he can throw them in jail. He has dozens of Pokémon held in a small holding cell so he can force them to attack Arceus. He even has Chikorita and Cyndaquil cooking his meals in the kitchen! Marcus is as cruel as they come.

BRONZONG

HEATRAN

TRICKS UP HIS SLEEVE

Marcus takes the real Jewel of Life, slips it in his robe, and replaces it with a fake. When Damos or Sheena tries to return the precious round orb to Arceus, it really is just a trap for the Mythical Pokémon. Marcus is so good at this trickery that, for thousands of years, Sheena's family has been protecting the fake.

TEAM ROCKET

Jessie, James, and Meowth have followed Ash and his friends to Michina Town. But luckily, their antics are contained in the present.

CROWNING ACHIEVEMENT

As the trio pokes around the temple, they find some relics from Damos' time. James dons a helmet. Meowth and Jessie find questionable crowns. But amazingly enough, Jessie also picks up Marcus' staff, the secret hiding spot for the real Jewel of Life. When the flower bud on top opens, revealing the glowing orb, the trio can't believe their luck. But their luck runs out pretty quickly because Sheena, Ash, and their friends soon return it to its rightful owner back in ancient times, Arceus. Then, in the present, the Jewel of Life disappears right out of their hands.

ALL TALK

However, they prove themselves to be more bark than bite. The first time Sheena presents the Jewel of Life to Arceus, Team Rocket has the opportunity to snag it. But perhaps they're very timid thieves because Jessie, James, and Meowth can't seem to muster the guts to grab it.

LEGENDARY AND MYTHICAL POKÉMON

DIALGA:
THE TEMPORAL POKÉMON

Height	17'09"
Weight	1505.8 lbs
Type	Steel/Dragon

As the Legendary Pokémon also known as the deity of time, Dialga's power transcends any clock or calendar. In fact, while Dialga fights in the present, it sends Sheena, Ash, Pikachu, Dawn, Piplup, and Brock back in time. Dialga understands the importance of helping Arceus. So, the Temporal Pokémon transports its human pals back in time not once, but twice. If at first you don't succeed, Dialga will help you try, try again.

PALKIA:
THE SPATIAL POKÉMON

Height	13'09"
Weight	740.8 lbs
Type	Water/Dragon

The Legendary Pokémon also known as the deity of space travels to Michina Town and fights alongside its former foe, Dialga. Amazingly enough, the Time-Space Axis told Sheena about the epic battle back in Alamos Town. It was one of the warning signs that Arceus would awaken and arrive soon. The whirlpools Ash and his friends saw first-hand at the river were the same kind that brought Dialga and Palkia—two Pokémon living in two different dimensions that never should have even met—together.

GIRATINA:
THE RENEGADE POKÉMON
ALTERED FORME

Height	14'09"
Weight	1653.5 lbs
Type	Ghost/Dragon

Giratina breaks through a black hole in the river and gets into a fight with Dialga. Before the battle gets out of hand, Ash wades in the water up to Giratina. When the Legendary Pokémon sees its old buddy Ash's face, it stops its attack.

However, the Renegade Pokémon returns when Arceus arrives. It joins Dialga and Palkia in an unlikely trio to stop the Alpha Pokémon from destroying the very town it helped create.

ARCEUS:
THE ALPHA POKÉMON

Height	10'06"
Weight	705.5 lbs
Type	Normal

Said to have created the entire world, Arceus is also known as the Alpha Pokémon.

ANCIENT HISTORY

When meteors threatened to destroy the world, the Mythical Pokémon risked its own life to save it. Although Arceus was able to break up the meteors, it lost its 16 Life Plates in the impact.

Luckily, a Michina Town local named Damos saw Arceus' sacrifice and ran over to help it. While Damos searched for a Life Plate, local wild Pokémon surrounded it to keep it warm. Damos successfully located one in the rocky terrain, giving Arceus the strength to recover them all. Then, as thanks for saving its life, Arceus selflessly lent Damos five of the Life Plates in the form of an orb called the Jewel of Life. Without those five, Arceus' power was reduced, and it was left weak to those types of attacks. But it trusted Davos, the human.

Damos was to return the Jewel of Life at the time of the solar eclipse. However, instead, Arceus was led into a trap and attacked. Robbed of its strength and its Life Plates, Arceus vowed to return for revenge on humanity after it got some rest.

FLASH FORWARD

A few thousand years later, Ash and his pals were there when the Alpha Pokémon finally awoke. Together with Sheena, Ash, Pikachu, Dawn, Piplup, Brock, and even Damos, they all worked together to help right the historic wrong.

When the Jewel of Life was finally returned to its rightful owner, Arceus freed all the Pokémon enslaved by Marcus. The Mythical Pokémon was restored, and it returned to its dimension.

However, when Ash and his pals returned to the present, Arceus was still fighting with Dialga, Palkia, and Giratina. So, Ash called out to Arceus to beg it to stop. When Arceus saw the face of the boy who had saved it thousands of years ago by giving it back the Jewel of Life, it listened. Ash had a bond with Arceus that not even an epic battle could break. There was justice, and now there was peace.

LIFE PLATES

These 16 angular slabs that look like they're made of diamonds are even more precious. They each draw on a different realm of Arceus' strengths. The Life Plates are its life force. When they are strewn across the winter wasteland, Arceus fears for its life. Luckily, Damos helps it recover them. In turn, Arceus helps Damos by lending him five Life Plates: Ground, Water, Grass, Electricity, and all increased by the added power of Dragon.

THE MYTH OF BETRAYAL

Sheena tells Ash and his pals about the historic event that took place right at the temple ruins. According to a local legend, the Mythical Pokémon Arceus saved the world from being destroyed by meteors. It used its own body as a force to stop the fiery shower from the stars. Although it saved people, Pokémon, and the planet, it nearly destroyed itself on impact. Arceus' Life Plates were scattered through a barren wasteland known as Michina Town.

With the help of the Jewel of Life, Michina Town was completely transformed into a prosperous farming community. The land was as rich as the people! Damos worried that if he returned the Jewel of Life, the land would go back to the sad years of struggle. Supposedly, he decided to keep the Jewel of Life and to destroy Arceus instead.

By the time of the solar eclipse, Damos had built a temple to honor Arceus. Legend has it that Damos welcomed the Mythical Pokémon inside an arena, pretending he would return the Jewel of Life. But Arceus soon found it was fake and was caught in a terrible trap. As dozens of Pokémon attacked it from the balconies of the arena, it was forced to flee.

One righteous inhabitant of the area, Damos, witnessed Arceus' sacrifice. He rushed to its side to see how he could help. Dozens of wild Pokémon kept Arceus warm while Damon looked for a Life Plate. With his help, Arceus was able to locate all 16 and restore its power.

Looking around at the rocks and craters, Arceus took pity on Damos and his neighbors in Michina City. It lent him the Jewel of Life, made of five of its Life Plates, to turn Michina Town into a fertile paradise. But the gift was a loan: Arceus made a deal with Damos to return the Jewel of Life during the next solar eclipse.

However, Arceus vowed to return to Michina Town someday for payback. It would rest to heal itself from its injuries and come back strong enough to destroy all of humanity because of this betrayal.

Arceus took a long slumber, too. Thousands of years went by before it woke up. But when it did, it immediately returned to Michina Town to settle the score. Luckily, Sheena, Ash, Pikachu, Dawn, Piplup, and Brock were there to change the course of history!

THE JEWEL OF LIFE

Back in ancient times, the people and Pokémon in the area were desperate for something that could transform the land. Luckily, Arceus lent them five of its 16 Life Plates: Ground, Water, Grass, Electricity, and all increased by the power of Dragon. Arceus shaped these Life Plates into a glowing green sphere called the Jewel of Life. Its power helped the locals turn the desolate, rocky desert into a rich, fruitful area.

FEATURED POKÉMON

INTERESTING ITEMS

TEAM ROCKET'S PEDAL-POWERED BLIMP

This primary-colored mode of sky travel would work well if Jessie could keep pedaling. Instead, it doesn't stay airborne very long, and they crash-land in Michina Town. Well, at least they made it this far!

WHIRLPOOLS AND WATERSPOUTS

Rising from the river into the sky, they look like tornados of water, but they're actually whirlpools of energy swirling to wake Arceus from its slumber. But that's not all they're up to. These swirling, twirling towers are also warping dimensions, bringing together powerful Pokémon that typically live apart, like Giratina, Dialga, and Palkia. And not even the Legendary Pokémon can stop them!

These whirlpools of energy are so strong, they suck up trees and even Piplup and Pikachu. Summoned by Sheena, Dialga bravely swoops in to save Ash and Dawn's Pokémon pals.

THE STONE TABLET

Above the fountain at the shrine, there is an ancient tablet carved with important advice. When Ash, Dawn, and Brock first arrive in Michina Town, Sheena reads the inscription to them. It says:

However, when they return from the past, having successfully given the Jewel of Life back to Arceus, they find a new carving. There is a picture of them all together with Arceus and quite a different message left by Damos. Now it reads:

> **"RETURN THUS TO ARCEUS— THE JEWEL OF LIFE. PLACATE ITS RAGE, LEST DESTRUCTION VISIT THIS LAND."**

SOLAR ECLIPSE

This rare event happens when a full new moon completely covers the sun.

In ancient times, Arceus had made a deal with Damos that he would return the Jewel of Life on the night of the solar eclipse. This is also the time that Sheena, Ash, Pikachu, Dawn, Piplup, and Brock arrive when they travel back in time.

FAKE JEWEL OF LIFE

For generations, members of Sheena's family have been protecting a green orb locked in a stone flower bud that they believed to be the Jewel of Life. Upon Arceus' return, she cannot wait to soothe its anger, restore its faith in humanity, and return what rightfully belongs to it. But when she presents Arceus with a proper apology and the green orb, it only enrages Arceus. The Alpha Pokémon smashes it with one stomp—it's a fake.

THE MAGICAL CREATURE'S ARMOR

Marcus made the Pokémon around the temple wear armor traps. With these contraptions on, they were forced to do his evil bidding (or sometimes even just his cooking). Their will and abilities were disrespected by the selfish Marcus, who thought only of his own comfort and power.

> "TIME TO RETURN TO THE FUTURE!" —SHEENA

TOTALLY AWESOME TECHNOLOGY
THE TIME-SPACE AXIS

Sitting in the shrine at the temple ruins is a very sophisticated instrument that reads the Time-Space continuum. The Guardians of the Ruins, Sheena and Kevin, use this technologically advanced tool to detect disturbances. Known as the Time-Space Axis, it has different-colored spheres for each dimension it tracks. Green is for Earth, teal is for Giratina, blue is for Dialga, fuchsia is for Palkia, and orange is for Arceus. This amazing machine has signaled major events like the hole in time and space opened near the glacier and Dialga and Palkia's showdown in Alamos Town. It has one chime that rings out to signal the arrival of Arceus.

POKÉ BALL AND POKÉMON

This might seem basic to a modern Trainer, but Poké Balls are a relatively new piece of technology. So, to prove to Damos that they're truly from the future, Ash shows him a Poké Ball, and Monferno appears. Damos couldn't believe his eyes when the "magical creature" appeared. But then, he also couldn't believe his ears when Ash added that they're also called "Pokémon." Wow! Can you imagine what amazing things will be invented a few thousand years from now?

P0KÉMON THE MuVIE: WHITE - VICTINI AND ZEKROM
POKÉMON THE MOVIE: BLACK - VICTINI AND RESHIRAM

THE STORY

POKÉMON THE MOVIE: WHITE - VICTINI AND ZEKROM

In the middle of the desert, an injured Blitzle cries out. Damon and his Pokémon pal Reuniclus find it and bring it home to a nearby village.

But Ravine, the leader of the village, isn't too happy to see him. Damon has been trying to convince him to move back to the land that belongs to their people, a group known as the People of the Vale. Ravine thinks the land is lost, but Damon believes the legend is true, and he vows to prove it.

Suddenly, their argument is halted by an even bigger disruption. A black tornado on the horizon has sent a stampede of hundreds of Bouffalant headed their way. Damon reaches his hand up to the sky and summons the Legendary Pokémon Reshiram. It fires a Fusion Flare explosion right into the tornado, causing it to go up in smoke. But the Bouffalant don't stop running, so Reshiram herds them with bursts of Blue Flare.

Riding on Reshiram, Damon then flies back over to the villagers. He tells them the time has come for the People of the Vale to reclaim their land. Reshiram agrees, promising that is where the truth lies.

Meanwhile, Ash, Pikachu, Iris, Axew, and Cilan have arrived in the town of Eindoak just in time for the Harvest Festival, featuring a Pokémon Competition. But on their way into the city, they spot a Deerling trying to save its pal from slipping off a rock ledge. Ash is able to grab them just in time, but then the rock under his feet breaks off, too. But an invisible force seems to hold them back from falling. Then, amazingly enough, that same force helps Ash (carrying both Deerling and Pikachu) jump across the valley to another mountain ledge.

"THERE IS NO SHORTCUT TO THE TRUTH..." —RESHIRAM

The ledge that Ash landed on leads to a tunnel. A vision shows him the way to a cave made of a large crystal web. Another vision shows the way through a hidden brick door and into a famous local castle—the Sword of the Vale.

Iris and Cilan can't believe what they just saw! But what they didn't see was that the invisible force was none other than the Mythical Pokémon Victini sharing some of its power.

From a balcony, Ash signals to Cilan, Iris, and Axew, who are happy to see he's found his way. Cilan tells them that according to legend, the castle actually flew through the air from the valley to the spot it's in now. Then, Cilan shares some of the macarons he's made with his friends. But two go missing, right out of Ash's hand. It's the work of invisible Victini, which seems to have a big sweet tooth.

On their way to the festival, Ash, Iris, and Brock meet a few new friends. First, Damon shows them the way to town. Then, Juanita teaches them about Victini, a Pokémon said to give people and Pokémon power. She also mentions that according to legend, Victini protected the Sword of the Vale. Then, she gives Iris a little wooden charm of the Mythical Pokémon.

Then, the Mayor of Eindoak, Mannes, steps onstage and kicks off the annual battle competition. Ash, Cilan, and Iris are all excited to enter. However, Iris and Cilan get eliminated in the first round, Ash makes it all the way to face a fourth opponent and his Pokémon pal Samurott. In true Ash style, he picks a Pokémon with a strong type disadvantage—Tepig. Although it looks like the Fire-type has no chance, with a little extra power courtesy of invisible Victini, Ash wins the match.

Next, Ash faces Juanita's daughter, Carlita, and her Pokémon pal Hydreigon. Scraggy is excited to battle, but it soon finds itself in the bushes. Victini steps in to give it some added power, and this time, Carlita spots it! When Scraggy returns to battle, it knocks Hydreigon clean off the field with a single super Headbutt.

After the battle, Carlita is curious to find out if Ash had been getting help from Victini. Ash puts together that the invisible force and visions he's been experiencing must be the Mythical Pokémon. So, Ash holds out a macaron up to the nearby trees and offers it to Victini. The group watches it excitedly disappear bite by bite in midair. Then, on the second macaron, the invisible snacker reveals itself to be Victini. Ash, Pikachu, Iris, Axew, Cilan, and Carlita introduce themselves. Then, Ash thanks it for all of its help. The two instantly become buddies.

As Ash and Victini lead their friends on a stroll through town, they find an incredibly tall pillar. Ash wants to get a closer look, but Victini can't cross a certain invisible barrier. A ball of flames bursts around its body. Pillars around the city glow with a purple light, revealing the barrier around the perimeter of town. Sad, Victini flies off.

Along the way to find Victini, the group encounters Juanita, her son Damon, and Mannes. Juanita explains that they encountered one of the Pillars of Protection, and it is said that the Mythical Pokémon can't travel beyond their barrier. They finally find Victini playing around a pool by the castle. Ash's apology is so heartfelt that he doesn't look where he's going and slips. Victini grabs him by his hood to try to save its friend from falling in, but Ash slips right into the water face first. Then, they play in the pool together, happy to be reunited.

Back inside the castle, Mannes shows them a book that tells the story of the local legend of the People of the Vale.

More than a thousand years ago, there was a kingdom that drew its power from the invisible force that flows through the planet—Dragon Force. The wise king ruled the land with the help of his best buddy, Victini, and people, Pokémon, and nature lived in perfect harmony. The king had two twin sons. One was called the Hero of Ideals, who had the support of Zekrom. The other was called the Hero of Truth, and he had a friend in Reshiram. But somehow, the country became divided, and there was a great war that pitted the two princes and Legendary Pokémon against each other. Their battle was so intense, they used up all of their Life Energy. So, Zekrom and Reshiram fell into a deep slumber and were turned into stone spheres.

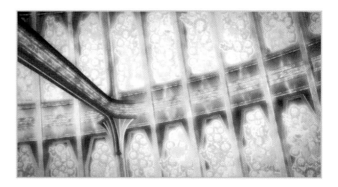

Damon adds that when the castle moved, the People of the Vale lost their connection to the land and scattered across the world. Just like his mother, Damon dreams of reuniting his people in their original homeland and bringing the Kingdom of the Vale back to life. From a balcony, Damon shows them the exact site where it used to be.

The two princes now realized the mistake of war, but the damage had been done. The Dragon Force became chaotic. The king called upon his Mythical Pokémon pal Victini, and it gladly shared its power with him. But in order to harness its power, the king had to create a barrier around the castle—the Pillars of Protection.

With the help of Victini and dozens of Duosion and Solosis, the king transported all the townspeople and the castle through the sky to a new mountaintop, where it sits to this day. Afterward, the king was left so weak, he was unable to take down the Pillars of Protection, and Victini has been trapped inside their barrier ever since.

Mannes tells them that three years ago, Damon brought him his plan to restore the kingdom. Along with his Pokémon pal Reuniclus, Damon has traveled all over to reconnect with the People of the Vale in their new villages around the globe. From tundras to deserts, Damon visited them all, but no one wanted to even listen to his idea. But when things were looking down, one voice lifted him up. One day, he heard, "There is no shortcut to the truth." It was coming from the Sword of the Vale.

Mannes and Damon follow the voice beneath the castle to a cave filled with crystal paths. While Mannes doesn't get very far, Damon magically makes it all the way to see the stone sphere of Reshiram. Mannes knows that the path chooses the one it allows to pass, and clearly Damon is the chosen one. Damon must go alone.

When Damon comes face-to-face with the Light Stone, it is glowing with red light. It rises into the sky and bursts into the Legendary Pokémon Reshiram.

Damon and Reshiram travel again to the tribes of the People of the Vale, and this time, they not only listen, but they also agree to follow Damon. He tells Mannes, his family, and the tribes that Reshiram has shown him how they can use the Sword of the Vale to gain complete control of the Dragon Force's energy.

Meanwhile, Ash and his pals are sleeping. Victini is using Ash like a pillow, but its dreams are a vision it shares with Ash. In it, Victini watches the years pass. Then, its old friend the king apologizes for trapping Victini. Ash realizes just how lonely Victini must feel after hundreds of years. Victini then shows Ash the ocean. It wants to go there more than anything! So, Ash vows to take it to the beach.

The next day, Damon begins to enact his plan to reunite all the People of the Vale and the Sword of the Vale with their original land. First, he calls on Sigilyph to power up his plan. Over a stone board with carvings, mini Pillars of Protection appear, and Damon manipulates them with his hands. The real pillars uproot and float toward the castle. Mannes, the villagers, and Ash and his pals are all amazed!

Now inside the top of the castle, Damon asks Victini to grant him its power. Victini agrees because it has a vision and thinks Damon is actually the old king. When it realizes its mistake, it's too late. Victini is trapped between four pillars and below Sigilyph. There, it is drained of its power, which is shared with the Psychic-type Pokémon lining the walls. The interior glows with purple power, and the Sword of the Vale is lifted into the air.

Damon is using the castle to change the flow of the Dragon Force. From the castle balcony, Ash, Pikachu, Iris, Axew, Cilan, Carlita, and Juanita can't believe their eyes, and they spot a glow flowing through the land.

But the celebration is cut short when Victini cries out in pain. Ash races into the castle and sees his Mythical Pokémon friend struggling. Ash begs Damon to release it, but he won't because he still needs its power. Then, Damon calls on Reuniclus to trap Ash, Pikachu, Iris, Axew, and Cilan. Carlita and Juanita ask Damon to stop.

Reshiram arrives on the scene to find Ash and his friends. Juanita calls on her Pokémon pal Golurk to stop it, but it's powerless against Reshiram's fiery Fusion Flare. Damon then has Reuniclus use Psychic again on everyone, including his mother and sister.

Victini shares a flashback with Ash to the last time the castle was moved by the king. Before he died, the king told Victini that the Sword of the Vale should not be moved again because it would upset the Dragon Force.

When Ash wakes, he warns his friends, Carlita, and Juanita that the castle can't be moved. Juanita tells them there is only one way to stop it—Zekrom. Ash knows just where to find it in the cave beneath the castle. He leads his pals down a crystal path, but just like Damon before him, he's the one who is chosen to pass.

As Ash races to find the stone sphere containing Zekrom, a voice rings out across the cave. "Is it within you, the will to pursue your ideals?" Zekrom asks. Then, the crystal beneath their feet begins to disintegrate. When they reach the bottom, the glowing sphere asks Ash what his ideal is. He replies that he wants to help lonely Victini get its freedom back so he can take it to the ocean. Then, Zekrom appears before them.

Meanwhile on top of the castle, Mannes comes in a plane to pick up his friends and take them to safety. He tells them that the Dragon Force is out of control, just as Ash had warned. Juanita, Carlita, Iris, Axew, and Cilan hop in Mannes' plane.

Ash and Pikachu appear, riding Zekrom. The two Legendary Pokémon again get locked in an epic battle. But this time, when Reshiram is knocked out, Zekrom swoops in to catch it. Not only is its faith restored in Zekrom, its strength is also restored by the Dragon Force.

Back atop the castle, Pikachu is battling Reuniclus while Ash tries to free Victini. When Reshiram shows up, Damon is surprised it's no longer on his side. The Vast White Pokémon frees Victini from the pillar trap.

Then, Zekrom and Reshiram show Damon, his family, and his friends that beneath the clouds, the Dragon Force is raging. Now that Damon can see that

the land is angry, he is full of remorse for what he has done. Reshiram and Zekrom tell him that he must use the Sword of the Vale to control it. So, he asks the Legendary Pokémon to lend their power and push the Sword of the Vale back into its original home.

The castle begins to crumble as the Dragon Force reverses. Mannes takes Juanita and Cilan in his plane. Iris and Carlita hop on Hydreigon. Ash, carrying Victini, tries to make an escape, but they can't cross the barrier. The Pillars of Protection are circling close to the Sword of the Vale.

When the ground shifts, Damon selflessly moves Ash, Victini, and Pikachu to safety before he goes sliding off the side of the Sword of the Vale. Then, the castle rises high in the sky above the clouds. It's so cold, all the Duosion abandon ship. Ash doesn't know what to do.

Help is on the way as Damon returns, riding Golurk and the Legendary Pokémon. Zekrom shoots its bright Fusion Bolt. Reshiram fires a red-hot Fusion Flare. Pikachu sends a tough Thunderbolt. But the Pillars of Protection link together, locking Ash, Pikachu, and Victini inside. Damon begs Ash not to give up because he is the one chosen by the great Dragon Pokémon.

But Ash is so weak, he can't move. As he apologizes to Victini that he won't be able to take it to the ocean, a single tear falls from his eye and shatters. The strength of Ash's heart revitalizes Victini. It bursts into a fierce Searing Shot. Then, it adds a scorching Victory Star. With that combination, the Pillars of Protection break open, and a purple bolt rises into the sky, releasing the Sword of the Vale. Victini is so powerful it breaks its own barrier, but it has disappeared into the night sky.

When Ash wakes up, Damon is back on board steering the Sword of the Vale into its original home to tame the Dragon Force. With Zekrom and Reshiram's help, the castle is returned to the exact right spot. The Dragon Force is instantly soothed.

Ash, Pikachu, and their friends all head down to the ocean. There, Ash cries with sorrow as he wishes his pal Victini were there to share the experience. He then tosses one of Cilan's macarons into the water as tribute, but it gets eaten in midair. Ash pulls out a second one, and Victini shows itself! Ash hugs his friend so tightly, it nearly chokes on its treat.

As thanks for their help, Victini flies around the valley, turning the rocky terrain into a lush landscape. All the people and Pokémon of the Kingdom of the Vale are once again in perfect harmony with nature.

IN BLACK AND WHITE

Between *Pokémon the Movie: Black - Victini and Reshiram* and *Pokémon the Movie: White - Victini and Zekrom*, there are both major and minor differences that a discerning Pokémon fan can pick out. Here's where *Pokémon the Movie: Black - Victini and Reshiram* diverges from the above story.

- The movie begins in a tundra. Damon is there to see the village chief, Glacine.

- Glacine's son, Luis, finds an herb in the snow and gives Damon a vial that contains a piece.

- When a glacier is headed toward some villagers and Beartic, Donuke and his Pokémon pal Stoutland try to help. Then, Zekrom swoops in to save the locals.

- Gothitelle is always by Damon's side.

- The crew spots Mandibuzz in the sky.

- Deep in the cave beneath the castle, Damon hears the voice of Zekrom speak of ideals.

- After following the crystal path down, Damon finds the Dark Stone. From it, Zekrom appears.

- Zekrom can hear the land's anger, and instead of stopping them, he helps Ash and Pikachu try to break through the pillars.

- Zekrom stops the herd of Bouffalant.

- Ash goes through the cave beneath the castle in search of the Light Stone. Along the way, he hears the voice of Reshiram speak of truth.

- One night, when Mannes and Damon think the scattered People of the Vale have rejected their proposal to reunite, they hear the voice of Zekrom ask, "Is that as far as you will go for your ideals?"

- Golurk battles Zekrom.

POKÉMON THE MOVIE
BLACK
VICTINI AND RESHIRAM

"THE PATH CHOOSES THE ONE IT WILL ALLOW TO PASS." —MANNES

LOCATIONS

EINDOAK

This peaceful town is perched on a mountaintop. Many people and Pokémon call Eindoak home, but perhaps its most famous resident is rarely seen—Victini.

THE SWORD OF THE VALE

Towering above the modest skyline of Eindoak is the giant Sword of the Vale. According to legend, the castle originally stood in another spot in the valley, but a powerful king moved it. It's hard to imagine a building so big and heavy lifting up into the sky, but with the help of Victini, Reshiram, Zekrom, Golurk, Damon, Ash, and Pikachu, it moved again!

But no matter where it's located, it's an important place to the local community. This sword-shaped brick castle is not just impressive in size: it also houses many incredible things inside.

THE LIBRARY

Inside the Sword of the Vale is a meeting room with cozy chairs and wall-to-wall books. One of the tomes is a pop-up book all about the ancient local legend. It is in this library that Ash, Pikachu, Iris, Axew, and Cilan learn about the Kingdom of the Vale and Damon's dream to reunite his people on their land. It's also where the scattered People of the Vale gather to show support for Damon's plan.

THE CAVE

Deep beneath the castle is a cave covered in a web of crystal paths. But not just anyone can reach the Legendary Pokémon hidden there. Zekrom and Reshiram are resting in stone spheres that the two twin princes of the Kingdom of the Vale placed in secret spots more than a thousand years ago. Of all the people there to help, only Ash and Damon were chosen to pass through this tricky cave and enlist the help of the powerful Legendary Pokémon.

THE DOME

At the very top of the Sword of the Vale is a dome. It is held up by a rim of columns, which gives a beautiful, nearly unobstructed view of

the surrounding area. From here, Damon steers the Sword of the Vale.

In the center, there is a structure specifically designed to harness the Psychic-type power of Sigilyph, Duosion, Solosis, and Victini. The dome pulses with a purple glow when it's charged up.

THE BALCONIES

There are many balconies on the Sword of the Vale. Notably, off the dome, there are steps that will lead to stone balconies. But perhaps the most impressive terraces are on each side of the Sword of the Vale. These grand balconies are pristine parks. Covered in greenery, they are so large that they can hold many people and plants.

THE STORAGE ROOM

This simple room might look like a repository for odds and ends, but it's a clever cover. Ash discovers that a brick wall inside the

storage room is a hidden door leading to the cave beneath the castle.

THE ORCHARD

Surrounding the Eindoak location of the Sword of the Vale is a beautiful area with fruitful trees. Mannes' family has owned that orchard in town for generations. The people and Pokémon are all welcome to help themselves to the delicious berries.

THE TOWN CENTER

From a stage in the middle of town, the Mayor of Eindoak, Mannes, welcomes everyone to the Harvest Festival and announces the rules for its Pokémon Competition. Nearby, Juanita has a cart covered in different toys, dolls, and masks celebrating Victini, the Mythical Pokémon of the local legend. It is here that Tepig surprisingly wins a round of the Pokémon Competition against Samurott.

TUNDRA

The People of the Vale have scattered across the globe. One tribe landed in an icy tundra by a frosty river. The people live in igloos made of ice bricks, and their neighbors are Beartic. Damon trekked through a lot of snow to visit them there and share his plan.

DESERT

Another tribe of the People of the Vale lives in tents atop orange rocks. Damon trekked through the orange terrain to talk to their leader—although initially, it seemed like Damon had more luck herding Bouffalant than convincing the people to move back to the original land.

CHARACTERS

ASH

After he arrives in Eindoak, Ash instantly makes a new friend—the Mythical Pokémon Victini. When it sees Ash go out on a ledge to save a couple of Deerling, Victini knows Ash is a trustworthy Trainer. While Victini initially saves Ash from falling off said rock ledge, Ash soon finds himself on a quest to rescue the lonely, powerful Pokémon.

WIN/WIN SITUATION

When Ash employs his typical against-type battle strategy during the Harvest Festival's Pokémon Competition, he seems doomed. How can teeny Tepig win against splashy Samurott? How can stumbling Scraggy beat mighty Hydreigon? Well, with Victini's help, the odds are in Ash's favor. There's a reason they call Victini the Victory Pokémon. The Mythical Pokémon powered up his Pokémon pals. Victini took a shine to Ash and sealed his success, no matter how nonsensical his wins were.

SHARING IS CARING

Ash happily shares macarons with Victini, and so much more! The Mythical Pokémon gives Ash the chance to look inside its mind. Victini sends Ash visions from its past and even its dreams. Beyond Ash getting a sense of just how lonely it has been for more than a thousand years, these glimpses into its thoughts help Ash truly understand how to help Victini.

POKÉMON THAT CHOOSE YOU

Not just anyone is granted access to pass through the cave beneath the castle. While Cilan complains that he feels he's just going around in circles, somehow Ash has made it farther down than his crew. As Mannes puts it, the path chooses who shall pass. Only Ash and Damon were able to travel all the way down to the hiding places where the stone spheres of the Legendary Pokémon Zekrom and Reshiram lie.

THE POWER OF A SINGLE TEAR

Ash would never leave his pal Victini behind, even when there is danger. He stays in the dome despite the offer of a ride from Mannes to safety. Then, when the Sword of the Vale rises so high into the sky that Ash is too weak to move, he feels he'll never be able to make good on his promise to take Victini to the ocean. He sheds a single tear. As it falls, it shatters, but it really is heartbreaking. Seeing Ash so upset motivates Victini to liberate its friends Ash and Pikachu and itself from the Pillars of Protection.

PIKACHU

SCRAGGY

OSHAWOTT

CILAN

Although Cilan enters the Pokémon Competition and loses in the first round, he wins big overall in Eindoak! The man with the macarons, Cilan has the perfect recipe to please the Mythical Pokémon Victini. It can't resist his sweet, handmade, delicious cookies. Luckily, he brought an entire basketful to share with his friends—people and Pokémon alike.

PANSAGE

IRIS

This Dragon Master in training gets a close look at some truly amazing Dragon Pokémon! In addition to Reshiram and Zekrom, Iris is excited to meet Carlita's Hydreigon. Although the circumstances are troubling at the castle, Iris does get to ride on the Pokémon.

EMOLGA

Iris also enters the Pokémon Competition. Although she chooses Emolga, Drilbur invites itself onto the battlefield, disqualifying her from the round.

AXEW

DRILBUR

DAMON

The son of Juanita and the brother of Carlita, Damon hadn't been home much. He had been on a quest to fulfill a dream his mother first shared with him—to reunite all the scattered People of the Vale on their land to revive the Kingdom of the Vale. So, Damon traveled the globe, speaking with all of the tribes and hoping to convince them to return. But even passionate and patient Damon couldn't get anyone to agree—that is, until he brought along a very persuasive friend with him, a great Dragon Pokémon. In *Pokémon the Movie: White - Victini and Zekrom*, that Legendary Pokémon was Reshiram. In *Pokémon the Movie: Black - Victini and Reshiram*, that Pokémon was Zekrom.

MAN WITH A PLAN

Three years ago, Damon presented Mannes with his mission to return his people to their homeland. At first, Mannes was the only one who supported him on his life's work to restore the Kingdom of the Vale. As he traveled the globe speaking to the scattered tribes of the People of the Vale, he returned rejected, but not defeated. Damon refused to give up. He was one of the chosen ones who could pass through the cave beneath the castle. Now, with a great Dragon Pokémon backing him, he returned to the tribes and was able to get their support.

A DOUBLE-EDGED SWORD

A major step in restoring the Kingdom of the Vale was to return the Sword of the Vale back to its original location. In order to move this gigantic monument, Damon had to assemble a team of Psychic-type Pokémon: dozens of Solosis and Duosion, his Pokémon pal Sigilyph, and the Mythical Pokémon Victini.

At first, Victini was on board because it thought it was dreaming of the time it helped its old friend the king. But once it realized that it was the present day and Damon was steering the Sword of the Vale, it got upset. It was in pain as it was drained of its power, but worse yet, Victini knew the Dragon Force would become chaotic again. Luckily, its new friends Ash and Pikachu were there to help!

But Damon isn't exactly a villain. He was hoping to do good, and he inadvertently did some bad. To him, hurting Victini was just a necessary evil, a small sacrifice to achieve something great. But even his mother, Juanita, didn't agree with his methods. They tried to reason with and even fight him, but Damon had his Pokémon pal use Psychic to stop them! It wasn't until Damon saw with his own eyes the destruction the Dragon Force was causing that he realized he'd gone too far. Just like that Dragon Force, Damon saw he was out of control.

Damon instantly changed his course and did everything he could to fix the problem he had created. He wholeheartedly apologized to his peers and his family for his misdeeds. They forgave the humble Damon for admitting where he went wrong. But, of course, they will always admire him for dreaming big!

Under Damon's leadership, Reshiram, Zekrom, and Golurk helped land the castle safely in the right spot. Now, the Sword of the Vale was back in its original place, and the Kingdom of the Vale was together again.

SIGILYPH:
THE AVIANOID POKÉMON

Height	4'07"
Weight	30.9 lbs
Type	Psychic/Flying

Damon's Psychic-type Pokémon pal helps him move the Pillars of Protection.

GOTHITELLE:
THE ASTRAL BODY POKÉMON

Height	4'11"
Weight	97.0 lbs
Type	Psychic

In *Pokémon the Movie: Black - Victini and Reshiram*, Gothitelle is always by Damon's side.

REUNICLUS

Height	3'03"
Weight	44.3 lbs
Type	Psychic

In *Pokémon the Movie: White - Victini and Zekrom*, Reuniclus is always by Damon's side.

MANNES

The Mayor of Eindoak, Mannes takes his job seriously. Damon first came to him three years ago to discuss his dream of reuniting the People of the Vale and reviving the Kingdom of the Vale. Mannes supported him and stuck by his side, even when it seemed impossible. He went with him on his journey to the cave beneath the castle. Although he didn't make it far, he realized Damon was the one chosen to pass. Mannes could see the special connection and even hired Damon to help restore the castle.

Mannes cares a lot about the community. He cheerfully hosts the Harvest Festival and welcomes everyone. But he makes a point of being a good neighbor every day. The orchard outside of the Sword of the Vale has been in his family for decades, and all are allowed to help themselves to its delicious fruit.

Mannes monitors the moving of the Sword of the Vale from his red plane. When there is trouble at the castle, Mannes helps Juanita, Carlita, Cilan, Iris, and Axew escape.

CARLITA

Juanita's daughter and Damon's sister, Carlita is a descendent of the People of the Vale and a fierce Pokémon Trainer. Along with her Pokémon pal Hydreigon, Carlita easily wins the round against Cilan and Pansage. Then, the pair is also poised to win their match with Ash and Scraggy. Invisible Victini gives Ash an unstoppable advantage, but Carlita puts together the clues.

Although Carlita acts like a good sport during the battle, afterward, she just has to ask Ash if he's gotten some help from the Victory Pokémon. As it turns out, he did without even knowing it. Carlita's hunch was right: Victini had taken to Ash! But perhaps even better than an award, Carlita and her new friends see the Mythical Pokémon for the first time…with Cilan's macaron in its mouth.

HYDREIGON

JUANITA

Juanita, a descendent of the People of the Vale, is the mother of Damon and Carlita. In fact, it is Juanita's dream to see the People of the Vale reunite and return to their land. It's that very seed of the ideal that she plants in Damon's head, which ultimately became his

passion in life. However, when Damon will stop at nothing to achieve the dream, including trapping Victini, Juanita begs her son to rethink what he's doing and calls on Golurk for backup.

Ash and his friends first meet Juanita at her cart in the center of town during the Harvest Festival. She has an incredible display of Victini-themed items. Juanita tells Ash, Pikachu, Iris, Axew, and Cilan all about the Mythical Pokémon. Then, she gives Iris a wooden charm of the Victory Pokémon from her cart. Later on, Juanita gets to see the real Mythical Pokémon, thanks to her new pals.

GOLURK:

THE AUTOMATON POKÉMON

Height	9'02"
Weight	727.5 lbs
Type	Ground/Ghost

Although Juanita loves her son, when she feels their dream of reviving the Kingdom of the Vale has gone too far, she calls on her Pokémon pal Golurk to fight back. While it's no match for a Legendary Pokémon opponent, it is able to lend a hand. Eventually, it even rescues Damon when he slips off the side of the Sword of the Vale.

TEAM ROCKET

Jessie, James, and Meowth originally come to Eindoak to try to steal all the Pokémon at the Harvest Festival. But when they see Victini, their ambitions focus on nabbing the Mythical Pokémon. Unfortunately for them, the only thing they get to grab is the side of the Sword of the Vale as they go sliding off.

THE TRIBE IN THE DESERT
(STORY MORE PROMINENTLY FEATURED IN THE WHITE MOVIE)

• In *Pokémon the Movie: White - Victini and Zekrom*, Reshiram saves them from the tornado and the stampede.

RAVINE

The leader of the People of the Vale who now live in the desert, Ravine is a proud man who initially believes that their original land is forever lost. He does not think Damon's plan to reunite all the tribes is wise, and he wishes Damon would stop trying to convince him otherwise.

Although Ravine first believes the legend is nothing more than a tall tale, Damon and his Legendary Pokémon pal help change his mind when they stop a black tornado and a Bouffalant stampede from hitting their homes.

MANUKE

Ravine's right-hand guy is Manuke. Along with Ravine, he watches a Legendary Pokémon help Damon stop a Bouffalant and the black tornado. Then, he joins him on his journey to Eindoak.

LUISA

More prominently featured in *Pokémon the Movie: White - Victini and Zekrom*, Luisa is the daughter of Ravine, the leader of their tribe. Damon rescues her injured Blitzle. As thanks, she gives Damon a charm featuring a little sculpture of the Electric-type Pokémon.

Luisa also gets the chance to travel with her father to Eindoak as a show of support for Damon's plan.

THE TRIBE IN THE TUNDRA
(STORY MORE PROMINENTLY FEATURED IN THE BLACK MOVIE)

• In *Pokémon the Movie: Black - Victini and Reshiram*, Zekrom saves them from the glacier.

GLACINE

Damon trekked all the way out through the tundra to come to see the village chief, Glacine. Although he thinks he'll make his case with words and ideals, Damon winds up convincing her with his courage and the company he keeps. When a giant glacier threatens the village, Damon swoops in just in time with a great Dragon Pokémon to save the day! From then on, Glacine concludes that Damon isn't a dreamer: he's a visionary with the Legendary Pokémon power to back his plans. So, she joins him back in Eindoak to show her support for the restoration of the Kingdom of the Vale.

LUIS

The son of the village chief, Luis is a smart kid who likes to help his mom. Along with his Pokémon pal Lillipup, he finds a rare herb buried in the snow. In *Pokémon the Movie: White - Victini and Zekrom*, Luis gives a clipping of the same herb in a vial as a parting gift to Damon.

DONUKE

The right-hand man to the village chief, Donuke chalks Damon's dream up to nothing more than a legend. He isn't happy to see Damon at first. However, when Damon (with the help of his Legendary Pokémon pal Zekrom) rescues the village chief, Luis, Beartic, the village, and Donuke from a giant glacier, he changes his mind about the dreamer.

STOUTLAND
Donuke's Pokémon pal speedily drives his sled through the snow.

LILLIPUP

LEGENDARY AND MYTHICAL POKÉMON

VICTINI:
THE VICTORY POKÉMON

Height	1'14"
Weight	8.8 lbs
Type	Psychic/Fire

THE WAY TO VICTINI'S HEART IS THROUGH ITS STOMACH

Victini typically travels under a cloak of invisibility, but it first reveals itself to Ash and his friends while noshing on a delicious macaron made by Cilan. It can't resist the sweet treat! And the playful Pokémon loves to take them right out of Ash's hand, even when there's a whole open basket full of macarons.

THE KING OF HEART

More than a thousand years ago, Victini was always by the side of the king of the People of the Vale. The two were great friends. With Victini's help, the king was able to make the emergency move of the Sword of the Vale to soothe the inflamed Dragon Force.

However, in order to harness Victini's power, he had to put it between the Pillars of Protection. The move was tremendously straining on the king, who was left too weak to remove them before he passed. In some of his last words, he apologized to Victini for trapping it in the barrier in town, where it would remain for centuries. The king also told Victini to make sure the Sword of the Vale was never moved again because the Dragon Force would become chaotic. According to legend, Victini protects the Sword of the Vale.

To this day, Victini still misses its best buddy, the old king. It thinks of him often and even sees him in its dreams. Victini grew very lonely without its pal.

NOW YOU SEE IT, NOW YOU DON'T

Victini has been hiding in plain sight. The Victory Pokémon was trapped between the invisible barrier of the Pillars of Protection, but not a soul in Eindoak had seen it in a very long time. (Well, that is, until it was munching on Cilan's macarons in midair.)

No wonder Victini had been so lonely. It lived like a ghost in a small land. But when it sees that Ash is a caring kind of guy, it keeps appearing before its new friend. Victini also shares what it's thinking. Ash can see its thoughts and dreams. The two are fast friends who really rely on each other's insights and vision. So, while Victini might appear and disappear, one thing remains—their bond.

WIN OVER

Victini first meets Ash when it watches Ash bravely wander out on a thin ledge to save a pair of wild Deerling. When the rock crumbles beneath his feet, Ash takes a dramatic leap with the two Deerling and miraculously lands on another mountain. How was he able to make that superhuman jump?

During the Pokémon Competition, Tepig is knocked off the battlefield by Samurott, and it looks like it's also knocked out. But somehow, Tepig returned even more powerful than it started and won the match with a single explosion of Ember. How did its Fire-type attack get so super-strong?

Ash's enthusiastic but inexperienced pal Scraggy seems out of its depths in a battle with Hydreigon. When Scraggy gets tossed into the bushes, it returns to win the round. How did Scraggy get so super-tough? Carlita, Hydreigon's Trainer, has a hunch that Victini might be helping. It is said that Victini brings victory, even when it doesn't seem possible! Whether Ash was jumping across a valley or facing a talented challenger, Victini was there to seal his success. What a pal! But Ash certainly wants to be Victini's champion, too. When it's trapped between the Pillars of Protection and its power is being sapped, Ash relentlessly works to free his friend.

In the end, Victini ensures its own victory! As the Sword of the Vale rises into the sky and Ash is too weak to help anymore, Victini finds the strength inside itself to break through the barrier, save the Sword of the Vale, and give itself the freedom it had dreamed of. Victini is victorious!

ZEKROM:
THE DEEP BLACK POKÉMON

Height	9'06"
Weight	760.6 lbs
Type	Dragon/Electric

One of the great Dragon Pokémon, the Legendary Pokémon Zekrom will assist anyone who wants to build an ideal world. In *Pokémon the Movie: White*, that person is Ash Ketchum. In *Pokémon the Movie: Black*, that person is Damon. But no matter who finds the stone sphere of Zekrom in the cave beneath the castle, it is a helpful force for good. Together with its foil, Reshiram, it tries to destroy the Pillars of Protection and uses its strength to move the Sword of the Vale back into place.

In *Pokémon the Movie: White*, Zekrom helps Damon save some People of the Vale and Beartic that are stuck in a chilling situation. When a glacier threatens their safety, Zekrom and Damon swoop in to save the day.

Since the time of the Kingdom of the Vale, Zekrom has been resting in the Dark Stone in the cave beneath the castle.

RESHIRAM:
THE VAST WHITE POKÉMON

Height	10'06"
Weight	727.5 lbs
Type	Dragon/Fire

This Legendary Pokémon's power is balanced by its fellow great Dragon Pokémon, Zekrom. The two team up to destroy the Pillars of Protection and help relocate the Sword of the Vale to soothe the Dragon Force. Reshiram is always willing to lend a hand to anyone who wants to build a world of truth. In *Pokémon the Movie: White*, that person is Damon. In *Pokémon the Movie: Black*, that person is Ash Ketchum. However, no matter who is allowed to pass through the crystal cave beneath the castle and release it from its stone sphere, Reshiram will remain a force for good.

In *Pokémon the Movie: Black*, Reshiram helps Damon stop a black tornado and a stampede of Bouffalant to protect a local tribe of the People of the Vale.

Since the time of the Kingdom of the Vale, Reshiram has been resting in the Light Stone in the cave beneath the castle.

FEATURED POKÉMON IN *POKÉMON THE MOVIE: WHITE*

FEATURED POKÉMON IN *POKÉMON THE MOVIE: BLACK*

POKÉMON FEATURED IN BOTH MOVIES

THE LEGEND OF THE KINGDOM OF THE VALE

More than a thousand years ago, all of the People of the Vale lived together. Their ruler, the king, relied on his Pokémon pal, the mighty Mythical Pokémon Victini. The Kingdom of the Vale was a place where people and Pokémon lived in harmony with nature. It was a flourishing community that wisely harnessed its power from the invisible Dragon Force energy that flowed through the land.

The king had two well-loved and courageous twin sons. One prince was known as the Hero of Truth, and he was accompanied by the great Dragon Pokémon Reshiram. The other prince was known as the Hero of Ideals, and he was aptly paired with the great Dragon Pokémon Zekrom. Both of the great Dragon Pokémon would only show their support for wise and righteous leaders. But somehow, the princes became enemies, and the People of the Vale turned against each other, sparking a terrible war.

Zekrom and Reshiram fought each other so bitterly that they were drained of their Life Energy. Too weak to continue the battle, the great Dragon Pokémon fell into a deep slumber and were transformed into stone spheres—the Light Stone and the Dark Stone.

Although the princes came to regret their feud and the war it started, the problems they had caused were beyond being solved by a simple ceasefire. The Dragon Force had become out of control and was destroying the land. To save his kingdom, the king called on his powerful Pokémon friend, Victini.

Happy to help, Victini lent its special power to the king. To harness it, the king had to build a barrier to keep its strength concentrated in the Sword of the Vale. These Pillars of Protection surrounded the castle. Together with the Psychic-type energy of dozens of Solosis and Duosion, Victini charged up the Sword of the Vale. The king now had the strength to command the castle (with all of his subjects safely inside) to move through the air and find a new home atop a mountain.

Now, the Dragon Force was soothed, but the king's strength was spent. He couldn't remove the barrier, and Victini has been trapped within the Pillars of Protection ever since. As for the princes, they hid the Dark Stone and the Light Stone deep beneath the castle in a secret cave. After all they had been through, many of the People of the Vale left the area and scattered across the land. But Victini, which had been stuck there, chose to remain invisible ever since—well, that is, until a righteous visitor named Ash arrived in town.

INTERESTING ITEMS

ANNUAL HARVEST FESTIVAL

The town of Eindoak is home to the yearly Harvest Festival. One of the highlights is the annual Pokémon Competition. Ash, Pikachu, Iris, Axew, and Cilan arrive just in time for the opening ceremony.

Mannes takes to the stage with Klink, Klang, and Klinklang to welcome all of the people and Pokémon there to enjoy the city's celebration. He then kicks off the Pokémon Competition.

THE POKÉMON COMPETITION

Ash, Cilan, Iris, and Carlita all enter the annual Pokémon Competition that takes place during the Harvest Festival. Mannes explained the rules. Each competitor is given a special necklace. Then, the Trainers pair up for one-on-one battles with no substitutions in locations across the city. The Trainer who loses the round passes their necklace on to their opponent. This set of events repeats until only one Trainer is left with their original necklace.

CILAN'S MACARONS

Victini adores these tiny cookies made by Cilan. But these macarons are more than just a snack: they buttered up Victini. The Mythical Pokémon had remained invisible for a thousand years, but Cilan's macarons helped Victini come out of hiding. Cookies make everything sweeter!

VICTINI CHARM

At the Harvest Festival, Ash, Pikachu, Iris, Axew, and Cilan meet Juanita. She is in charge of a cart filled with Victini dolls, toys, masks, and goodies. Iris loves a little wood carving of the Victory Pokémon. Juanita gives her the charm off her cart and wishes Iris luck in the Pokémon Competition. While the real Pokémon has lots of charm, this trinket is pretty cute, too.

THE LIGHT STONE AND THE DARK STONE

After their epic battle long ago, the great Dragon Pokémon fell into a deep slumber. They were then transformed into stone spheres. To protect the Legendary Pokémon, the twin princes hid them separately in the cave beneath the castle. In a thousand years, only Ash and Damon have located the Light Stone and the Dark Stone. They are the ones of pure heart that the path has allowed to pass.

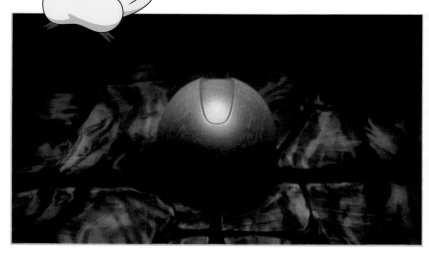

THE PILLARS OF PROTECTION

These tall stone pillars have detailed carvings on each side. More than a thousand years old, they surround the Sword of the Vale. When the king or Damon moves the Sword of the Vale, they also manipulate the location of the Pillars of Protection. When in motion, or charged with energy, or if Victini tries to cross them, the carvings give off a purple glow.

The king initially used these barriers to harness Victini's power so he could calm the Dragon Force. However, after the difficult move, the king was too weak to remove them, and he left the Victory Pokémon trapped in a small radius in town.

As if it weren't a small enough space, the Pillars of Protection close in on Ash, Pikachu, and Victini when the Sword of the Vale rises high into the sky. With barely a few feet to move, Victini uses an explosive Victory Star to break their bond and finally frees itself and the Sword of the Vale.

THE STONE TABLET

The Sword of the Vale doesn't have a steering wheel, but beneath the dome, there is a square stone tablet. It has a starburst-like carving, and mini stone Pillars of Protection swirl above it. When Victini's strong Psychic-type power is added, both Damon and the king are able to manipulate the location of the Sword of the Vale.

THE POP-UP BOOK

In the library at the Sword of the Vale, there is a special book that illustrates the legend of the Kingdom of the Vale. Each page has a pop-up illustration of the scene. It's an incredibly detailed and beautiful book that has been treasured through the ages. Mannes and Damon show it to Ash, Pikachu, Iris, Axew, and Cilan.

TOTALLY AWESOME TECHNOLOGY

THE MOST MUSICAL CART

Providing music for the Harvest Festival is an amazing musical instrument that features horns, harps, flutes, and even accordions. This portable cart is very colorful. Powered by Klink, Klang, and Klinklang, it plays the most terrific tunes.

MANNES' HELICOPTER

From the sky, Mannes can survey the situation and keep an eye on the Dragon Force. The mayor's red flying machine is easy to jump into in an emergency because it has no top; it's like the convertible car of planes. But make no mistake—it is a sturdy ship that can carry a whole lot of passengers. Cilan, Iris, Axew, Juanita, Carlita, and Mannes were all comfortable flying in it together. There was even plenty of room for Ash, too, but he wouldn't leave his Pokémon pal Victini.

Amazingly enough, Mannes' helicopter is powered by his Pokémon pal Klinklang.

POKÉMON THE MOVIE: GENESECT AND THE LEGEND AWAKENED

THE STORY

Red Genesect instructs the other Genesect—Electric Genesect, Fire Genesect, Ice Genesect, and Water Genesect—to follow it. Their eyes glow red as they obey their leader. They land on an icy mountainside. Suddenly, an avalanche threatens their safety. From across the land, Water Genesect signals the Legendary Pokémon Mewtwo that they're in danger. Mewtwo swiftly speeds through the sky and uses Psychic to lift four Genesect out, but it sadly couldn't help Red Genesect.

Mewtwo feels connected to Genesect because they were also man-made in a lab from fossils. Just like Mewtwo, Genesect broke free from the lab and the scientists who created them. Now, Genesect think everyone is their enemy. Mewtwo knows what it's like to feel that fear, and it wants to help them find a new home. But Red Genesect doesn't trust anyone, and when it returns, it starts firing at Mewtwo.

Mewtwo tries to explain that it's been 300 million years since Genesect walked the planet, but Red Genesect is focused on making Mewtwo history. It coordinates an attack with the other four Genesect, which fire a big ball of Techno Blast and make their escape.

> "ALL POKÉMON BELONG SOMEWHERE. THERE'S A PLACE FOR EVERY POKÉMON!" —ASH

Genesect arrives in a big city. Coincidentally, Ash, Pikachu, Iris, Axew, and Cilan are visiting, too.

In the center of the city is a new amazing Pokémon habitat called Pokémon Hills. It hasn't opened to the public yet, but Professor Oak was able to get Ash and his pals a private tour with Eric. As they follow Eric across the footbridge, they see a spiraling dome with lush trees and waterfalls that flow into the river below.

Inside, Pokémon Hills has all kinds of different environments to suit all the various Pokémon that call this magical facility home. In fact, the incredible indoors look the same as the great outdoors. Wooper and Lotad are paddling in the lake. Sewaddle and Sableye are hanging by the shady trees. Golem and Geodude are going around the rock formations. Ash, Iris, and Cilan take out their Pokémon so they can get in on all the fun!

The grounds around the dome include a colorful flower garden, a hedge maze, and another beautiful lake filled with a special ancient flora that still flourishes—Panna Lotuses. But there, Ash and Pikachu are surprised to find a Pokémon that dates back just as far, Genesect. Pikachu and Ash run over to check it out, but its body closes up to hide. Ash isn't even sure it's really a Pokémon since it looks like a metal machine. But when he steps onto it, Water Genesect goes flying, carrying Ash and Pikachu across the lake like a hovering surfboard. Water Genesect gives them an awesome ride!

Suddenly, Red Genesect returns. When it sees Ash pat Water Genesect, the pair of Genesect assumes its in trouble and launches a coordinated attack. Iris, Axew, Cilan, and Ash run for it, but Pikachu tries to fight back. Unfortunately, it takes a hit so hard, it flies into the bushes. Ash races to his best friend's side. Water Genesect stands before the other Genesect and begs them to stop. But Red Genesect questions its loyalty and tells it to destroy the enemy. Water Genesect's eyes glow red as it is forced to follow the leader.

As the bright blue Techno Blast flies through the sky, Mewtwo speedily swoops in to block it from hitting Pikachu and its pals. The impact is so great that it blows a hole through the ground, and now Mewtwo and the crew find themselves in a tunnel beneath the city. Red Genesect leads the others out of there.

Back on land, Water Genesect opens up and stands. It tells Ash the same thing it told Mewtwo—it wants to go home. It's happy for its new friends Ash, Pikachu, Iris, Axew, and Cilan, but they can sense its sadness. So, Ash vows to help it find its home.

Mewtwo asks if they're okay, but it doesn't care about the humans. It is only concerned about its fellow Pokémon. Before Mewtwo leaves, Ash asks about Genesect. It tells them that the species of Pokémon have been extinct for 300 million years, only to be brought back to life in a lab. Genesect now find themselves in a world they don't know and don't trust. Then, Mewtwo flies back up into the sky before they can ask any more questions.

Ash carries Pikachu to the Pokémon Center. There, he and his crew, along with Eric, discuss the day's events with Nurse Joy. Hanging at her desk is a picture of Panna Lotuses that Eric took. He tells them he transplanted the flowers in Pokémon Hills from a preserve called Absentia Natural Park. Eric adds that the lotuses are the most ancient flowers in existence today, and they date back 300 million years to the time of Genesect. Then, Nurse Joy's assistant, Audino, wheels out Pikachu, which is feeling a whole lot better.

While Eric, Ash, and his crew are at the Pokémon Center, trouble is brewing (or rather, exploding) at Pokémon Hills. Genesect have decided to fight their  way in, attacking all the wild Pokémon that live in the habitat. They are running out, trying to escape the coordinated takeover. Feraligatr tries to fire back, but two Genesect nearly blow the water out of the lake. In the middle of Pokémon Hills, Genesect are building another habitat—a massive brown nest.

Suddenly, Sableye arrives at the Pokémon Center to ask for help. Eric worries about what's going on at Pokémon Hills. They all drop their dinner to check it out. When they arrive, the Pokémon inhabitants are outside the habitat. Ralts is badly injured, so Cilan rushes it to the Pokémon Center. Team Rocket decides to go inside to catch Genesect, but they soon find themselves under attack by Red Genesect. Their launcher gets caught in the giant nest, and they race for the door with fire at their heels.

Ash, Pikachu, Iris, and Axew follow Eric's lead to the Transformer Substation, the place that controls the electricity for the whole city. There, they see electricity surging as Genesect's nest string has wrapped itself around parts of the system.

Two Starly seek out Mewtwo. They tell it there's trouble at Pokémon Hills, and Mewtwo snaps into action. It feels it must help its fellow lab-created Pokémon find a home.

Eric, Ash, Pikachu, Iris, Axew, and Sableye return to Pokémon Hills to find that the giant nest crafted by Genesect is now covering most of the Pokémon habitat. Water Genesect greets them and apologizes because it can't disobey Red Genesect, but it doesn't mean any harm. Then, it shows them that its favorite flower is floating in the river there—the Panna Lotus. Since the flower was around back when Genesect roamed the planet, it's no wonder they feel most at home here in Pokémon Hills where they're in abundance.

Suddenly, Feraligatr sends a scorching signal to a couple of Genesect. It's still ready to fight for its home. Red Genesect sneaks up behind it and knocks it over the railing. Feraligatr goes flying, falling fast toward the ground. Lucklly, Mewtwo swoops in and lifts the Big Jaw Pokémon to safety.

The lights inside Pokémon Hills begin to flicker as the nest short-circuits the city's transformers. Eric races to a control panel to try to get it all back online. He worries the Genesect nest will not only hurt Pokémon Hills, but it could also cut off the power for the entire city.

Then, Mewtwo reaches out to Red Genesect. It asks for a ceasefire, and in return, Mewtwo promises that it will help them find a new home. But Red Genesect refuses to follow anyone and begins to battle Mewtwo.

While their battle rages, Team Rocket's launcher (which was lodged in the nest) comes loose and is headed straight toward Water Genesect's head. Ash thinks fast and has Pikachu knock it out of the way with Iron Tail. Water Genesect hugs Pikachu in thanks.

Red Genesect chases Mewtwo through the city skyline. Mewtwo begs Genesect to listen to reason, but it just wants to fight. When Mewtwo dodges its fire, the blast hits a building. Mewtwo reminds Red Genesect that people live in the city and could be hurt, but Genesect doesn't care. It rams into Mewtwo, slamming it against another skyscraper. Seeing it has no choice but to battle, Mewtwo Mega Evolves in Mega Mewtwo Y. Now, it is so speedy, not even Genesect's attacks can catch it.

In the Transformer Substation, Eric scrambles to get the city's power back online.

Meanwhile, back at Pokémon Hills, the other Genesect fire at Ash and his friends, but Water Genesect steps up to defend them. At first, it's three against one, but  Cilan rushes back in with all the wild Pokémon, and they're ready to stand up for their home. Facing a fight from all of those angry Pokémon, the trio isn't sure what to do. They communicate telepathically with Red Genesect, which instructs them to destroy everyone. But Water Genesect doesn't want to follow those orders or be under its control.

Before a single attack can be fired, Ash runs between all the inhabitants of Pokémon Hills and the trio of Genesect. He begs the wild Pokémon to understand that Genesect just want their own home. But Genesect believe they're all their enemies and plan to destroy them all. Water Genesect gets caught in the battle and thrown against a railing. Ash rushes to his side, but there's even more trouble as the fighting escalates to a war inside Pokémon Hills.

Just when the wild Pokémon seem to have the three Genesect surrounded, Red Genesect returns. Then, all four at once leave nearly all the Pokémon weak, except Persian. As Genesect set their sights on the Classy Cat Pokémon, Ash again jumps in front of it to try to reason with Genesect. They again fire a coordinated attack at Ash, but Water Genesect swoops in to protect its pal. But it's badly hurt now. Ash rushes to its side, but the light in its eyes is gone.

The other four Genesect plan to attack the other wild Pokémon together, but this time, Mega Mewtwo Y holds all their fire in one hand. Ash, Pikachu, Iris, Axew, and Cilan can't believe its incredible power!

The four Genesect now focus their attention on Mewtwo, but it's not afraid. It warns them that if they don't stop, it will defeat them. The Genesect refuse to give up. Instead, they fold up like flying saucers, zooming around and trying to keep up with Mewtwo. Mewtwo again Mega Evolves into Mega Mewtwo Y.

"DESTORY THE ENEMY!" —RED GENESECT

Through all the fighting, the Panna Lotuses have also taken a blow. Their petals are strewn across the water. Water Genesect picks a broken one up, and a tear streams down its face. It wants to go home. All of the wild Pokémon in Pokémon Hills see its sorrow and feel bad for Genesect, even the ones still fighting Mewtwo.

The lights suddenly go out in Pokémon Hills and the Pokémon Center. The city is in a total blackout. Worse yet, now an electrical fire is rising up the nest. Ash asks Oshawott to use Hydro Pump to put out the fire. Feraligatr helps, too. Golem, Graveler, Deerling, and Sawsbuck all find a way to send sand to take down the flames. Everyone wants to help save the nest from the fire—even Sableye.

When the fire surrounds the Genesect trio, Persian and Feraligatr step up to save them. They can't believe the Pokémon they were trying to destroy would help them. Their eyes stop glowing red.

Sadly, Water Genesect is scorched by the flames and falls from the nest into the river. Ash races to rescue it, but a loose piece covered in flames is headed to hit him. The Genesect trio teams up to blast it away just in time. But as the other Pokémon are coming together, Red Genesect is still trying to destroy Mega Mewtwo Y.

A blast sends Mega Mewtwo Y flying into a railing. Ash and his friends grab it by the hand so it doesn't fall. Then, it snaps back into action as Mewtwo.

Back on the ground, Mewtwo and Red Genesect fire another round of attacks. Then, Ash jumps between them. He tries to reason with Red Genesect one more time. Ash promises to help them find a real home because he knows there is a place for everyone on the planet.

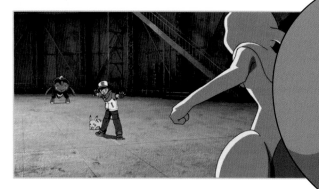

Red Genesect pauses but begins to fire up another booming Techno Blast. So weak it can barely stand, Water Genesect again jumps before Ash to plead with Red Genesect to stop. The Genesect trio races to its side to support its cause. Then, all of the wild Pokémon of Pokémon Hills show their support, too.

But Red Genesect now thinks that everyone is its enemy and fires a vicious Techno Blast at them. Mewtwo Mega Evolves again into Mega Mewtwo Y to stop its attack. Then, it carries Red Genesect up beyond the planet and takes it where no one else exists. With the awe-inspiring view, Mewtwo explains to Red Genesect that they were both created on this planet, and it is their home. People and Pokémon alike live here as friends. Then, Mewtwo reaches its hand out to Red Genesect, explaining that it is still its friend. Together, they return to their home. But on their way back, Mewtwo passes out, so Red Genesect holds it in its arms, and they fall together.

From Pokémon Hills, Genesect can sense that Red Genesect and Mewtwo are in trouble. The four Genesect act fast and form a stringy net, but the pair falls right through it. Iris calls on Dragonite and Ash calls on Charizard to help, but the pair again falls right through.

Ash thinks fast and creates a water bubble using a technique he learned to master from his friends from the Marina Underwater Pokémon Show. He has Feraligatr and Oshawott combine their Hydro Pump with Psychic by Ralts, Kirlia, and Sableye. The result is one gigantic water bubble cushion that Mewtwo and Red Genesect safely fall right into. On impact, the bubble bursts into the river around Pokémon Hills. Ash and Oshawott jump in to rescue Mewtwo. Feraligatr swims out to help Red Genesect. But they're both A-Okay.

"THIS IS THE PLANET WE BOTH COME FROM, THE PLANET ON WHICH YOU AND I WERE CREATED. CREATED BECAUSE THERE IS A REASON FOR US TO BE HERE. THE INHABITANTS OF THIS PLANET, PEOPLE AND POKÉMON ALIKE, LIVE TOGETHER AS FRIENDS. HERE, WE ARE ALL FRIENDS. YOU AND I ARE FRIENDS."
—MEWTWO

Mewtwo then grabs Red Genesect's hand again and lifts it up. Red Genesect speaks. It tells them everyone on the planet is a friend. Ash, Pikachu, Water Genesect, Oshawott, and all the wild Pokémon couldn't agree more!

Looking at a Panna Lotus in the river, Ash thinks of the perfect home for Genesect—the inspiration for Pokémon Hills, Absentia Natural Park. Relieved the city's power is back, Eric helps Ash, Pikachu, Iris, Axew, Cilan, and Mewtwo show Genesect the way to their new home.

LOCATIONS

THE BIG CITY

This urban sprawl expands in every direction, as far as the eye can see. There are tall skyscrapers, billboards covered in light, and sidewalks filled with lots of people and Pokémon!

At the heart of this big city is a nature preserve. Inside the lush park is a new Pokémon habitat, Pokémon Hills. While it hasn't been opened to the public yet, Professor Oak secures a sneak peek for Ash, Iris, and Cilan.

POKÉMON HILLS

A river surrounds the giant spiral dome, and its grounds include a colorful flower garden and hedge maze.

Inside, there are stained-glass windows lining its many tiers. There are all kinds of different environments for all the various kinds of Pokémon. From forests to rock formations, it has everything, including a river that runs through the bottom floor.

Many wild Pokémon call this preserve home…and a few more try to have it all to themselves. Luckily, Ash and his pals were there to help their tour guide Eric protect Pokémon Hills.

THE NESTS

Genesect built a new home for themselves right inside the dome. The stringy nest took shape quickly as Genesect scared the other Pokémon out. This brown oval structure is suspended from many tough strands attached on all sides to different railings, posts, and even the Transformer Substation below, which provides electricity to the entire city.

When the nest's support strands begin to cause power surges, the stray bolts set the structure ablaze. However, with the help of Ash, Pikachu, Iris, Axew, Cilan, Eric, and Mewtwo, Genesect are able to build a new nest in their perfect home, Absentia Natural Park.

CORRIDOR

Typically used by the workers, Eric leads Ash and his pals through a special corridor that connects all the way to Pokémon Hills. However, they head to the Transformer Substation.

TRANSFORMER SUBSTATION

Beneath the ground by Pokémon Hills lies the multi-level Transformer Substation. From the row of metal boxes, electricity flows through the city. This is the main hub of power for every skyscraper, every apartment, all the billboards, and even the street lights in town.

But not just anyone can waltz in—Eric has the special code to open the door. There are also control panels and dials on the inner wall. There is a larger computer connected to the system that Eric is very adept at working. Galleys line both sides of the corridor of each floor, keeping the workers and visitors a safe distance from the metal power boxes in case there's a problem—like a bunch of Genesect stringing a nest to it.

THE POKÉMON CENTER

Nurse Joy and her helper, Audino, are busy in the big city. At the front desk, Nurse Joy greets her patients.

The lobby is decorated with photos Eric took of the beautiful Panna Lotuses and the rock formations at Absentia Natural Park.

The Pokémon Center also has an outdoor seating area with tables, string lights, and umbrellas, perfect for dining al fresco with friends day or night.

ABSENTIA NATURAL PARK

This incredible nature preserve features tall orange rock formations, lush greenery, soft grass, patches of wildflowers, a crystal blue lake,

and most importantly, plenty of Panna Lotus flowers. It's so breathtaking, Nurse Joy hung photos that Eric took of the area in the lobby of the city's Pokémon Center.

THE LAB WHERE MEWTWO WAS CREATED

Surrounded by scientists, the Legendary Pokémon was created in a lab. It was born in a test tube and mistreated by the very people

who worked to bring it to life. But it broke free, and now, because of its experience, Mewtwo feels responsible for helping all the Pokémon that were also created in a lab.

THE CAVE

After escaping the lab, Mewtwo was angry and alone. It didn't trust anyone, not even other Pokémon. But when a terrible storm knocks it out of the sky, it seeks shelter in a cave on a mountainside. There, wild Pokémon inside warm it up and nurse it back to health. But they not only restore its strength, they also restore its heart.

CHARACTERS

ASH

Our hero makes a good friend in Water Genesect. After Ash and Pikachu meet it by the lake, they aren't sure what to make of the mechanical-looking Pokémon. But when Water Genesect takes them on a ride across the river, they know they've met a fun-loving friend!

HOME STRETCH

When Water Genesect opens up to Ash and tells him that it wants to go home, Ash vows to help it. Little did he know at the time that Water Genesect was created in a lab and doesn't really have a true home. But Ash won't give up on his new buddy! Ash knows that there's a home for everyone on the planet.

When Genesect build a huge nest at Pokémon Hills and kick out all of the wild Pokémon inhabitants, it is Ash who tries to stop the fighting. Ash bravely stands between both sides (not once, but twice) to explain that all Genesect are after is a home.

BUBBLE OVER

When Mewtwo arrives to help with the situation at Pokémon Hills, Ash is there to help Mewtwo. Ash catches Mewtwo as it falls, along with the support of his friends Iris and Cilan. Then, when Mewtwo is in free fall with Red Genesect, it is Ash who thinks fast and remembers the water bubbles from the Marina Underwater Pokémon Show. He instructs Oshawott and Feraligatr to use Hydro Pump, and Ralts, Kirlia, and Sableye to shape it with Psychic. Combined, they create a big water bubble cushion to catch Mewtwo and Red Genesect.

CHARIZARD

When Mewtwo and Red Genesect are in free fall, Charizard teams up with Iris' Pokémon pal Dragonite and Genesect to try to catch them.

PIKACHU

Pikachu is always ready to help a Pokémon in need. It quickly uses Iron Tail to swat away Team Rocket's falling weapon before it hits Water Genesect.

OSHAWOTT

Using Hydro Pump, Oshawott helps put out the electrical fire inside Pokémon Hills and assists in creating the water cushion for Red Genesect and Mewtwo.

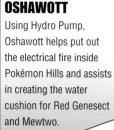

SNIVY

LEAVANNY

PIGNITE

CILAN

The caring Pokémon Connoisseur is most at home in the kitchen, but he'll stand up to any heat! He rallies the wild Pokémon inhabitants of Pokémon Hills to return and stand up to Genesect.

His main concern is a Pokémon's wellbeing. He drops everything to take an injured Ralts to see Nurse Joy.

PANSAGE

CRUSTLE

STUNFISK

ERIC

The guy who greets Ash, Pikachu, Iris, Axew, and Cilan at Pokémon Hills, Eric knows all the ins and outs of this Pokémon preserve. At Professor Oak's request, he takes Ash and his friends on a special tour, even before it's open to the general public. Eric shows them all the amazing features of the incredible Pokémon habitat, from the different environments housed inside to the colorful grounds outside and even the Transformer Substation below.

JACK OF ALL TRADES

An important figure at Pokémon Hills, Eric is often tapped to perform many tasks. He is knowledgeable in all kinds of science, both natural and computer.

Eric has learned a lot about the world's various terrains and the variety of Pokémon. In fact, he's been very hands-on and a key part of Pokémon Hills' development. For example, Eric helped transplant the Panna Lotus flowers from Absentia Natural Park.

When he's not enjoying the natural wonders of Pokémon Hills, he's helping maintain its artificial intelligence. Eric is a tech-savvy guy who can direct the computer system and the various panels around the structure. When the giant nest threatens the city's power, it is Eric who mans the controls.

Eric also has an artistic side. An avid photographer, Eric took beautiful photos of Absentia Natural Park. Those photos now hang in the lobby of the local Pokémon Center.

IRIS

Plucky Iris is there to lend her buddy Ash a hand as they protect the wild Pokémon of Pokémon Hills, help Genesect, and aid Mewtwo.

AXEW

EXCADRILL

EMOLGA

DRAGONITE

When Mewtwo and Red Genesect are in free fall, Dragonite springs into action with Ash's Pokémon pal Charizard and Genesect to try to catch them.

TEAM ROCKET

Jessie, James, and Meowth have followed Ash and his friends all the way to the big city. And when they sneak in and get a good look at Pokémon Hills, they think it's their big chance to catch Genesect and Mewtwo. However, before they can even aim their weapon, Red Genesect is right there to scare them away.

While they look for an exit, the power goes out, and they make a misstep. They fall into an area where city workers have been making repairs, and a group of Durant send them blasting off of the jobsite!

NURSE JOY

Caring Nurse Joy helps Pikachu and Ralts recoup their strength after their scuffles with Genesect.

AUDINO

LEGENDARY AND MYTHICAL POKÉMON

MEWTWO:
THE GENETIC POKÉMON

Height	6'07"
Weight	269.0 lbs
Type	Psychic

Born in a lab, Mewtwo broke free from the scientists who created it. Mewtwo understands what it's like to feel alone in the world, like everyone is your enemy. So, the Legendary Pokémon feels that it has a responsibility to help Genesect understand there is also a place for them here on the planet. It feels a kinship with its fellow man-made Pokémon.

DEPENDED ON THE KINDNESS OF STRANGERS

After escaping the lab, Mewtwo was on its own. Angry and exhausted, it got caught in a big storm and struck by lightning. Barely able to walk, Mewtwo slipped into a cave for shelter. Once inside, it realized it wasn't alone. At first, it was nervous to see all the wild Pokémon inside. But when another bolt struck and sent it flying, Tangrowth caught it in its arms.

Then, all of the Pokémon, even though they were complete strangers, huddled around Mewtwo to warm it up and help restore its energy. When Mewtwo woke up, it was so touched by their care that both the hurt it felt from the lightning bolt and the hurt it felt from its past in the lab were healed. From that day forward, Mewtwo felt like it had a place on the planet and friends in its fellow Pokémon.

Now, Mewtwo regularly keeps company with Flying-types. It loves to soar through the sky with Swanna, Unfezant, Swellow, Staraptor, and Braviary.

MEGA MEWTWO Y:
THE GENETIC POKÉMON

Height	4'11"
Weight	72.88 lbs
Type	Psychic

During its struggle to reach Red Genesect, Mewtwo Mega Evolves into Mega Mewtwo Y a few times. In the temporary Mega Evolved form, it speedily dodges a flurry of attacks from three Genesect at once, fiercely battles back, and even carries Red Genesect up into space like a rocket.

PEOPLE PROBLEMS

Although Mewtwo is a friend to all Pokémon, it still does not trust humans completely. When Genesect attack Ash, Pikachu, Iris, Axew, and Cilan, Mewtwo speeds in and rescues them. However, it makes it clear that it is only concerned about the safety of Pokémon.

GENESECT:
THE PALEOZOIC

Height	4'11"
Weight	181.9 lbs
Type	Bug/Steel

A species of Mythical Pokémon that roamed the world 300 million years ago, the five featured in this film were brought back to life from fossils. These man-made Pokémon then had weapons added above their heads by humans.

Led by Red Genesect, Water Genesect, Fire Genesect, Ice Genesect, and Electric Genesect now find themselves in a world they don't recognize. They are fearful of people and Pokémon alike. Scared, mad, and alone, all they have is each other. They stick together, a band of Genesect against the world. But when they try to take over a new nature preserve known as Pokémon Hills, they wind up making friends with everyone they think are their enemies. Genesect can stand tall or fold into flying saucers.

RED GENESECT

The leader of the Genesect pack, this fierce, trigger-happy Mythical Pokémon doesn't trust anyone. It thinks everyone is its enemy, both people and Pokémon. It even thinks the Legendary Pokémon Mewtwo is its foe and fires right at it despite Mewtwo's pleas that it's there to help. Worse yet, when its fellow Genesect do not want to continue battling the wild Pokémon inhabitants of Pokémon Hills, Red Genesect calls them traitors and continues cruelly fighting everyone on its own.

GENERAL GENESECT

Every time someone pleads with Genesect to stop fighting, it replies, "Don't give me orders!" Red Genesect is large and in charge. It won't listen to reason. Anyone who disagrees with it can talk to its cannon.

In an attempt to hit Mewtwo, Red Genesect freely fired throughout the city, striking buildings with no regard for the people and Pokémon that might get hurt in the crossfire.

Red Genesect also has the ability to give its fellow Genesect orders. It can communicate with them, even when they're in different locations, and give them instructions on how to handle the situation. And, of course, Red Genesect always advises them to respond with fire!

WATER GENESECT

When Pikachu first spots Water Genesect, it folds up into a flying saucer to hide. Ash runs up to see what the transforming thing is. When they step on it like a surfboard, Water Genesect takes Ash and Pikachu for a ride over the lake.

Back on the shore, Water Genesect opens up and tells Ash it wants to go home. Ash promises to help his new Pokémon pal!

FIRE, ELECTRIC, AND ICE GENESECT

At first, this trio follows Red Genesect's orders and tries to destroy all of the people and Pokémon at Pokémon Hills. But when Ash tries to protect Water Genesect and even jumps in the river to rescue it, they soon see with their own eyes that Ash is a true pal. So, when a beam covered in flames is falling right above Ash, the trio teams up to come to his aid and blast it away.

Then, even more surprisingly and importantly, when Ash takes a stand and asks Red Genesect to stop the fighting, the three Genesect (along with Water Genesect) back him up. Unfortunately, this makes Red Genesect temporarily turn on its fellow Genesect, although it eventually sees the light.

When their pal Red Genesect is free-falling back to the ground with Mewtwo, the other four Genesect quickly create a net to help catch it.

In the end, all of the Genesect make a new nest together in their peaceful new home, Absentia Natural Park.

FLOWER POWER

Water Genesect is a sensitive soul that truly appreciates the beauty of its favorite flower—the Panna Lotus. It introduces Ash, Pikachu, Iris, Axew, and Cilan to the blossom as it floats in the river.

When the battle blasts a few buds apart in Pokémon Hills, peacenik Water Genesect is upset by the destruction.

FINDING PEACE

When nothing in the world could seem to stop Red Genesect, Mega Mewtwo Y did something out of this world. It flew like a rocket ship straight up into space, carrying the stubborn Pokémon with it. Amazingly enough, by breaking out of the planet, Red Genesect has a breakthrough. Mega Mewtwo Y is able to finally get it to see that the world is home to many inhabitants, and one of them is Red Genesect. Then, Mewtwo extends its hand and reaches out to Red Genesect, offering its friendship. With its newfound perspective and its new pal, Red Genesect is ready to return to the planet and make a new home for itself.

In fact, on the return trip, when Mewtwo passes out, Red Genesect grabs its pal and hugs it for safety the whole way home.

BREAKING RANK

Before Ash can aid his new friend, four more Genesect show up and begin to attack under Red Genesect's command. Even Water Genesect is ordered to fire on its new pals. Mega Mewtwo Y swoops in and stops the attack...But that certainly isn't the last time Red Genesect will lead them into battle.

When Ash and his crew return to Pokémon Hills, they find a giant nest in the middle and Water Genesect. It apologizes to them for firing, but it can't disobey Red Genesect. Ash accepts its apology and wants to get to know his new Mythical Pokémon pal.

Water Genesect doesn't want to fight the inhabitants at Pokémon Hills or Ash and his friends. It doesn't want to be under Red Genesect's control. Water Genesect wants to stop the war and bring the peace back to Pokémon Hills, and it's willing to be the first Genesect to stand up.

FEATURED POKÉMON

FERALIGATR: THE BIG JAW POKÉMON

Brave Feraligatr doesn't run when Genesect attack its home, Pokémon Hills. The Water-type Pokémon fights back and won't back down. But when Genesect aims its fire at Feraligatr, it takes a fall from a balcony. Luckily, Mewtwo is there to catch it with Psychic. But the exchange doesn't stop Feraligatr from standing its ground.

Feraligatr is always looking for a way to help protect its home. When Pokémon Hills catches fire, Feraligatr adds its Hydro Pump to Oshawott's. The pair again uses Hydro Pump together to create the water bubble cushion that breaks Mewtwo and Genesect's fall from space.

SABLEYE: THE DARKNESS POKÉMON

Small Sableye is able to sneak around Pokémon Hills undetected by Genesect. Although it is initially shy when it meets Ash, Sableye rushes to get him and his friends for backup when Genesect start to fight its wild Pokémon pals. The Psychic-type Pokémon also helps Ash create the bubble cushion that catches Red Genesect and Mewtwo when they fall back to the world.

INTERESTING ITEMS

PANNA LOTUS

You don't have to worry about overwatering this lovely flora—the Panna Lotus lives right in the river. This beautiful blossom has a rich history. It is said to be the most ancient flower that is still found in the Pokémon world today. Eric told Ash and his friends that they have been budding for 300 million years! In fact, Genesect are drawn to them because they also existed back when the Paleozoic Pokémon roamed the planet.

> "FINALLY, I HAD DISCOVERED A PLACE WHERE I BELONG. THE GENESECT DESERVE AS MUCH!"
> —MEWTWO

THE GIANT WATER CUSHION

After getting a behind-the-scenes view of the Marina Underwater Pokémon Show, Ash knows just how to make a giant water bubble. Ash's friends Lizabeth, Shep, Meredith, and Kyle showed him how they use the bubbles created by combined attacks from Poliwhirl, Poliwag, Medicham, and Meditite to do the impressive tricks in their performances. And while their traveling show is a total hit, Ash is counting on their bubble technique to absorb the other kind of hit—direct impact.

When Mewtwo and Red Genesect are plunging down to the ground, Genesect's net and even Dragonite and Charizard can't seem to stop their free fall. So, Ash thinks fasts and has Oshawott and Feraligatr combine their Hydro Pump with Psychic by Ralts, Kirlia, and Sableye. Together, they create a gigantic water bubble that makes the perfect cushion to catch both Pokémon safely.

Although it's clear Ash has mastered the Marina Underwater Pokémon Show's bubble-building technique, it doesn't seem like he'll be trying to match their aquatic acrobatic skills any time soon.

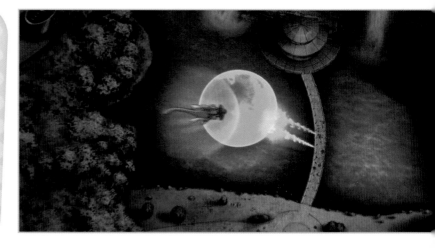

TOTALLY AWESOME TECHNOLOGY

TEAM ROCKET'S LAUNCHER

This cannon fits snugly over James' shoulder, but he never even gets the chance to fire it. Red Genesect is even fiercer than this launcher. The second the Mythical Pokémon sees that Team Rocket is ready to attack, it beats them to the punch and fires the first shot.

The launcher lodges right in a strand of the nest. When it's rattled by an impact, the launcher falls down and is headed straight for Water Genesect's head. Luckily, Pikachu quickly uses Iron Tail to knock it out of harm's way.

THE CONTROL ROOM AT POKÉMON HILLS

Inside the habitat on the main floor, there is a metal box that contains a very important control panel. From the readings on the screen, Eric can tell there is trouble brewing in the Transformer Substation. But when it sounds an alert, Eric knows things have gone from bad to worse and that the city is in danger of losing power. So, he races over to the main computer.

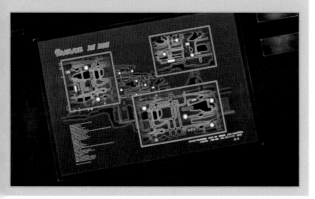

THE KEYPAD AT THE CORRIDOR

You not only have to know about the corridor, but you also need to know the combination to get inside. Forget an old-fashioned key: Eric types a unique sequence into the keypad to unlock the side door.

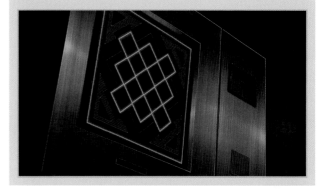

> ## "EVERYTHING'LL WORK OUT. I'LL MAKE IT WORK OUT!"
> ## —ASH

THE MAIN COMPUTER

The main computer at Pokémon Hills has multiple screens, dials, and buttons. Eric is a computer whiz who quickly directs the keyboard to try to avert a crisis from the fire in the Transformer Substation. The whole city's power is at stake, but Eric doesn't think about the pressure—he keeps his focus on the mission.

PUKÉMON THE MUVIE: HOOPA AND THE CLASH OF AGES

THE STORY

A long time ago, in a village in the desert, a giant gold ring appeared in a clear blue sky. Inside, a rippling beam of light swirled, and soon after, a massive purple Pokémon with two horns poured out upside down. It was none other than the Mythical Pokémon Hoopa.

"Alahooparing!" Hoopa shouted, sliding two gold bracelets off of its wrists.

The rings hovered in the sky as Hoopa transported Legendary Pokémon Kyogre and Groudon. The villagers in the town below couldn't believe their eyes, and it seemed neither could the Legendary Pokémon! Groudon opened its mouth to send a fiercely defensive Fire Blast at Hoopa, but it deflected the attack by catching it in one ring. Then, it released the blast out of its other ring, landing a direct hit on Kyogre.

"Were you surprised? Why? Hoopa can do anything!" Hoopa bragged.

But Hoopa wasn't done fighting. The villagers ran for the hills, afraid of what Hoopa would do next. Through its rings, it brought yet more Legendary Pokémon to battle: Regigigas, Reshiram, and Zekrom. The trio teamed up and tried to stop Hoopa, but even together, they couldn't seem to control the wild ringmaster's rampage.

"See? Hoopa is strong!" it said, celebrating its victory.

Who would be powerful enough? Who would be brave enough? Who could stop Hoopa?

Then, a man with a white cape and a gold medallion necklace walked through the deserted town and right up to Hoopa. With his arm outstretched, he uncapped a special ringed urn he had brought called the Prison Bottle. A glowing light peeked out of the bottle and surrounded Hoopa. The Mythical Pokémon struggled to resist it, but it was no match for this powerful container. The massive Pokémon was pulled into the tiny ringed Prison Bottle. The man quickly sealed it again, locking up Hoopa inside.

Hoopa stayed there for 100 years until Baraz, a young man with the same gold medallion, decided to go looking for it deep in a dark cave. With outstretched arms, he used his unique powers to release the ringed bottle from its ancient bonds. But the minute he held the bottle, purple smoke surrounded him. He struggled against it, but it overcame him, and his eyes began to glow red.

Meanwhile, on the other side of town, Ash, Pikachu, Bonnie, Dedenne, Clemont, Pancham, Chespin, and Serena are visiting a nearby Pokémon Center with a cool pool. Serena surprises her pals with a sweet treat—donuts and Poké Puffs. "Yummy!" Bonnie declares.

But Chespin does not even get a taste before a mystery hand appears through a gold ring and switches out its Poké Puff for a spicy Tamato Berry. Unaware of the quick trick, Chespin goes to take a big bite. Its face immediately turns red, and flames shoot out of its mouth—which is shocking behavior for a Grass-type.

Another ring appears, and a mystery hand tries to take Pikachu's donut. However, tough Pikachu won't let go of its treat. Ash steps in to try to help it, but the mystery hand winds up dragging them both through the ring, donut and all. Then, the ring disappears from the Pokémon Center. Bonnie, Clemont, and Serena can't believe what they just witnessed.

On the other side of the ring, Ash, Pikachu, and the donut reappear before the Mythical Pokémon Hoopa in its Confined form. It might be smaller and sillier than Hoopa in its Unbound form, but it's still full of mischief. The ring slips back on one of Hoopa's horns. Ash and Pikachu see famous Dahara City in the distance, and they try to figure out how they traveled through the ring to a completely different place so far away.

"WERE YOU SURPRISED?" —HOOPA

"Are you surprised?" Hoopa says with delight at their confusion.

Ash and Pikachu introduce themselves to Hoopa, but it decides to call its new friends Pikan and Ashkan. Excited to have company, Hoopa wants to play another game. It holds out a pair of golden rings and summons dozens of Pikachu. The whole area fills up with Pikachu, including Pikachu Rock Star, Pikachu Belle, Pikachu Pop Star, Pikachu PhD, and Pikachu Libre. Hoopa then asks Ash to find his best friend, Pikachu, in the crowd. But Ash knows immediately where his Pokémon pal is. Upset that it lost its own game, Hoopa throws itself into a temper tantrum that sparks all the Pikachu to zap Ash with electricity.

Just then, Hoopa's friend Meray comes running over, embarrassed by its bad behavior. She insists that Hoopa return all of the Pikachu, and Ash's pal can't agree more. It helps round up its fellow Pikachu. Then, Hoopa reopens its rings. One by one, they hop through the rings and are returned to where they came from.

Rather than travel back to the Pokémon Center, Ash and Pikachu ask Hoopa to help bring their friends here. A ring appears poolside, and Ash pops his head out.

"I'm back!" Ash jokes as he pulls his pals through the gold ring.

Serena, Bonnie, Dedenne, and Clemont look around their new location with awe. They are very impressed they could travel by ring!

"Were you surprised? Come on, were you surprised?!" Hoopa asks with glee.

Ash and Pikachu laugh at their new Pokémon pal's playful nature. Serena spots Dahara Tower in the distance and suggests they all go visit the landmark together. Bonnie adds that if they use Hoopa's rings, they could be there in a jiffy. But there's a hitch, and it has Hoopa feeling pretty down.

"Unfortunately, Hoopa can't travel through its own ring just yet," Meray explains.

Serena feels bad for bringing up the touchy subject, so she offers Hoopa a delicious Poké Puff she baked. It turns Hoopa's frown upside down, but not for long.

Two evil forces are about to threaten their trip to Dahara Tower. Up in the clouds, Team Rocket is spying on the crew from their hot air balloon. Down on the ground, red-eyed Baraz arrives, riding on Braviary and holding the antique Prison Bottle.

"You found the Prison Bottle!" Meray cheers.

But her celebration ends quickly as he opens the bottle, releasing a powerful purple smoke. Hoopa screams at the smoke that covers it. Then, suddenly, its eyes glow red, and it grows into its giant Unbound form.

"Hoopa!" it shouts, letting everyone know it's back.

After the huge change, Ash, Serena, Bonnie, and Clemont wonder if Hoopa just Evolved before their very eyes. Meray explains that this is actually Hoopa's true form.

"That's so great, Hoopa! You're back to normal!" Meray says, happy for her old Pokémon pal.

Hoopa celebrates, "Yes, yes, this power! Hoopa is strong!"

But Baraz looks confused. His eyes are no longer red, and he's not quite sure what happened or how he got there. Now, Meray is confused. But their conversation is cut short by Hoopa, which has started a rampage and is smashing buildings and columns. Then, with its eyes glowing red, Hoopa sets its sights on the Prison Bottle. It reaches to grab it out of Baraz's hand, but a bright blue glow protects the precious bottle from Hoopa's grip.

Angry, Hoopa throws a gold ring off its wrist and toward Dahara City. It drops it on a building and pulls the spire right off of it and through the ring. Then, it chucks the building top off at the whole crew.

Ash thinks fast and yells, "Pikachu! Thunderbolt, let's go!"

"Piiiiikachuuuuuu!" it shouts, turning the solid spire into a light rock rain.

Baraz warns everyone to run, but Meray refuses to. She wants to guard the Prison Bottle since it was her idea to restore Hoopa's full power. When Hoopa tosses  another ring to steal another building's spire, they all make a break for it. Hoopa chases after them. Just when they've cleared the rubble, Meray bravely turns around and uncaps the Prison Bottle, pointing it right at Hoopa.

Hoopa cries out as it struggles to keep its strength, but it's no use. The Prison Bottle sucks the purple smoke right back into it, leaving small Hoopa behind.

Meray caps the bottle quickly, but the rage inside rattles, and it drops the bottle to the ground. Baraz is afraid if someone picks it up, it will take over their mind—the same way he felt he was under its wicked spell.

"Don't touch it! The bottle contains something evil," Baraz warns.

Clemont has the perfect solution: one of his Clemontic Gear inventions.

"I call this my Fully Automatic Lifting Machine!" Clemont says, taking the technology out of his backpack with his robot arm. "I designed it to use the principles behind the Pokémon move Magnet Rise."

Amazingly enough, his machine gets a good grip and lifts the bottle off the ground, protecting its powers from touching anyone and adding a metal handle.

"Way to go!" Serena cheers.

"Science is so amazing!" Ash adds.

Baraz apologizes to Ash, Serena, Clemont, and Bonnie for getting them mixed up in Hoopa's struggle. Ash reminds him that they're always happy to help a Pokémon in need, and Hoopa certainly needs their aid.

But one day, the wishes turned into battle challenges. The villagers love to watch the super-strong Mythical Pokémon Hoopa in action. Eventually, all the victories went to its head. Hoopa wanted to test its power and began to use its rings to summon Legendary Pokémon to battle, like Regigigas, Kyogre, Groudon, and more!

It had to be stopped. As it turns out, the brave man with the white cape and gold medallion who brought the ringed bottle is actually Baraz and Meray's great-grandfather. He made the Prison Bottle himself on the spot that is now Dahara Tower. After sealing Hoopa's power in the bottle, he hid it deep in a cave for safety.

"Hoopa's afraid," it whimpers. "Disappear. It's getting dark. So afraid. Hoopa is disappearing…"

Worried about Hoopa, they decide to rush it to the Pokémon Center. On their way across the river, Meray and Baraz admit they're concerned that Hoopa will again destroy the city the way it did 100 years ago. Baraz tells them the story that's haunted his village ever since.

According to legend, a century ago, Hoopa arrived through its ring and stole the villagers' food. To pay them back for filling its belly, it dropped gold coins like rain from the sky, showering them with riches. So, the grateful villagers built it a special home. In return for gifts of delicious delicacies, Hoopa would grant everyone's wishes.

Then, their great-grandfather returned home to Arche Valley with the smaller Hoopa in its Confined form and treated it like part of the family. Since Meray and Baraz were born, they have cared for Hoopa. It's been like a sibling to them.

Speaking of trouble, make it double! Nearby in the sky, Team Rocket has been watching from their hot air balloon, and Meowth thinks that Prison Bottle will give it superpowers. The trio decides to steal it. Baraz tries to warn them not to take it out of Clemont's contraption.

"You're a little late for that, pal!" Meowth replies, holding it in its paws with a smile.

Suddenly, Meowth's eyes glow red. In a daze, it opens the Prison Bottle, releasing a strong purple smoke that slithers down to Hoopa. Hoopa struggles to fight the evil power that's been trying to control it.

"Hoopa! Don't give in!" Ash cheers it on. "You can defeat it!"

At dinner that night, Baraz and Meray reveal that just like their ancestors, they wear a gold medallion to show that they possess a great power that is said to come from the Alpha Pokémon itself, Arceus. Their great-grandfather had mastered that power and could even communicate with the Mythical Pokémon Arceus. Baraz and Meray are still training hard in the hopes of reaching that level.

Hoopa is also trying to understand its power. Their great-grandfather told Hoopa that until it learned why it was confined, it wouldn't be able to pass through its own rings. It still struggles with its punishment, the loss of its full strength, to this day. After all these years, Meray and Baraz felt that it was time to try to give Hoopa back its true power.

"So, I set out on a journey to find the Prison Bottle, but this was the end result," Baraz said. "I'm sorry for causing trouble. Still, I want to do something for Hoopa."

In an incredible show of will, Hoopa stays strong. With the help of Meray's and Baraz's special power, they fend off the purple smoke.

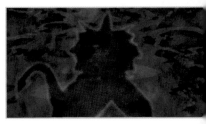

However, the bottle has a mind of its own. It slips out of Meowth's grip and shatters in midair. The rings and cap fall to the ground. The purple smoke rises to the sky. It takes shape and turns into a shell of Hoopa in its Unbound form.

"The anger's trying to become the real Hoopa," Baraz worries. "Hoopa, yet not Hoopa. It's a shadow of Hoopa."

The first move the shadow makes is Hyperspace Fury, using one of its rings to punch Team Rocket's balloon right out of the sky. Then, it shouts at Hoopa, "Disappear!"

"No!" Hoopa yells. "I won't disappear!"

Baraz sends Braviary to battle the shadow Hoopa, but a Dark Pulse blast leaves it unable to fight.

Hoopa steps up and uses its ring to summon some backup in the form of Legendary Pokémon Lugia. While the Diving Pokémon fends off the larger Hoopa with a flash of Aeroblast, Baraz tells everyone to run for safety.

Baraz knows he must remake the Prison Bottle at Dahara Tower. Meray says they'll need the same materials their great-grandfather used: fire, water, and ground, the three great forces of nature.

"For water power, I've got Frogadier!" Ash volunteers.

"For fire power, I've got Braixen!" Serena offers.

Short a Ground-type Pokémon friend, Bonnie thinks fast and suggests that Hoopa uses its ring to bring over one of the local wild Hippopotas.

"Alahooparing!" Hoopa cheers, tossing its ring and putting Bonnie's idea into action.

Now, all they need to do is get to Dahara Tower. The shadowy Hoopa is hot on their trail! The group decides to divide and conquer. Baraz, Meray, Clemont, Bonnie, and Serena continue on to Dahara Tower, traveling as fast as they can through the smaller Hoopa's ring. Ash and Pikachu stick with Hoopa to help it hide out. Hoopa is very touched that its new pals Ashkan and Pikan have its back. As they walk through the city to find a safe place to hide, Ash thinks about Hoopa's predicament. The purple shadow and his new Pokémon pal are both Hoopa.

"It's like you're having a battle against yourself or something. But since both of you are you, I think you should get along," Ash says, suggesting they try to make up.

But before they can take another step, two giant gold rings appear. The shadow Hoopa pokes its head and hand through in an attempt to catch Hoopa. Luckily, Lugia is still on the case and is able to hold it off. Ash, Pikachu, and Hoopa flee to find another hiding spot.

Over at Dahara Tower, Baraz and the team have started firing a new Prison Bottle with the combination of attacks from their Pokémon pals Frogadier, Braixen, and Hippopotas. But the real thing heating up is the epic battle between Lugia and the larger Hoopa through the city. Locals are shocked to see the Legendary and Mythical Pokémon locked in battle, their stray attacks destroying buildings. Hoopa wants to help it come to an end.

"Do you think Hoopa and Shadow can make up?" Hoopa asks his pal Ashkan.

"Sure you can! Then you'll get your old power back," Ash adds.

Hoopa is happy to hear that it not only has hope, it also has a plan. However, Hoopa in it's Unbound form has found them again. They try to flee, but in the middle of the street, the shadow Hoopa surrounds them with rings to unleash Hyperspace Fury. There is nowhere to run. However, Lugia swoops in and flies them right out of there!

The shadowy Hoopa strikes Lugia down from the sky. Ash, Pikachu, and Hoopa fly off its back and onto a building rooftop. Lugia picks itself up and flies back into the battle, but the larger Hoopa cleverly uses a gold ring to transport it back home.

"Hoopa, we've got to fight, too!" Ash says to rally his Pokémon pal.

"Hoopa fight with you!" it promises. "Alahooparing!"

With that, it uses its rings to summon Legendary Pokémon Latias, Latios, and Rayquaza. Ash asks for their help. Ash on Latios and Pikachu on Latias ride into battle together. Ash asks all three Legendary Pokémon to fire Dragon Pulse, but Hoopa doesn't even flinch. It uses every single one of its rings to drop dirt on the city that it swirls into a sandstorm. Latios, Latias, and Rayquaza cry out. Ash asks them to use Psychic to put a stop to the sandblasting. It works, but the sand drops over the city, landing on the local people and Pokémon.

Then, Hoopa in its Unbound form uses its rings to summon its own super group of Legendary Pokémon: Dialga, Palkia, Kyurem, Primal Groudon, and Primal Kyogre. They fire at Hoopa and its pals in unison. Ash asks Latias, Latios, and Rayquaza to use Dragon Pulse together again with the added blow of Pikachu's powerful Thunderbolt. They are able to cancel out the hit, but all power behind this battle causes a chain reaction. Rayquaza, Latias, and Latios Mega Evolve in midair. Kyurem becomes Black Kyurem.

The battle turns even uglier as both the Legendary Pokémon and the city's buildings take massive hits as they chase each other through the streets. Black Kyurem becomes White Kyurem, then knocks Ash off Latios' back. Hoopa thinks fast and uses a ring to transport him safely up onto the Legendary Pokémon's back again.

As the epic battle wages on, the citizens are forced to run out of town to look for safety. This town belongs to Legendary and Mythical Pokémon now.

Sensing that a new Prison Bottle is being created, Hoopa in its Unbound form focuses its attention on Dahara Tower. It throws a ring toward the landmark to set up an attack.

'Oh no, you don't!" Ash yells.

Then, he asks Mega Latios to fire Dragon Pulse to stop its hand, but they don't see Dialga's fierce attack coming. It lands a direct hit, breaking the building's iconic ring.

Ash asks Mega Rayquaza to use Twister around the landmark. Then, Ash asks Mega Latios and Mega Latias to add Psychic to the storm. Together, the shadowy Hoopa and his team of Legendary Pokémon combine their attacks to try to destroy the swirling shield, but even their six-pronged attack can't break through. This Hoopa won't give up. It places a set of rings in front of each of its Legendary teammates and a set of rings around Dahara Tower to deliver their attacks in close range. Its strategy pokes holes in the shield, and Hoopa is able to land its next attack. The Twister comes crashing down. Dahara Tower might look defenseless, but Mega Rayquaza, Mega Latios, and Mega Latias are still in the fight.

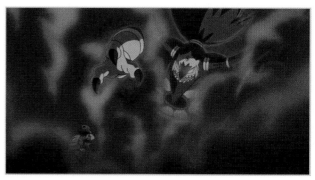

With its teammates focused on the battle, shadow Hoopa zeroes in on Ash and Hoopa. After they fall off Mega Latios' back, shadow Hoopa's hand is right there to scoop them up. But to everyone's surprise, the powerful Pokémon can't quite get a grip.

The darkness lifts over the city, and the sunshine reveals Baraz standing there with his arm outstretched, holding the new Prison Bottle. All of the Legendary Pokémon summoned by Hoopa in its Unbound form are freed from its mind control, and their eyes stop glowing red. The battle is over, but there is still some unfinished business.

Baraz opens the new Prison Bottle. As expected, Hoopa in its Unbound form returns to purple smoke and gets drawn back in. But the force of its anger is so great that the bottle goes flying into the air. Ash jumps to catch it, but he gets engulfed in purple smoke, and his eyes begin to glow red.

Possessed by the shadow, Ash yells at Hoopa, "It is over. Disappear! Away! / am Hoopa!"

But Hoopa won't be intimidated. It remembers its pal Ashkan told it to try to reconnect with its other half. So, Hoopa decides to share its story of all the happy memories it had with Baraz and Meray. It uses its Psychic powers to communicate all the good times in Arche Valley playing with its friends.

"Come on, were you surprised? Shadow has fun life now, too!" Hoopa promises. "Shadow, Hoopa waited for you."

The purple smoke can feel the love, and its heart changes. Suddenly, a beam of light shoots straight up into the sky. Ash and his eyes return to normal. Baraz confirms that the evil power is gone. All of the Legendary and Mythical Pokémon rejoice!

But perhaps the celebration begins too soon—the Dahara Tower is suddenly swallowed by dark purple smoke. Baraz can sense that time and space are being warped, possibly by the number of Legendary and Mythical Pokémon that were summoned. The dark smoke begins to close in on the tower. The people inside are beginning to panic.

Ash asks Pikachu to try to stop it with Thunderbolt, but it's too powerful. The Legendary Pokémon outside also try to stop it with their combined attacks, but they have no effect on whatever this space and time warp is.

Hoopa thinks fast and has Ash open the Prison Bottle. Hoopa in its confined form becomes Hoopa in its Unbound form.

"Here and now, the true, true power of Hoopa!" Hoopa announces proudly, ready to use its power for good.

It lays down rings so all of the people trapped in Dahara Tower can escape. The only ones still inside are Meray, Baraz, Serena, Clemont, Bonnie, Ash, and Pikachu. Meray tells them to get out as soon as they can because the ring is shrinking.

Not wanting to leave their new friend behind, Bonnie reminds them that, "Hoopa's not able to go through the ring!"

"We don't know, and we won't unless Hoopa tries!" Ash says. "Hoopa, here's my wish: for you to escape from this place!"

Ash then opens the Prison Bottle again, returning Hoopa to its Confined form. Ash holds his Mythical Pokémon pal and vows to try together. Meray and Baraz also use all of their power to help them get through. Ash and Hoopa together charge at the ring, but they get bounced back. Meray joins them on their second attempt, but only she makes it through. Baraz tries to help on their third attempt, but only Ash makes it through. They're running out of time, and the warp is seconds away from closing in on them.

Suddenly, the time and space rift stops. Baraz's medallion glows. They charge the ring together again, and he asks Meray to also use her power to help. Hoopa reflects on a particularly happy memory when Baraz's and Meray's great-grandfather said it was part of the family. The strength of that love breaks through the ring and releases the seal that trapped Hoopa. It doesn't waste a second reaching back through the closing ring to save its brother, Baraz.

The space and time warp closes in on itself, and the Alpha Pokémon appears in the sky.

"Arceus!" Meray calls out in awe at the sight.

Order has been restored, perhaps in no small part because of the Mythical Pokémon Arceus. All of the Legendary and Mythical Pokémon begin their journey to return to their homes. Hoopa is really happy to have been able to help and to finally have its full power restored. Now, Hoopa plans to use its true strength to rebuild the land where Dahara Tower stood. Proud of his new Pokémon pal, Ash vows to continue on his journey to become a Pokémon Master with all the lessons he learned on this adventure.

LOCATIONS

DAHARA CITY

Dahara is a huge hub in the desert surrounded by sparkling rivers. Long ago, it was just a small village, but a visit from Mythical Pokémon Hoopa changed all of that. To thank the locals for sharing their food, Hoopa showered them with gold coins. The citizens used that wealth to build a big, beautiful city covered in tall skyscrapers.

DAHARA TOWER

The architectural jewel of Dahara City, this unusual monument features a tall arch banded with two golden rings. A famous tourist attraction, it sits along the river, shining in the sunlight. It marks the spot where the unusual and powerful Prison Bottle was made and remade.

THE POKÉMON CENTER WITH A POOL

Nurse Joy and Clefairy have quite a spread at their Dahara City location. In addition to the typical medical center, it also

has an amazing outdoor pool and deck area. This Pokémon Center is more like a resort, a total paradise for people and Pokémon that love to swim. But the visitors aren't the only ones having fun in the sun! Nearby, there are a lot of Hippopotas relaxing in the sand.

One funny prank that Hoopa played involved this very pool. When Ash, Serena, Clemont, and Bonnie said they were thirsty, Hoopa used a ring to transport all of the pool water from the Pokémon Center and drop it on the crew. They were soaked, Meray was mad, and Nurse Joy didn't know what happened, but Hoopa thought it was hilarious.

ARCHE VALLEY

Just outside the city, there is a lush valley. Our heroes Meray, Baraz, and Hoopa all call this precious part of the desert home. Their family has lived there for generations.

THE CAVE

A century ago, Meray's and Baraz's great-grandfather hid the Prison Bottle deep down in a cave outside Arche Valley. Baraz made it his mission to locate this special underground site.

THE DONUT SHOP

Ash and Pikachu are first transported by Hoopa's ring to a park in front of the local donut shop. Dahara City is known for the sweet treat.

HOOPA: ASHKAN!

ASH: NO, IT'S ASH!

HOOPA: PIKAN, ASHKAN, PIKAN, ASHKAN, PIKAN, ASHKAN!

CHARACTERS

ASH

When Ash gets transported through a gold ring, he not only changes locations, but he also finds a new mission. Ash and his pals just have to help their new pal, the Mythical Pokémon Hoopa, restore its true power.

FROGADIER

Ash calls on his Water-type buddy Frogadier to help remake the Prison Bottle. He asks Clemont to care for it while he helps protect Hoopa. In Dahara Tower, Frogadier makes a big splash with Baraz, adding the force of water to forge the new Prison Bottle.

PIKACHU

It doesn't matter how many Pikachu Hoopa playfully summons: Ash's best friend Pikachu is one of a kind. Ash can pick it out of a crowd, and it stays by Ash's side to help protect Hoopa.

SERENA

Amazing baker Serena wows her pals with a delicious round of donuts and Poké Puffs. They are so delicious, they tempt Hoopa to steal one, and so begins their friendship.

BRAIXEN

Serena asks her Fire-type Pokémon friend to help remake the Prison Bottle.

PANCHAM

Pancham loves hanging out poolside at the local Pokémon Center.

CLEMONT

Inventor extraordinaire Clemont saves the day with one of his Clemontic Gear inventions, the Fully Automatic Lifting Machine. Since Clemont's happy to help, Ash also entrusts him with temporarily watching his Pokémon pal Frogadier.

BONNIE

Credit where credit is due, Clemont's little sister is one smart girl. She thinks fast and has Hoopa use its rings to transport one of the Hippopotas she spotted to Dahara Tower to help forge the Prison Bottle.

DEDENNE

BARAZ AND MERAY

Meray and Baraz are the great-grandchildren of the brave man who first made the Prison Bottle that contained Hoopa's Unbound form. They also wear the same gold medallions their ancestors have worn for generations. It connects them to the amazing Alpha Pokémon, Arceus. From this Mythical Pokémon, they draw a special power that they use to help their Pokémon sibling, Hoopa.

GREAT-GRANDFATHER

One hundred years ago, this incredibly courageous man restored order to Dahara City. He took the care of Hoopa on himself. He brought Hoopa back to his own home and treated it like a member of his family. He passed this important responsibility on to his great-grandchildren, Meray and Baraz. According to their great-grandfather's wishes, the pair was raised with Hoopa and formed an unbelievably strong bond.

Legend has it that the great-grandfather and his ancestors were able to communicate directly with Arceus. He too wore the gold medallion that shows their deep familial connection.

BARAZ

Baraz is the brave brother of Hoopa, who dared to find the Prison Bottle and unlock its true power. So, he is the first to be possessed by the evil shadow in 100 years.

Wise Baraz has been working with his sister to master their connection to Arceus. He also has a mysterious connection to the evil shadow inside the Prison Bottle and is able to sense its thoughts and feelings. He uses this special sight to protect his hometown, Dahara City, and also to forge a new Prison Bottle with the help of some Pokémon pals.

MERAY

After her great-grandfather passed, Meray was tormented by the notion that her lifelong Pokémon pal Hoopa had been cut off from its true power. So, Meray initially encouraged her brother to travel to find the Prison Bottle.

Although she loves her Pokémon sibling, Hoopa, she is often embarrassed by its silly pranks. She keeps a close eye on it to be sure it doesn't get into too much trouble. Unfortunately, her compassion gets it in the most trouble it's ever been in as Hoopa's Unbound form is unleashed on her town.

SOLROCK: THE METEORITE POKÉMON

Solrock was an important part of Baraz's hunt to find the Prison Bottle. It not only lowers Baraz safely into the cave, but it also lights up the dark depths.

BRAVIARY: THE VALIANT POKÉMON

Baraz's Pokémon buddy Braviary is also there to help him travel through the sky. He rides on Braviary from the cave back to Dahara City and also into the epic Legendary Pokémon Battle. But his friend Braviary is also a fierce fighter that always wants to gets in on the action.

TEAM ROCKET

When Team Rocket sees Hoopa transform into its Unbound form after the Prison Bottle is opened, Meowth becomes obsessed with getting it for itself. Meowth imagines it will make it an unstoppable, super-strong giant. However, when Jessie and James help Meowth get its paws on the Prison Bottle, all the evil shadow does is use Meowth to open the cap. Once it gets Meowth to release it, the shadow sends Team Rocket and their hot air balloon flying with a single punch.

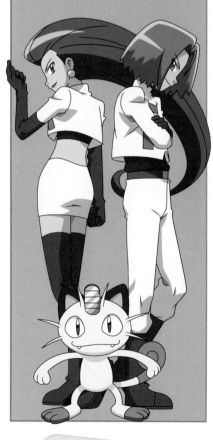

"WHAWASSAT? WHAT'S UP?!" —MEOWTH

FEATURED POKÉMON

HIPPOPOTAS: THE HIPPO POKÉMON

When Baraz needs a Ground-type Pokémon to help remake the Prison Bottle, Bonnie remembers Hippopotas hanging out near the local Pokémon Center. So, Hoopa uses its ring to bring one over.

COSPLAY PIKACHU

When Hoopa plays a trick on Ash and summons dozens of Pikachu through its rings, several costumed Pikachu show up, too!

• Pikachu Belle

• Pikachu Libre   • Pikachu Pop Star   • Pikachu Rock Star   • Pikachu PhD

MYTHICAL POKÉMON

ARCEUS:
THE ALPHA POKÉMON

Height	10'06"
Weight	705.5 lbs
Type	Normal

According to legend, Arceus began in an egg. When it emerged, it shaped everything in the world. Locals in Dahara City believe that Baraz's and Meray's family are somehow connected to Arceus. Their ancestors claim to have communicated with the Mythical Pokémon and even draw power from it. Because of their devotion to Arceus, they all wear a gold medallion in the shape of its gold belt.

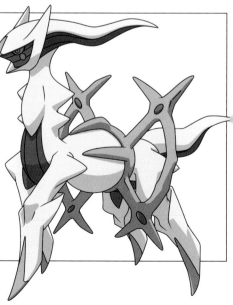

HOOPA:
THE MISCHIEF POKÉMON

The star of the movie (or rather, stars) is the Mythical Pokémon Hoopa! It has two forms: Confined, a small Pokémon with a silly side, and Unbound, a large Pokémon with an even bigger ego.

On Hoopa's arms, wrists, and horns are gold rings. They might look like jewelry, but they're actually a very important part of its power. Hoopa can slip them off and transport people, places, things, and even attacks right through them. It can catch a foe's attack in one ring and unleash it out of another. It can even simply stick its own hand through a ring to grab something or someone. However, Hoopa has struggled with being able to travel through its own ring ever since the Prison Bottle was forged.

HOOPA (CONFINED)

Height	1'08"
Weight	19.8 lbs
Type	Psychic/Ghost

Hoopa loves to play pranks, and perhaps that's why it's called the Mischief Pokémon. It uses its rings to create illusions and always asks, "Were you surprised?" Nothing makes it happier than impressing people with its clever use of power.

However, the reason its true strength has been stored in the Prison Bottle is simply because it misused its power. For a century, Hoopa has lived with the family of the man who made the Prison Bottle, and it has grown up with Baraz and Meray. They love Hoopa like a sibling, so they want to help it regain its true strength.

HOOPA (UNBOUND)

Height	21'04"
Weight	1080.3 lbs
Type	Psychic/Dark

Considered Hoopa's true form, Hoopa's Unbound form possesses incredible power. Dahara City witnessed the depths of its strength 100 years ago. At first, Hoopa was considered the benefactor of the city. In exchange for delicious food, Hoopa gave the town a ton of gold coins. The grateful villagers built Hoopa a home, and it became a wonderfully generous neighbor. The citizens could always count on Hoopa to use its power to grant their wishes. However, with the adoration of the townspeople and on a winning streak in Pokémon Battles, Hoopa became an egomaniac. It was impressed with its own strength, and it liked to show off by using its rings to bring Legendary Pokémon over and challenge them to battles. During these epic matches, it turned the whole city into its personal battlefield, and Hoopa truly showed it had no bounds.

LEGENDARY POKÉMON
SUMMONED BY HOOPA - CONFINED FORM

To aid in the battle against the dark shadow that possessed Hoopa in its Unbound form, Hoopa summoned some serious backup.

LUGIA:
THE DIVING POKÉMON

Height	17'01"
Weight	476.2 lbs
Type	Psychic/Flying

With the flap of its wing, Lugia can destroy an entire building. The Diving Pokémon lives deep in the sea, saving its power for the right situation—like offering Ash and his pals a ride to escape Hoopa.

LATIOS:
THE EON POKÉMON

Height	6'07"
Weight	132.3 lbs
Type	Dragon/Psychic

Intelligent Latios can share the picture that it sees in its mind with others. Latios flew Ash through the epic battle.

MEGA LATIOS

Height	7'07"
Weight	154.3 lbs
Type	Dragon/Psychic

During the epic battle, Latios Mega Evolved.

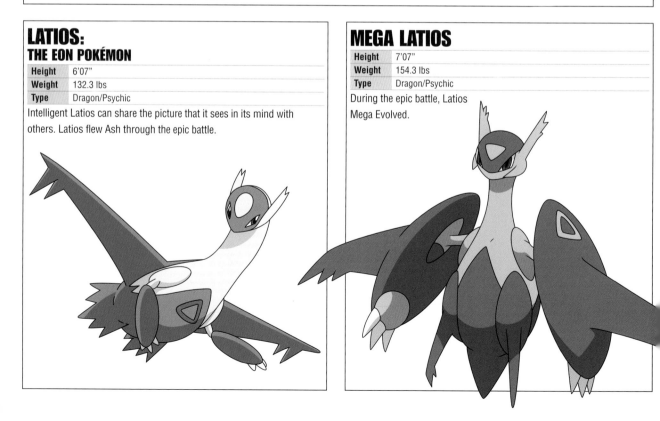

LATIAS:
THE EON POKÉMON

Height	4:07"
Weight	88.2 lbs
Type	Dragon/Psychic

Sensitive Latias can clearly feel people's emotions. It generously offers Pikachu a ride during the epic battle.

MEGA LATIAS

Height	5'11"
Weight	114.6 lbs
Type	Dragon/Psychic

During the epic battle, Latias Mega Evolved.

RAYQUAZA:
THE SKY HIGH POKÉMON

Height	23'00"
Weight	455.2 lbs
Type	Dragon/Flying

Ancient Rayquaza has supposedly been alive for hundreds of millions of years. According to legend, it was also responsible for ending the conflict between Kyogre and Groudon. In this epic battle, it was extremely helpful in protecting Hoopa.

MEGA RAYQUAZA

Height	35'05"
Weight	864.2 lbs
Type	Dragon/Flying

During the epic battle, Rayquaza Mega Evolved.

SUMMONED BY HOOPA - UNBOUND FORM

KYUREM:
THE BOUNDARY POKÉMON

Height	9'10"
Weight	716.5 lbs
Type	Dragon/Ice

This powerful Legendary Pokémon is actually missing a few pieces. It is waiting for a hero to fill its emptiness with truth and principles.

BLACK KYUREM:
THE BOUNDARY POKÉMON

Height	10'10"
Weight	716.5 lbs
Type	Dragon/Ice

During the epic battle, Kyurem became both its Black Forme and White Forme.

WHITE KYUREM:
THE BOUNDARY POKÉMON

Height	11'10"
Weight	716.5 lbs
Type	Dragon/Ice

KYOGRE:
THE SEA BASIN POKÉMON

Height	14'09"
Weight	776.0 lbs
Type	Water

Kyogre can cause storms so severe that the sea level rises. It is known to battle Groudon for the power of nature.

PRIMAL KYOGRE:
THE SEA BASIN POKÉMON

Height	32'02"
Weight	948.0 lbs
Type	Water

During the epic battle, Kyogre became Primal Kyogre.

GROUDON:
THE CONTINENT POKÉMON

Height	11'06"
Weight	2094.4 lbs
Type	Ground

Groudon is considered the living embodiment of the land. It often battles Kyogre to gain ground—literally.

PRIMAL GROUDON:
THE CONTINENT POKÉMON

Height	16'05"
Weight	2204.0 lbs
Type	Ground/Fire

During the epic battle, Groudon became Primal Groudon.

GIRATINA:
THE RENEGADE POKÉMON

Height	14'09"
Weight	1653.5 lbs
Type	Ghost/Dragon

This legendary Pokémon lives in a world on the other side of ours. Knowledge there is weird and warped to our way of thinking.

DIALGA:
THE TEMPORAL POKÉMON

Height	17'09"
Weight	1505.8 lbs
Type	Steel/Dragon

According to legend, time began ticking at the birth of Dialga.

PALKIA:
THE SPATIAL POKÉMON

Height	13'09"
Weight	740.8 lbs
Type	Water/Dragon

According to myth, Palkia lives inside a cranny in the spatial dimension parallel to our own home.

REGIGIGAS:
THE COLOSSAL POKÉMON

Height	12'02"
Weight	925.9 lbs
Type	Normal

Using natural materials like rock, magma, and a special ice mountain, Regigigas is said to have made Pokémon that resemble it.

ZEKROM:
THE DEEP BLACK POKÉMON

Height	9'06"
Weight	760.6 lbs
Type	Dragon/Electric

Zekrom is always there to lend a hand to those who want to build an admirable world. On the other hand, it can also strike down with lightning.

RESHIRAM:
THE VAST WHITE POKÉMON

Height	10'06"
Weight	727.5 lbs
Type	Dragon/Fire

White-hot Reshiram can sear the world with fire and turn anything it touches to ash.

"ALAHOOPARING!" —HOOPA

THE LEGEND OF HOOPA

According to locals in Dahara, 100 years ago, the city was destroyed by an angry Pokémon that possessed incredible power: Hoopa.

One day, a gold ring appeared in the sky. A giant hand slipped through and grabbed a bunch of food from the local market. At first, the vendor was angry that Hoopa didn't pay for what it took. But shortly after its snack, Hoopa showered the town with gold coins as a thank you. It was riches beyond their wildest imagination!

The grateful locals built Hoopa a regal home and brought it food. Hoopa gladly granted their wishes in return. With a Mythical Pokémon friend like Hoopa, the town grew and prospered.

One day, a citizen challenged Hoopa to Pokémon Battle. At first, it started battling Pokémon like Steelix and Dragonite and easily won. The locals loved to watch the powerful Pokémon fight, and Hoopa loved showing off its strength. It seemed like a winning situation for all. However, the biggest battle would come with Hoopa's ego. It became so invested in its victories, it kept upping the stakes. It even began to use its rings to summon Legendary Pokémon simply so it could battle them. It would even challenge two or three of them at a time!

At first, the locals were impressed that it could summon Groudon and Kyogre to their city. However, the damage from the attacks started to really cause problems. During a battle with Regigigas, Zekrom, and Reshiram, Hoopa was so destructive, the locals headed for the hills to get away from the attacks.

Although Hoopa won the battle against the trio of Legendary Pokémon, one human was still willing to stand up to it.

To make the city safe again, a brave man appeared, bearing a Prison Bottle he made with the three forces of nature: water, fire, and ground. He was Meray's and Baraz's great-grandfather and claimed to have a connection to the Mythical Pokémon Arceus. Willing to face the powerful Hoopa to protect the city he loved, he stood in the center of town and uncapped the Prison Bottle. A bright blue beam of light surrounded big Hoopa and sucked it into the Prison Bottle, leaving its smaller Confined form behind.

The man made it his mission to care for Hoopa and hide the Prison Bottle to protect the city. Someday, the man hoped Hoopa would be righteous and respect its power. Only then would he agree to release the Prison Bottle and restore Hoopa's true power again.

As part of its confinement, Hoopa also couldn't travel through its own rings anymore. This punishment frustrated Hoopa more than anything else. However, it was the only way it could prove it had learned its lesson. If it could understand why it was confined, it would earn the ability to travel through its rings again. The man tried to guide it to find that self-awareness, but he never lived to see that day. So, the man entrusted his great-grandchildren, Meray and Baraz, with the responsibility of caring for Hoopa. Their life's work would also be to help their Pokémon sibling learn and earn its true power.

INTERESTING ITEMS
THE PRISON BOTTLE

This antique has an unusual shape and an even more interesting past. According to legend, Meray's and Baraz's great-grandfather created it with the three forces of nature: water, fire, and ground. To mark the land where it was made, the spectacular Dahara Tower was built.

The bottle holds the power to turn Hoopa from its Confined form to its Unbound form. However, when a person or Pokémon touches the bottle, it can control their mind, as Baraz, Ash, and Meowth learned the hard way.

The cap looks like Hoopa and has eyes that can glow brightly with power or red with its anger. When someone is possessed by it, their eyes also turn red.

Another notable feature of the bottle is its gold rings. Similar to Hoopa, the body and cap of the Prison Bottle have a handful of gold rings that are immune to Hoopa's attacks.

NICKNAMES

Hoopa speaks its own language. When it first meets Ash and Pikachu, it gives them pet names and refuses to call them anything else. From here on out, Ash and Pikachu shall also be known as Ashkan and Pikan.

THE GOLD MEDALLION

Worn by people in Meray's and Baraz's family, including their great-grandfather, it is said to resemble the gold belt on Arceus. It supposedly signifies their familial link to the Mythical Pokémon. According to their great-grandfather, their lineage has drawn power from their relationship to Arceus and can even communicate with it. When they need its strength to fight the good fight, or even help seeds sprout instantly, the medallion glows.

TAMATO BERRY

Red and spiky, the Tamato Berry is super-spicy! It gives off so much heat that Clemont's friend Chespin shot fire out of its mouth, and it's a Grass-type! It was all a trick, a switcheroo by Hoopa. It used its ring to steal a green-glazed, donut-shaped Poké Puff baked by Serena and replace it with a Tamato Berry right before Chespin sunk its teeth in.

EVERYONE WHO WAS POSSESSED BY THE POWER IN AND OUT OF THE PRISON BOTTLE

- Hoopa
- Baraz
- Meowth
- Ash
- Primal Kyogre
- Primal Groudon
- Kyurem, Black Kyurem, and White Kyurem
- Giratina
- Dialga
- Palkia

TOTALLY AWESOME TECHNOLOGY
THE FULLY AUTOMATIC LIFTING MACHINE

A prized invention by Clemont, this piece of Clemontic Gear is actually based on the move Magnet Rise. The C-shaped Fully Automatic Lifting Machine came right out of Clemont's backpack to save the day. Hoopa's angry power was safely stored inside the Prison Bottle, but no one could touch it to pick it up off the ground, or they would become possessed by it. So, Clemont offered his mechanical wonder to lift and carry the Prison Bottle safely.

After Hoopa fends off the angry purple smoke that had escaped from the Prison Bottle, it turns into a separate shadow of Hoopa in its Unbound form. This Hoopa is unmerciful and nearly unstoppable as an epic battle of Hoopa versus the shadow Hoopa begins. The angry power shadow wants to get ahold of Hoopa's Confined form for good. Luckily, Ash, Clemont, Bonnie, Serena, Meray, and Baraz aren't going to let that happen without a fight!

EPIC BATTLE

BRAVIARY VS. HOOPA

Baraz calls on Braviary to cut through Hoopa's Dark Pulse stream with Air Slash. But the strength of Hoopa's attack overpowers Braviary and knocks it out in a single round. It's clearly not a fair fight, so Hoopa in its Confined form thinks fast and calls on a Legendary Pokémon to stand up to Hoopa in its Unbound form. It tosses a ring in the air and summons Lugia, the Diving Pokémon.

LUGIA VS. HOOPA

Hoopa in its Unbound form fires the first shot, a glowing purple Dark Pulse, but Lugia dodges it. Then, Lugia knocks Hoopa out of the sky and down to the sea with a powerful shot of blue Aeroblast. While Lugia has Hoopa's full attention, the crew decides to split up. Meray, Baraz, Serena, Bonnie, and Clemont head to Dahara Tower through the ring provided by Hoopa in its Confined form. Ash and Pikachu stay to help Hoopa hide.

It's like Hoopa in its Unbound form can sense its other half because it soon finds it and Ash. One ring appears, and it pokes its head through, grinning at the sight of the other Hoopa. So close to getting it in its clutches, another ring arrives, and Hoopa in its Unbound form uses Hyperspace Fury to slide its hand through to try to get ahold of Hoopa.

Just before it can get its hands on Hoopa in its Confined form, Lugia surprises the shadowy Hoopa from behind with a strong Sky attack. It swoops down and around, striking it again with Sky attack. Hoopa slams into a building, smashing the side. Black smoke billows above the city.

Meanwhile, Ash, Pikachu, and Hoopa hide behind some boxes in another building, but soon, shadow Hoopa uses Hyperspace Fury to send its hand through a ring in an attempt to capture Hoopa again. Ash grabs his Legendary Pokémon pal, and they run into the street. There, shadow Hoopa surrounds them with six rings and unleashes Hyperspace Fury fists through each one.

Luckily, Lugia swoops in again to fly Ash, Pikachu, and Hoopa out of the ring of rings. Hoopa in its Unbound form wastes no time firing an intensely bright Charge Beam, knocking Lugia down to the ground. Ash, Pikachu, and Hoopa in its Confined form are thrown off its back, but Lugia gets right back into the fight. It flies straight for the shadowy Hoopa, glowing a bright blue with its wings outstretched in Sky attack. Then, it follows up with a powerful ball of light that grows into Aeroblast. Hoopa catches the bright beam in a ring, and then, it quickly surprises Lugia with another ring that sends it back to its deep sea home.

"THAT'S SO WEIRD. IT'S LIKE YOU'RE HAVING A BATTLE AGAINST YOURSELF OR SOMETHING." —ASH

RAYQUAZA, LATIOS, AND LATIAS VS. HOOPA

Hoopa in its Confined form doesn't waste time calling in some backup. Using three rings, it summons more Legendary Pokémon: Rayquaza, Latios, and Latias. They arrive ready for action. Hoopa in its Unbound form swoops down to come face-to-face with its opponents. While it works up a devastating Dark Pulse, Ash leads the Legendary Pokémon out of close range. Then, he asks them to fire Dragon Pulse in unison to block the purple stream of Dark Pulse. The strength of their combined efforts goes up in smoke (black smoke, that is), as Hoopa seems unaffected.

It traces the trio of Legendary Pokémon through the city. Then, it heads them off by dropping tons of sand from its rings and swirling it into a full blast storm. Ash asks Latios and Latias to use Psychic to swallow up the storm. Their eyes glow blue, and the sandstorm recedes into one big final blast, spraying the city with dust.

Even Hoopa in its Unbound form knows when to admit it needs help. So, it calls on its own army of Legendary Pokémon: Dialga, Palkia, Kyurem, Giratina, Primal Groudon, and Primal Kyogre. Their eyes glow red, proving that the same power that controls Hoopa is also in possession of their minds. This Hoopa's army is twice the size of the one on the side of Hoopa in its Confined form.

RAYQUAZA, LATIOS, LATIAS, AND PIKACHU VS. HOOPA, DIALGA, PALKIA, KYUREM, GIRATINA, PRIMAL GROUDON, AND PRIMAL KYOGRE

They fire their first round at their foes in unison. Dialga opens its mouth and unleashes Roar Of Time. Palkia's arm glows purple as it strikes with Spacial Rend. Giratina sends Energy Ball. Kyurem balls up Dragon Rage. Primal Kyogre shoots a series of orbs with Origin Pulse. Primal Groudon lets out a fierce Fire Blast. And Hoopa blasts Dark Pulse from its chest.

Ash thinks fast and asks Latios, Latias, and Rayquaza to again fire Dragon Pulse, but this time, he also asks Pikachu to add its electrifying Thunderbolt. All of their attacks meet in midair and cause a huge explosion. Black smoke and orange flames appear in the sky instantly. Out of the powerful blast, Ash's team finds new strength as they emerge from the smoke all having Mega Evolved.

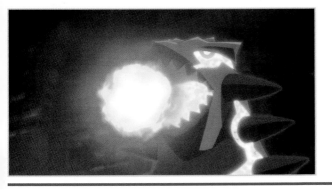

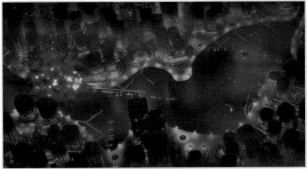

MEGA RAYQUAZA, MEGA LATIOS, AND MEGA LATIAS VS. HOOPA, DIALGA, PALKIA, BLACK KYUREM, GIRATINA, PRIMAL GROUDON, AND PRIMAL KYOGRE

Not to be left behind, Kyurem's body is bathed in a blue glow as it becomes Black Kyurem. With its newfound strength, its entire body is surrounded in a glowing ball that pulses with purple zaps. It fires Freeze Shock at Latias and Pikachu, but they dodge it. The Ice-type attack hits a building and turns it into a skyscraper glacier.

Palkia then tries Spacial Rend, throwing a purple slash at Mega Latias and Mega Latios. The pair of Legendary Pokémon dodges the attack, and instead, a building gets cut clean through. They don't get far before Primal Groudon tries to scorch them with fiery Flamethrower. As they dodge that blast, they are headed straight for Black Kyurem. Before Ash can plan their strategy, Primal Groudon accidentally hits Black Kyurem with another Flamethrower.

Meanwhile, Giratina and Mega Rayquaza are locked in battle. Mega Rayquaza is covered in a green glow as it rockets toward Giratina with Dragon Ascent, slamming it into the side of a skyscraper. Then, it lets out a loud Roar to let Giratina know it's not done with it yet. Giratina tries to respond with a powerful Energy Ball, but slippery Mega Rayquaza easily avoids it. So, it turns its attention to Mega Latios and Mega Latias, shooting a dark Shadow Ball. It comes very close, but Ash's Legendary Pokémon pals are quick enough to dodge it.

MEGA RAYQUAZA, MEGA LATIOS, AND MEGA LATIAS VS. HOOPA, DIALGA, PALKIA, WHITE KYUREM, GIRATINA, PRIMAL GROUDON, AND PRIMAL KYOGRE

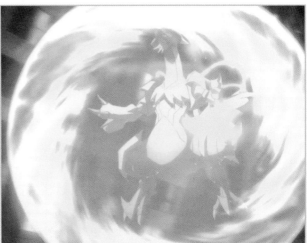

In midair, Black Kyurem becomes White Kyurem. It surrounds itself in a glowing orb with orange talons and fires Hyper Beam at Ash, knocking him off of Mega Latios. As he plunges to the ground, Hoopa quickly tosses a couple of rings to transport him back to Mega Latios' back.

"BECOMING A POKÉMON MASTER CAN'T JUST BE GIVEN TO ME. IT'S SOMETHING THAT I HAVE TO ACHIEVE! I HAVE TO DO IT ON MY OWN!" —ASH

MEGA RAYQUAZA, MEGA LATIOS, AND MEGA LATIAS VS. HOOPA, DIALGA, PALKIA, BLACK KYUREM, GIRATINA, PRIMAL GROUDON, AND PRIMAL KYOGRE

Mega Rayquaza swirls around now Black Kyurem to prevent it from attacking its pals. But now that it's close, Black Kyurem gets a good grip on Mega Rayquaza and drags it down into the river, which ices over as soon as they pierce the water. But their battle is heating up! Black Kyurem and Mega Rayquaza shoot back up into the air. Mega Rayquaza then blasts its foe.

Still on Mega Latios' and Mega Latias' trail, Black Kyurem tries to knock them out of the sky with frosty Ice Beam, but Groudon is the one that gets iced out. By the time Groudon breaks out of its icy shell, they're all long gone.

With a sharp turn, Mega Latios and Mega Latias shake off Black Kyurem, but now, Primal Kyogre is on their tail. It sends multiple blasts their way with Origin Pulse, but the city is the only thing that takes the hits.

Mega Rayquaza spots the battle explosions in the distance and heads over to help. It gets between Ash's team and Primal Kyogre, and then it fires a fierce Hyper Beam. It dodges the attack, but now, Ash and his team have to turn their attention to an even bigger problem.

Hoopa is set to destroy the Dahara Tower. Using Hyperspace Fury, it sends one of its rings close to the landmark, then pushes its hand through. Before it can strike, Ash quickly has Mega Latios use Dragon Pulse to slap it on the wrist.

Then, Ash, Pikachu, Hoopa in its Confined form, Mega Latios, Mega Latias, and Mega Rayquaza all line up in front of Dahara Tower to protect it. On the other side of the river, Hoopa's Legendary army lines up, too. Dialga makes the first move, firing a powerful ringed beam Roar Of Time. It hits the giant gold ring of Dahara Tower, and rocks shower down.

Furious, Ash quickly hatches a plan to protect the sacred building. He asks Mega Rayquaza to use Twister. It flies up into the clouds and gets them to swirl down around the entire tower. Then,

he asks Mega Latios and Mega Latias to charge the protective layer with Psychic currents.

Hoopa in its Unbound form and its Legendary army try to all fire their attacks together, but they prove no match for the swirling Psychic-charged Twister.

The shadowy Hoopa tries a second time, this time using two sets of rings. It puts one in front of each member of its army and the second set all

around Dahara Tower. When they fire their attacks again, it uses the rings to transport them to close range. The strength of the Twister begins to weaken. Then, Hoopa fires dark Shadow Ball directly at Mega Rayquaza. The hit immediately drops Dahara Tower's protection.

Mega Latios and Mega Latias immediately go on the offensive, blasting Dragon Pulse. Palkia responds with a Spacial Rend Slash that knocks Ash right off Mega Latios' back again. But there's no time to pick him up—Mega Latios, Mega Latias, and Mega Rayquaza have to fight back against Hoopa and its army, which have come even closer to them and reaching their evil goals.

Mega Rayquaza takes a direct hit that sends it falling to the ground with a thud so hard, the sidewalk tile turns to rubble. Ash tries to run, holding Hoopa in its Confined form in his arms, but he can't seem to hide. Hoopa emerges from the smoke of the battle and is so close it can reach them. Its big gray hand wraps around them, and just when it looks like they've lost the epic battle, the sky turns blue.

Hoopa is shocked that its hand can't get a grip. It is very close, so why can't it grab them? Behind Hoopa stands Baraz with a new Prison Bottle, just in the nick of time! Hoopa in its Unbound form is powerless against it. Ash escapes from its hand, and it slips back into its Prison Bottle. Giratina, Primal Groudon, Primal Kyogre, Kyurem, Dialga, and Palkia are all freed from the evil power that possessed them. Now, it's Hoopa's turn.

POKÉMON THE MOVIE: VOLCANION AND THE MECHANICAL MARVEL

THE STORY

Volcanion lets out a roar as it lands on a giant flying ship. Levi steps onto the deck, ready to battle with Glalie and Alakazam. He makes them Mega Evolve with his special Key Stone. Then, Levi throws two bands. One wraps around Volcanion's front leg. Volcanion stomps on the other one. But before Volcanion can fight back, Levi instructs Mega Glalie and Mega Alakazam to turn it into an ice cube and send it flying with Freeze Dry.

While Ash and Clemont are having a fun practice battle with their Pokémon pals, Volcanion comes crashing down at their campsite. The loose band lands right around Ash's waist, tethering our hero to the Mythical Pokémon. Volcanion tries to throw Ash off of it, but the band just reels him back in. Ash slams right into Volcanion again. Clemont informs the pair that they're attached by an electromagnetic pulse, whether they like it or not.

But Volcanion doesn't have time any time to waste. It races through the forest and flies up into the air. Ash tries to keep up and winds up hanging onto its leg in midair. It lands them at the Tower Wall of the Azoth Kingdom, right next to the flying ship that belongs to the mad scientist Alva.

Atop the Tower Wall, Alva's goons Levi and Cherie reveal the precious item they were guarding on their ship—Magearna. Prince Raleigh is very excited to meet the Mythical Pokémon that is so important to the history of his kingdom. But Volcanion has come to take Magearna back to its home.

Alva forces Alazkazam, Glalie, and Gengar to Mega Evolve with a special golden staff he crafted. Before Volcanion can strike, Glalie turns it into an ice cube again.

Suddenly, Volcanion breaks out of its ice shell. The blast sends Ash flying, and he lands right on Magearna. Of course, that tether pulls him right back to Volcanion, and Ash takes Magearna with him. Then, Volcanion jumps off the ledge, leaving its foes in a thick mist so they can't follow it. From the air, Kimia sees the whole scene unfold.

Meanwhile, at the castle, Raleigh's sister (Princess Kimia) catches wind of the struggle with Volcanion and Magearna from her close advisor Flamel. She hops on her transforming jetpack and heads to the Tower Wall.

Back on the deck, Raleigh apologizes for the attack and explains why Magearna is so important to his kingdom. Five hundred years ago, a famous master of Arcane Science named Nikola created many revolutionary gadgets to improve Azoth Kingdom, including Magearna. Sadly, Magearna was lost during a war. So, Raleigh is just too happy that it's now been returned to its home.

Down on the street, Magearna is happy to be reunited with its friend and hugs Volcanion. Ash introduces himself, but Volcanion doesn't trust humans and pushes him away. But soon, even more humans arrive—Clemont, Serena, Bonnie, Luxray, Dedenne, and Squishy are finally reunited with their friend, too!

Clemont is so thrilled to meet his hero Nikola's greatest invention, Magearna. Then, he tries to use his own Clemontic Gear Aipom Arm to break through the tether, but it can't. Magearna tries to cheer Clemont up by opening its hand to reveal a bouquet. But Volcanion doesn't like it hanging out with humans, so it sends a Hydro Pump blast their way. Then, Magearna unveils two bouquets to try to cheer up Volcanion. But as they make their way to Nebel Plateau, Volcanion continues to spar with Ash.

Back at the castle, Kimia tries to reason with her little brother. In Raleigh's mind, he's learning about Nikola and Arcane Science. But Kimia worries about his involvement with Alva.

Meanwhile, Team Rocket has made their way to Azoth Kingdom. They arrive at the Tower Wall and offer their services, bragging that they know Ash and his pals. So, Alva gives them their first assignment working for him: track down Ash, Volcanion, and Magearna.

After watching his pal be on the receiving end of Volcanion's attacks Clemont builds Ash a special suit of armor he calls Mr. Iron Defense.

In the middle of the night, Team Rocket sneaks up on Ash and his pals' campsite. Using special Key Stones Alva gave them, they force Pinsir and Heracross to Mega Evolve. Volcanion instructs Serena, Bonnie, and Clemont to hide Magearna in the forest. Ash and Volcanion stay back to battle Mega Pinsir and Mega Heracross.

Ash closes the helmet on his armor and tells Volcanion to let their foes have it. Volcanion forms a Focus Blast so powerful it turns the lush forest area into a crater. Thanks to the suit of armor, Ash and Pikachu are completely unaffected. But it doesn't look like they'll be hearing from Pinsir and Heracross any time soon. Ash is impressed with Volcanion's power. It tells Ash it can level an entire mountain.

However, Magearna, Clemont, Bonnie, and Serena accidentally walk right into Team Rocket's trap. Luckily, Kimia arrives on her flying machine with her Pokémon pal Gardevoir. Using her Key Stone and the friendship she earned, Kimia helps her friend Mega Evolve. Then, Mega Gardevoir blasts Team Rocket off with an explosive Dazzling Gleam.

Aboard Kimia's flying machine, she tells Ash and his pals she's concerned about her brother. Raleigh believes everything Alva says because he is a top Arcane Science researcher who has taught Raleigh a lot. But Kimia knows Alva is up to something.

Suddenly, Starly flies up to Volcanion to inform it of an injured Amaura nearby. They rush to its aid. While Ash removes the net around its neck, Volcanion is surprised by a blast from the evil Pokémon Hunter behind Amaura's suffering. But as he speeds over in his truck to catch Volcanion, it quickly uses Mist to block his vision, and he slams into a rock.

"AND THAT'S THE REASON I CAN'T TRUST HUMANS. POKÉMON ARE INCAPABLE OF LYING, BUT HUMANS ARE, AND DO!" —VOLCANION

It was a close call, but Volcanion shrugs it off because it is used to this kind of horrible behavior from humans.

Carrying the injured Amaura on its back, Volcanion leads Ash, Pikachu, Clemont, Serena, Bonnie, Dedenne, and Kimia to its home, the Nebel Plateau. The sprawling natural wonder is filled with wild Pokémon, but they're all afraid of the visitors because they've all been hurt by humans in the past.

With Amaura lying down on the grass, Serena treats its injuries with medicine and ties its bandages into bows. Amaura begins to feel better. It opens its eyes, and Volcanion welcomes it to its new home. Then, Magearna serenades them all with a beautiful melody. All the Pokémon around the plateau sway to the song.

The next day Clemont is also doing what he loves: tinkering with technology. While he's working on a repair for Kimia's flying machine, he finds Gulpin's Acid Spray to be quite helpful in cutting through metal. So, he immediately thinks of applying the trick to Ash and Volcanion's bands. Now free of the tether, Ash is so happy that he hugs Gulpin. But Gulpin gets so scared, it squirms out of his arms and hides behind Volcanion. The Steam Pokémon still doesn't trust Ash (or any humans, for that matter) and tells Ash to go. But Ash vows that he is there to help.

Nearby, Serena has made a big batch of her famous Poké Puffs as a sweet treat for all of the Pokémon. Ash brings a plate to Volcanion, but the Steam Pokémon serves him bitterness. It tells Ash that every Pokémon in Nebel Plateau has been lied to and hurt by humans. Pikachu promises Volcanion that Ash doesn't lie and he fights with all he's got to protect those he loves. Volcanion replies that while it's grateful for what Ash has done to help, he and his friends need to leave. Ash doesn't take it personally—he just leaves the plate of Poké Puffs for his new friends. Even Volcanion can't resist a taste of the delicious pastry.

But the wild Pokémon of Nebel Plateau are still nervous because they are afraid of people. So, Serena, Clemont, and Ash decide to call their Pokémon pals to act as ambassadors. Before they know it, all the Pokémon are playing together.

Injured by the Pokémon Hunter, Volcanion decides to take a reviving bath in the nearby hot springs. Because they're tethered, Ash follows him in. However, his Mr. Iron Defense suit swells with water and bursts into pieces.

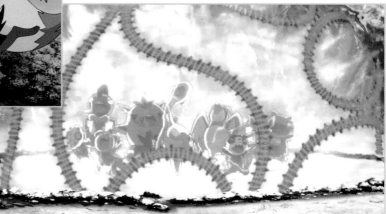

Suddenly, a thick black smoke cloud caused by Mega Gengar covers Nebel Plateau. The Pokémon try to run, but they soon find themselves trapped in charged chains. Volcanion arrives on the scene and clears the smoke, but something even darker is revealed—Alva's goons. Levi demands that Magearna be handed over. With his hand on the trigger, he zaps all of the Pokémon in chains and promises more pain if they don't comply.

Volcanion tells Magearna not to listen to the goons. So, Levi and Cherie make good on their nefarious promise. Manectric surrounds Ash and Volcanion in a jolting  Electric Terrain. Next, Steelix adds a Stealth Rock. Then, Levi zaps all the Pokémon again. They cry out from the shocks. Magearna doesn't want to be the reason they're hurt, so against Volcanion's pleas, it turns itself over to Alva.

On the deck of the flying ship, Alva and Raleigh are there to greet Magearna again. Raleigh shouts down to his sister that this will be good for their kingdom. Then,  he asks Alva to explain his plan to them. But the mad scientist instead surprises Raleigh by having Mega Gengar use Mean Look so he can steal Magearna's precious Soul-Heart. When Raleigh tries to stop Alva, Levi holds him back.

Without its Soul-Heart, Magearna is a shell of its former self. Alva has Gengar throw its body overboard. Then, Alva orders Houndoom, Swampert, Tyranitar, Aggron, and Banette to fire Hyper Beam to finish Volcanion. Raleigh can't believe that his hero has completely betrayed him. From inside the bridge, even Team Rocket can't believe the evil Alva! The flying ship makes its escape, although no one seems able to stop Alva.

When the smoke clears, Clemont is impressed to see that the wild Pokémon banded together and used a combination of Dig and Safeguard to protect Volcanion from the blast. The Steam Pokémon thanks its friends and rushes over to Magearna. It's lying limp in the grass. Volcanion puts it on its back and carries it onto Kimia's flying machine. Ash and his crew follow. They head out on a mission to find Alva and get Magearna's Soul-Heart back.

On the flying ship, Meowth can sense Magearna's sorrow through the Soul-Heart now in Alva's evil hands. Team Rocket decides to do something decent and plans to take back the Soul-Heart and return it to Magearna. But before they can get close, Alva has Gengar use Psychic to stop them. Then, he throws Jessie and James off the side of his ship. Meowth remains his prisoner inside.

As the flying ship passes over the beautiful Field of Flowers, Volcanion remembers meeting Magearna there for the first time 500 years ago. The Steam Pokémon talks about its friend that cared for all the troubled Pokémon of the plateau and vows to save it! Team Rocket spot Kimia's flying machine from the woods and uses a grappling hook to hitch a ride to save their pal Meowth.

Flamel calls Kimia with an important update: a previously unknown design diagram by Nikola was found in Raleigh's room. The drawing shows how the Tower  Wall could be turned into a Floating Fortress. Nikola's intended it to protect the kingdom, but it caused a war over who would control the design diagram. To stop the struggle, Nikola hid both the drawing and Magearna because its Soul-Heart ignites the transition).

> **"SO NOW, SINCE MY BROTHER IS INVOLVED IN THIS, THAT MEANS THAT I AM, TOO."**
> **—KIMIA**

Unfortunately, Alva now has everything he needs to carry out his evil plan. Back at the Tower Wall, he put the final piece of his plan into place. The Soul-Heart starts the gears spinning. The Tower Wall rises and turns into the Floating Fortress, just as Nikola's design diagram described.

Alva spots Kimia's flying machine on the horizon and decides she'll be his first target. But when he instructs the Floating Fortress to fire, the contraption fizzles out because Magearna's heart won't let it happen. With tears in its eyes, Meowth tells Alva that Magearna is suffering and doesn't want to fight.

On the top deck of the Floating Fortress, Levi and Cherie have lined up their army of forced Mega Evolved Pokémon: Mega Camerupt, Mega Manectric, Mega Houndoom, Mega Glalie, Mega Banette, Mega Alakazam, Mega Swampert, Mega Pidgeot, Mega Tyranitar, Mega Beedrill, Mega Steelix, Mega Salamence, and Mega Aggron. Volcanion leads Flying-types Noivern, Hawlucha, and Talonflame, and all arrive ready to battle. Kimia's flying machine soon lands on the Floating Fortress, and Ash, Greninja, Serena, Pancham, Sylveon, Braixen, Bonnie, Clemont, Chespin, Bunnelby, and Luxray join the fight. Squishy jumps out of Bonnie's bag, and bathed in a green glow, it becomes Zygarde 10%.

While the Pokémon distract Alva's goons, Volcanion blasts into Alva's command center and leads Kimia, Gardevoir, Ash, Greninja, and Pikachu down. But right as they arrive, shocking chains slither up from the floor, tying them all up.

The evil Alva has a plan to make sure Magearna can no longer resist his plans. First, he has Mega Gengar use Mean Look on the Soul-Heart. Then, to break the Mythical Pokémon's spirit, it uses the Soul-Heart's power to set fire to the Nebel Plateau. However, the blast misses its target and strikes another part of the forest. Meowth begins to cry because it can no longer hear Magearna's voice coming from the Soul-Heart. Alva is pleased to hear that his plan to break the Mythical Pokémon's heart worked. Now, nothing stands in Alva's way...or so he thinks!

Alva again asks the Soul-Heart to destroy Nebel Plateau. But the fierce single beam is met with a group of fiery resisters! The wild Pokémon of Nebel Plateau have banded together, and their combined attacks are keeping the beam at bay.

Squishy speedily arrives on the scene. It transforms into Zygarde Complete and breaks the beam.

Back at the Floating Fortress, Alva doesn't understand how a group of little Pokémon could stop him. Volcanion is so enraged by Alva's mean words and actions against its friends that its anger explodes, breaking the charged chains.

Suddenly, an alarm goes off. The Floating Fortress is on course to crash-land into Nebel Plateau, and the control system isn't responding. Kimia knows that this is the evil work of Alva. Raleigh says the only way to stop it would be to blast the Floating Fortress into dust. Volcanion steps up, reminding them that explosions are its specialty. But Volcanion is out of water. They have to hurry to get it to the Floating Fortress' water tanks.

Free again, Ash quickly has Pikachu use a powerful combination of Thunderbolt and Electro Ball to disarm Mega Gengar. Ash quickly grabs Alva's golden Key Stone staff and jumps off the bridge, ramming it into the contraption that's caging the Soul-Heart. As the staff shatters, so do Levi and Cherie's fake Key Stones. Mega Gengar returns to Gengar and flees from Alva through the floor. All of the Pokémon forced to Mega Evolve are freed from Alva's control. The battle that was raging on the top deck instantly ends! Seeing the writing on the wall, cowardly Alva slips on a jetpack and makes his escape.

Ash, Pikachu, Raleigh, and Volcanion race through the Floating Fortress to find the tanks, but the handle to turn them on is stuck. Ash asks Pikachu to loosen it with Iron Tail. Soon, the basin floods with water, and Volcanion is able to fill up. While they wait, Raleigh tells Ash he feels so bad for trusting Alva. He loves science, but maybe he needs to spend some time out of the lab. Ash encourages Raleigh to become a Pokémon Trainer and begin a journey of his own.

Ash grabs the Soul-Heart from its circular cage and places it back where it belongs, with Magearna. The Mythical Pokémon awakens, but it still seems vacant. Meowth tells them it can sense Magearna's heart is still broken.

"IN THAT CASE, IT'S RETRIEVE THE SOUL-HEART OR BUST!" —JAMES

As the Floating Fortress nears the plateau, it's a race against time. Volcanion lifts Ash, Pikachu, and Raleigh back to the upper deck. But Volcanion doesn't get in the flying machine with everyone else. With a blast of steam, it selflessly sends the flying machine far away to protect everyone.

Then, Volcanion goes back into the depths of the Floating Fortress to blast it into bits to protect its friends and the plateau it loves. With a great bursting Explosion, the entire brick fortress becomes nothing but little rocks and dust. Nebel Plateau is safe, but Ash is upset that Volcanion tricked them into leaving it behind. He and his friends fear for what happened to the Steam Pokémon inside the Floating Fortress.

Back at Nebel Plateau, all of the wild Pokémon surround Magearna and try to warm its heart, but it still seems vacant. Suddenly, a mist sweeps in, and Magearna walks right into it. There, it finds its best friend, Volcanion. Magearna hugs its buddy, and its heart is full again.

Volcanion collapses, exhausted. Ash and his pals try to help it, but Magearna simply unveils two bouquets from its hands. Volcanion lets out a sneeze so strong, it wakes itself up and even clears away the mist across the plateau.

When Volcanion sees that Ash, Pikachu, Serena, Clemont, Bonnie, Dedenne, Kimia, and Raleigh are all still there, it is impressed. With a big smile, it dubs them all Honorary Nebel Plateau Pokémon! All the wild Pokémon cheer, and Pikachu gives Volcanion a big hug. Then, the Steam Pokémon asks Pikachu to take extra-good care of its good friend Ash.

> "SINCE WE'RE STUCK TOGETHER NOW, WE MAY AS WELL HAVE FUN!" —ASH

LOCATIONS

AZOTH KINGDOM

A very famous Arcane Scientist named Nikola designed this incredible mechanized city. Although it was originally built nearly 500 years ago, his techniques were so advanced and precise that it is still exactly as he planned it.

The streets are filled with all kinds of helpful machines like elevators, people-moving treadmills, and lifts. Everything churns like clockwork on gears—even some of the buildings. Inventor Clemont is in complete awe of this impressive city.

THE CASTLE

Home to siblings Princess Kimia and Prince Raleigh, the castle is full of Nikola's amazing decorative and mechanical touches. There is a basket elevator, steps that magically appear with each step that lead Kimia to her hidden garage, a great hallway covered in churning gears, and even beautiful artwork.

KIMIA'S GARAGE

A painting of Kimia and Raleigh is the door to Kimia's secret garage. Inside is her ride, a power cycle that transforms into a sophisticated jetpack. She can exit the castle through the garage door that opens up quickly like a drawbridge instead of rolling up like a typical one.

FLAMEL'S OFFICE

Flamel's office is covered in computer screens, and she keeps it dark so she can best see them. Flamel's desk is just a keyboard console to help her conduct her research.

RALEIGH'S ROOM

In his lab, Raleigh spends most of his time at his desk, tinkering with technology and studying the Arcane Scientist Nikola. There are stacks of books and gears everywhere. It is here that Raleigh tries his hand at replicating some of Nikola's inventions and gets advice from Alva.

THE TOWER WALL/FLOATING FORTRESS

Most ancient cities have a wall for protection, but Nikola didn't just stop at the bricks. He invented a special mechanism that would move a part of the wall and lift it into the air, turning it into a Floating Fortress.

Nikola developed all of his inventions with the safety of the city and the happiness of its citizens in mind. So, when the Arcane Scientist announced this special Floating Fortress, he thought people would be excited for the security blanket. Instead, a power struggle erupted over who would control the Tower Wall and the use of the Floating Fortress. The city descended into war. Supposedly, it was during this time that Magearna, one of Nikola's most beloved inventions, was lost.

In actuality, Nikola was so disheartened by the vicious battle between his countrymen that he sent Magearna away to prevent anyone from ever being able to use the Floating Fortress. Magearna holds a key part to its function: the Soul-Heart. It is this precious piece that powers the whole mechanism that Magearna guards in its chest.

While everyone had assumed for the past five centuries that this genius invention was lost to the ages, a previously unknown design diagram of the Floating Fortress was discovered in Raleigh's room. It explained the inner workings of that piece of the Tower Wall. Unfortunately, it became Nikola's worst nightmare, and the instructions fell into the wrong hands—the power-hungry scientist Alva's.

THE BRIDGE

The multi-tiered room holds a very special mechanism. In the center of the room, there is a set of gears that spin once the Soul-Heart is placed in the middle.

On the top tier, Alva instructs the main computer, barks orders at Mega Gengar, and keeps Meowth tied up. Right behind his computer console, there is a secret door out of the Floating Fortress. Alva keeps his escape jetpack next to it.

On the bottom floor, there are trap doors that open to trap invaders like Volcanion and Ash with charged chains. From this command center, Alva carries out his evil plan.

THE WATER TANKS

In the belly of the Floating Fortress, there are two water tanks. Pikachu opens the rusty faucet with Iron Tail. Then, Volcanion fills up in the basin below.

THE TOP DECK

The top of this ancient structure has been covered in grass over the years. Some of the bricks have crumbled. It is multi-tiered and provides plenty of space for the epic

battle that unfolds between the Pokémon that Cherie and Levi force to Mega Evolve and the Pokémon pals of Ash, Serena, Bonnie, and Clemont.

FLYING SHIP

This green ship looks like it might be better suited for sea travel, but it's Alva's  airborne mode of transportation. From high up in the sky, he doesn't really have to get his hands dirty down on the ground with his goons.

From the helm, Alva's goons Levi and Cherie steer the ship. Their chairs look like they're  made from bony spines. There are many dials and a screen that all glow green. There, Levi and Cherie once stored their stolen treasure, Magearna.

The flying ship has many decks. On the main hull, giant Volcanion battles Levi with Mega Alakazam and Mega Glalie.

From the deck in front of the helm, Alva attacks the Nebel Plateau to get Magearna back. Gengar and Raleigh are by his side as Alva asks Magearna to turn itself over for the greater good of the kingdom. Raleigh shouts over the side, promising his sister down on the ground below that Alva has a great plan, but he is too naïve to realize that power-hungry Alva has tricked him. When Magearna turns itself over to Alva to spare its friends, it is on this front deck that he rips out the Artificial Pokémon's Soul-Heart and then tosses its body overboard.

ALVA'S OFFICE

Sitting in his pointed red chair, behind his big desk and a hologram of Nebel  Plateau, Alva interviews Team Rocket. After they tell him they know Ash well, Alva decides he can use them on his team and even gifts them his faux Key Stones so they can force their Pokémon to Mega Evolve.

NEBEL PLATEAU

Just outside the Azoth Kingdom lies a natural wonder called the Nebel Plateau. The lush landscape is lined by a crystal blue river. It is home to many wild Pokémon that have been wronged by humans in the past. They arrive injured, tired, hurt,  or just plain fed up with people. Then, at the Nebel Plateau, they receive loving care from the Mythical Pokémon residents Volcanion and Magearna to restore their spirit.

Surrounded by a community of understanding Pokémon with similar pasts, these lost souls find a happy future together at the plateau. So, when Alva threatens to destroy the land they all love, it's no wonder their guardian Volcanion is willing to risk everything to destroy the Floating Fortress before it crash-lands into the plateau.

THE HONORARY KNIGHTS OF THE PLATEAU

In the end, Ash and his friends help Volcanion see that not all humans are bad. In fact, the Mythical Pokémon even learns to trust again because of their dedication to helping the wild Pokémon and their beautiful community. As thanks for all of  their bravery and efforts, Volcanion dubs Ash, Serena, Clemont, Bonnie, Kimia, and even Raleigh Honorary Nebel Plateau Pokémon.

THE HOT SPRINGS

In a mountainside at Nebel Plateau, there is a lovely hot spring that is kind of like a natural spa. Volcanion loves to visit the waters and even uses them to heal its wounds from fighting a Pokémon Hunter. There, in the warm bath of the hot springs, a Pokémon can really relax and restore its energy.

However, if you're a human wearing a suit of special armor, beware. When Ash is accidentally dragged in wearing the Mr. Iron Defense suit Clemont built for him, the armor is too absorbent, and it soon bursts off of Ash like a water balloon.

THE FIELD OF FLOWERS

The Field of Flowers is covered in every shade of pink blossom. The wild flowers are so dense in this patch, you can hardly even see the grass they grow out of. It is in this beautiful garden that Volcanion first met its best friend Magearna 500 years ago.

CHARACTERS

ASH

Ash is a leader, not a follower. But when he accidentally gets shackled to the Mythical Pokémon Volcanion, Ash gets dragged along for the ride. Wherever Volcanion goes, Ash must follow. Neither Ash nor the Steam Pokémon seems pleased about it initially. But when Ash finds out it needs help saving Nebel Plateau and Magearna, he vows to prove to Volcanion that it can rely on humans. After all, being a Pokémon Trainer is about protecting Pokémon and showing them that you're trustworthy. So, since Ash is always ready to help a Pokémon in need, this is a challenge he gladly accepts!

Eventually, Clemont and Gulpin are able to cut Ash free from his tether to Volcanion. But their bonds now don't rely on a band with an electromagnetic pulse. Even when he regains his freedom, Ash, along with his best friend Pikachu, bravely backs Volcanion in its important mission.

MADE TO MEASURE UP

Ash does so many different clothing changes in this movie, he might want to consider becoming a member of Team Rocket— just kidding! Of course, Ash stays on the up and up, no matter what his outfit is.

When his clothing gets dirty from being dragged through the forest by Volcanion, Serena goes shopping in Azoth Kingdom. She styles him in a fancy outfit, complete with a hat and tie. It's not his style, but it'll do until laundry time.

Then, Clemont steps in with yet another custom outfit, but this one is at least practical. To protect Ash from Volcanion's attacks, Clemont builds him a special suit of armor he names Mr. Iron Defense. While it does shield Ash from Volcanion's Focus Blast burst, it is not waterproof. When Ash is dragged into the hot springs with the Mythical Pokémon, the suit explodes right off of him.

STRAIGHT TO THE HEART

Ash doesn't waste a single second when Magearna's Soul-Heart is on the

line. The minute Pikachu puts Mega Gengar on pause, Ash seizes the opportunity to snag Alva's staff and use it to break the swirling gears surrounding the Soul-Heart. He leaps from the top tier to drive it deep between the gears. With that bold leap, all of Alva's faux Key Stones shatter, and the Pokémon they controlled are instantly freed. Then, Ash replaces the Soul-Heart in its rightful owner, Magearna.

TALONFLAME

ASH'S GRENINJA

NOIVERN

HAWLUCHA

PIKACHU

Ash's brave best friend Pikachu stops Gengar with a great combination of Thunderbolt and Electro Ball. And its Iron Tail is so strong, it can even move metal. It opens the rusty faucet to the water tanks on the Floating Fortress.

CLEMONT

Just like Raleigh, Clemont admires the amazing Arcane Scientist Nikola. The inventor from Lumiose City feels right at home in the city he designed, Azoth Kingdom. Clemont is just in awe of all the amazing gadgets, inventions, and innovations that Nikola created around town. Clemont is thrilled he also gets to meet Magearna and ultimately will do whatever he can to protect one of Nikola's greatest creations!

However, Clemont is also a pretty awesome inventor himself. He builds Ash a special suit of armor, Mr. Iron Defense, to protect his pal from Volcanion's attacks.

With the help of a wild Gulpin, Clemont also fixes Kimia's flying machine and is able to cut through the bands on Ash and Volcanion.

BUNNELBY

LUXRAY

CHESPIN

DEDENNE

BONNIE

Clemont's little sister treats Serena like she's her big sister. Together, they help dry off Magearna when it falls in the river. Then, she helps Serena dress up the Artificial Pokémon with beautiful bows. She also helps her bake delicious Poké Puffs for all of the wild Pokémon at Nebel Plateau.

Bonnie also carries a very important Pokémon in her purse—the Zygarde she nicknames Squishy. It transforms not once, but twice to protect Nebel Plateau and its wild Pokémon community.

FLAMEL

Kimia's right-hand woman is a highly intelligent researcher. Flamel follows the clues on her fact-finding missions. From her impressive computer, Flamel gathers information and keeps Kimia updated with all of her important discoveries about Alva's evil plan.

SERENA

Skilled Serena is a great girl to have around in good times and bad. She is so caring and thoughtful that before you can even ask her to lend her expertise, she's already doing what she can.

When Magearna falls in the river, she helps dry it off. When Magearna needs to be cheered up, she gives it some new fancy bows so it feels good. When an injured Amaura crosses their path, Serena applies medicine and bandages to its wounds. When a Pokémon Hunter scares the wild Pokémon at Nebel Plateau, she bakes them all a batch of delicious Poké Puffs. It seems the only thing sweeter than Serena are her pastries!

SYLVEON **BRAIXEN** **PANCHAM**

KIMIA

The bold princess of the Azoth Kingdom, Kimia isn't afraid to speak her mind. But she doesn't just talk the talk—she definitely also walks the walk. Kimia is resourceful and brave, so she stays one step ahead of Alva. When the evil Neo-Arcane Scientist threatens her brother and her kingdom, Kimia is on the scene with her Mega Evolving Gardevoir, ready for action.

GARDEVOIR

ON THE FLY

Kimia has more than one mode of transportation and a secret garage at the castle where she parks her pride and joy. When Kimia wants to travel alone and be stealthy, she drives a power cycle with giant wheels that can conquer any terrain. Kimia also has a flying machine that's similar to a winged convertible airbus, which can transport many people and Pokémon.

MEGA GARDEVOIR

The Embrace Pokémon blasts Team Rocket off with a bright Dazzling Gleam.

MEGA EVOLUTION ACCESSORIES

Kimia keeps her Key Stone in a gold dial on a bracelet next to her wristwatch.

Gardevoir keeps her Mega Stone, Gardevoirite, on a gold charm necklace.

NIKOLA

Nikola was an incredibly gifted inventor and a master of Arcane Science. Around 500 years ago, his vision of a mechanized city came to life in Azoth Kingdom. Still to this day, his sophisticated designs incorporating gears to guide just about everything around keep the city moving and grooving.

THE HEART AND SOUL OF AZOTH

Nikola had an eye for detail and a big heart for his home. He innovated with the idea that everything he made would bring security and happiness to his fellow citizens of Azoth Kingdom. Nikola's inventions made the whole town prosper. Perhaps his greatest invention is the Mythical Pokémon Magearna. He gave it to the Royal Family as a gift, but even they did not truly know its power.

Magearna's Soul-Heart was the link that would transform Nikola's Tower Wall into his most ambitious design—the Floating Fortress. However, when a war broke out over who would control this power, Nikola hid both his design diagram and Magearna to protect the place he loved.

For centuries, no one knew where either the drawings or the Artificial Pokémon had gone. But when an evil scientist named Alva makes it his personal mission to find out, Nikola's best-intended inventions fall into the wrong hands. Luckily, Volcanion, Ash, Pikachu, and their friends are all there to defend Nikola's legacy!

JOLTEON

SPRITZEE

AMPHAROS

SKITTY

RALEIGH

Raleigh is the prince of Azoth Kingdom. However, he is probably better defined not by his title, but by his passion for his mechanical city and the Arcane Science that makes all of its hustle and bustle possible. His hero is the famous innovator and Arcane Scientist Nikola, who designed his entire kingdom.

As a member of the Royal Family, Raleigh wants to do what is best for his people. When Neo-Arcane Scientist Alva proposes that finding Magearna, one of Nikola's most beloved and important inventions, would help the kingdom, Raleigh is all too happy to help him in his mission. The naïve boy would never suspect that his friend and advisor Alva would be using him as part of his evil power grab.

NO AMOUNT OF WRONGS EVER MAKE A RIGHT

When his sister, Princess Kimia, warns Raleigh not to trust Alva, he tells her not to worry. In fact, Raleigh still stands by Alva even after he and his goons have bullied the people and Pokémon in Nebel Plateau, forced Pokémon to Mega Evolve, and put innocent Pokémon and people in charged chains. Raleigh thinks it's just what he has to do to get Magearna back. But when he witnesses Alva rip the Soul-Heart right out of the Artificial Pokémon and then toss its body off the side of the flying ship, he finally realizes his sister was right.

Raleigh tried to protest, but Alva just had Levi hold him back. Unfortunately, Raleigh learned the hard way that the end never justifies the means, especially if the means are totally mean.

Now, Raleigh wants to help right his wrong, and he's just the guy to help! He knows the Floating Fortress inside and out and leads Volcanion to the water tanks where it can power up its Explosion.

FOLLOW YOUR HEART

Although he was able to help save the day, Raleigh can't seem to shake the guilt he feels for trusting Alva. Raleigh tells Ash that he feels that if he didn't spend all his time trying to be book-smart, he might have had the street smarts to see Alva for the evil trickster he was. So, adventurous Ash encourages Raleigh to become a Pokémon Trainer and begin a journey of his own. After all, there's nothing like learning to rely on yourself!

HIDDEN TREASURE

An important and previously unknown design diagram for the Tower Wall and the Floating Fortress was found in Raleigh's room. He studied the drawing so hard that he knew his way around the Floating Fortress, even though no one had ever stepped foot on it—not even Nikola.

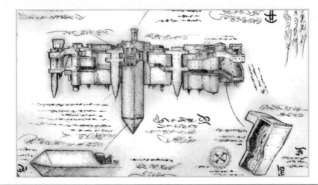

SWIRLIX

SLURPUFF

ALVA

Self-important Alva fancies himself an Arcane Science researcher and a master of Neo-Arcane Science. He has studied Nikola thoroughly, and while he's adapted his methods, he certainly lacks Nikola's intentions. Alva does it all for the glory of Alva.

FRIEND BY FORCE

Alva always has his golden staff and Gengar with him. But while Alva's invented a way to make faux Key Stones, there's no way to fake friendship. The minute Ash breaks Alva's staff and his faux Key Stone shatters, Gengar realizes it's finally free from doing Alva's evil bidding and disappears into the floor. Alva doesn't have a single real friend in the whole world. So, while Alva greedily wants to control everyone and lead the kingdom, he can't even seem to make one real buddy.

CRASH COURSE

When Ash breaks his golden staff, Alva escapes in a jetpack. Although Magearna and the kingdom are freed from his clutches, the petty villain makes sure that his plans will still be carried out. Alva set the Floating Fortress for an irreversible course—a crash landing into precious Nebel Plateau. But Volcanion and its new friends put their heads together to come up with the perfect solution. The Floating Fortress and Alva's final plan all go up in smoke with Volcanion's super-strong Explosion.

HAVE A HEART!

Power-hungry Alva wants to control and reshape Azoth Kingdom to be his ideal land. And he doesn't care who or what he destroys along the way. He tricks the young Prince Raleigh into trusting him for just long enough that he's able to use him to capture Magearna. Then, once he has the Mythical Pokémon, Alva rips out its Soul-Heart and throws Magearna's body overboard. There's no invention that can stop him from being so heartless!

GENGAR: THE SHADOW POKÉMON

Alva always takes Gengar with him. For example, the powerful Pokémon was able to break Magearna's heart with a single Mean Look. But it's not helping Alva because it wants to—the Shadow Pokémon is being forced to do his bidding. The second Ash breaks Alva's staff, the freed Gengar slips away into the floor to escape the evil scientist.

MEGA GENGAR

ALVA'S GOONS

LEVI

Alva's goon Levi has no problem doing his boss' dirty work. He will stop at nothing to get him Magearna, the Mythical Pokémon he needs for his evil plan. Cruel Levi doesn't care who he hurts, whether people or Pokémon.

Levi steps out on the deck of the flying ship to greet Volcanion with a battle. He forces Glalie and Alakazam to Mega Evolve with the faux Key Stone that Alva gave him. Then, he instructs them to turn Volcanion into a flying ice cube with Freeze Dry.

Then, Levi and Cherie follow Volcanion back to Nebel Plateau. There, they unleash charged chains, and Levi holds the trigger. He threatens Magearna that if it doesn't turn itself over to Alva, he'll zap all of the Mythical Pokémon's friends, including Volcanion. It's a promise he meanly makes good on until Magearna finally agrees.

Back on board the flying ship, Levi holds a disillusioned Raleigh back as Alva rips Magearna's Soul-Heart out.

Then, aboard the Floating Fortress, Levi leads an army of Pokémon that he and Cherie forced to Mega Evolve.

CHERIE

Levi's partner in crime, she's there every step of the way to help him carry out Alva's evil plans.

ALAKAZAM

MEGA ALAKAZAM

GLALIE

MEGA GLALIE

CAMERUPT

MANECTRIC

MEGA MANECTRIC

STEELIX

MEGA STEELIX

MEGA CAMERUPT

HOUNDOOM

MEGA HOUNDOOM

BANETTE

MEGA BANETTE

PIDGEOT

SWAMPERT

MEGA SWAMPERT

TYRANITAR

MEGA TYRANITAR

MEGA PIDGEOT

BEEDRILL

MEGA BEEDRILL

AGGRON

MEGA AGGRON

SHARPEDO

MEGA SHARPEDO

SALAMENCE

MEGA SALAMENCE

"YOU'RE
EVEN LESS
THAN
USELESS
TO ME."
—ALVA

TEAM ROCKET

Jessie, James, and Meowth arrive in Azoth Kingdom with their usual plans to poach Pokémon. But when Ash crash-lands into their desert strapped to Volcanion, they see a new business opportunity. Wanting to work for the wealthy prince in the hopes of getting rich, they go to meet with Alva and brag about knowing Ash. So, Alva gives them his manufactured faux Key Stones and sends them out to track Magearna down.

When they find Magearna with Volcanion, Ash, and his friends, Team Rocket tricks them into falling right into their trap, literally. Magearna lands right in a hole they dug as it tries to escape an attack from Mega Heracross and Mega Pinsir. But Kimia arrives at the scene with Mega Gardevoir just in time to send Team Rocket blasting off with Dazzling Gleam.

CHANGE OF HEART

When Team Rocket sees Alva in action, even this pack of thieves can't believe just how ruthless he is. After he rips Magearna's Soul-Heart out, they suddenly realize they have a heart. Jessie, James, and Meowth decide to try to steal it back from Alva so they can return it to the Mythical Pokémon. But Alva sees them coming and has Gengar stop them in midair with Psychic. He throws Jessie and James out, but Meowth is kept as his prisoner.

While the Soul-Heart is caged inside the Floating Fortress, Meowth can sense Magearna's suffering and sorrow. It pleads with Alva to stop with tears in its eyes, but it's no use. Alva's cruelty is senseless, so you can't reason with him.

In the end, Jessie and James use a grappling hook to hitch a ride on Kimia's flying machine back to the Floating Fortress so they can be reunited with their buddy Meowth. They might not always be good, but at least they're good to each other.

HERACROSS

MEGA HERACROSS

PINSIR

MEGA PINSIR

POKÉMON HUNTER

This greedy guy will stop at nothing to catch Pokémon he can sell on the black market, and he doesn't think twice about whom he hurts. He barrels through the forest, tearing it up with his big truck. When he sees a Pokémon he thinks will fetch him a good price, he just fires his weapons out the window.

The injured Amaura that Volcanion encounters was a victim of this selfish jerk. When Volcanion stands up to protect the wounded wild Pokémon, the hunter turns his attention to catching Volcanion. But he is no match for the Mythical Pokémon. Volcanion unleashes Mist so he can't see where he's driving and he slams into a big rock, the only thing harder than the Pokémon Hunter's head.

MYTHICAL AND LEGENDARY POKÉMON

VOLCANION:
THE STEAM POKÉMON

Height	5'07"
Weight	429.9 lbs
Type	Fire/Water

The Mythical Pokémon Volcanion protects all the wild Pokémon at Nebel Plateau. The Steam Pokémon selflessly looks after the Pokémon that arrive at the sanctuary, hurt by humans. Volcanion has always made sure that every Pokémon has a safe home at Nebel Plateau. But when Alva attacks, Volcanion learns that its Pokémon pals are there to protect it, too. When Alva commands Houndoom, Swampert, Tyranitar, Aggron, and Banette to fire crushing Hyper Beam directly at Volcanion, Kimia, Ash, and his friends, a group of courageous and clever wild Pokémon of the plateau acts fast and uses a combination of Dig and Safeguard to shield them.

GOOD OLD FRIENDS

Volcanion first met Magearna 500 years ago in the beautiful Field of Flowers. Like the other wild Pokémon of the Nebel Plateau, Magearna was a Pokémon refugee looking for a safe home to hide from humans. At Nikola's request, it had fled the war in the Azoth Kingdom. Ever since, the pair has been inseparable. Volcanion admires caring Magearna, which spends its day nurturing all the Pokémon at Nebel Plateau. When Alva steals its best friend, Volcanion will stop at nothing to save the kind soul.

THE TIE THAT BINDS

Volcanion does not like humans. It hates them so much, it doesn't even trust Pokémon that like humans. After centuries of caring for Pokémon that have been injured, hurt, or abandoned by people, it has a very negative view of humanity. And when it is accidentally shackled to Ash, it isn't even going to give him a chance. Volcanion drags Ash along, even through the dirt, because it's on too important of a mission—to save Magearna.

Ash sees first-hand just how cruel people like a Pokémon Hunter can be to Pokémon, but he is committed to standing up for what is right and helping every Pokémon in need. As Volcanion sees Ash adopt its important cause and continue to stay by his side even after Clemont frees them from their bands, the Mythical Pokémon comes to depend on

---

POWERHOUSE

Volcanion's strong will is backed up by its incredibly powerful attacks. The Mythical Pokémon can blast itself out of blocks of ice. And with its impressive Explosion, it burst the bricks of the Floating Fortress into dust. To get the Steam Pokémon's power pumped up for its awesome blow-ups, just add water.

its new friend. In fact, together with Ash and his pals, they form an unstoppable team that saves Nebel Plateau, the Azoth Kingdom, Magearna, and even each other. To honor Volcanion's new buddies, it gives them the special title of Honorary Pokémon of Nebel Plateau.

MAGEARNA:
THE ARTIFICIAL POKÉMON

Height	3'03"
Weight	177.5 lbs
Type	Steel/Fairy

Five hundred years ago, the amazing master of Arcane Science, Nikola, built this one-of-a-kind Pokémon. Magearna was a treasured gift and friend to the Royal Family, and it enjoyed spending its days in the castle with the princess. But Magearna was more than just a wonderful companion—it also held the powerful missing piece to create the Floating Fortress, its spherical Soul-Heart.

When war broke out in the kingdom, Nikola felt he had no choice but to hide his most beloved invention to protect it and the city. So, the Mythical Pokémon lived happily with Volcanion in the Nebel Plateau for centuries—that is, until greedy Alva sought to steal its precious Soul-Heart.

ALL HEART

Magearna has spent hundreds of years caring for its fellow Pokémon at Nebel Plateau. It loves its friends with all its heart. Giving Magearna is so devoted that it even hands itself over to Alva in the hopes he will stop hurting the Pokémon of the plateau. To Magearna, there is no sacrifice too great when the Pokémon it cares for are at stake.

Magearna truly is all Soul-Heart, in both its personality and its power. When Alva rips the Soul-Heart out of Magearna's chest, it is a shell of its former self. Volcanion carries the lifeless metal body on its back and sets out to fight for its friend.

IN FULL BLOOM

Magearna loves to greet people and Pokémon alike with a bouquet of flowers that springs from its hands. While most simply smile, they make Volcanion sneeze with such gusto that it gets the Pokémon back up on its feet after it collapses from exhaustion from creating the Explosion that destroyed the Floating Fortress.

LOST SOUL

Even when the Soul-Heart is separated from Magearna's body and trapped powering the Floating Fortress for Alva, Meowth can sense its struggle and its sadness. Magearna tries its hardest to resist, even when it's reduced to a sphere. But Alva breaks its spirit by having Mega Gengar use Mean Look.

Sadly, even when Ash returns the Soul-Heart to Magearna, it powers its body back up, but it still doesn't seem like itself. It's like the lights are on, but nobody's home. Meowth can tell its heart is still broken. When it returns to Nebel Plateau, some Pokémon friends try to connect with it, but it isn't until Volcanion returns safely that its heart is full again. There's just nothing like seeing an old friend to warm the heart!

BURST INTO SONG

When morale in the plateau is low after the Pokémon Hunter's sneak attack, Magearna cheers everyone up by playing a pretty song. The melody chimes across the whole Pokémon sanctuary, restoring peace and joy.

SQUISHY
ZYGARDE CORE FORME

Bonnie nicknamed her Zygarde travel companion "Squishy." She typically carries it in her bag in its Core Forme. However, when Alva's goon army attacks atop the Floating Fortress, it knows its friends are outnumbered. So, Squishy steps up and transforms into its 10 Percent Forme to battle. Then, when the Floating Fortress fires at the plateau, it helps the local Pokémon fight back. Squishy transforms into its Complete Forme to help stop the destructive beam.

ZYGARDE 10% FORME:
THE ORDER POKÉMON

Height	3'11"
Weight	73.9 lbs
Type	Dragon/Ground

ZYGARDE COMPLETE FORME:
THE ORDER POKÉMON

Height	14'09"
Weight	1344.8 lbs
Type	Dragon/Ground

FEATURED POKÉMON

AMAURA: THE TUNDRA POKÉMON

When Amaura arrives at the Nebel Plateau, it's in pretty bad shape. There's a net around its neck, and it's all bruised. Volcanion rushes to its side, but it isn't surprised to see another poor Pokémon hurt by humans. Ash helps remove the net, while Serena bandages its wounds. They all soon find out exactly who is responsible—a horrible Pokémon Hunter!

GULPIN: THE STOMACH POKÉMON

Wild Gulpin offers Clemont a hand (or rather, some of its special spit) when it sees he's having a hard time repairing the flying machine. Its harsh Acid Spray not only helps cut through a metal part, but it also aids in slicing the bands off Ash and Volcanion.

Although its spit is strong, it gets weak around humans because it was so hurt by its former Trainer. But not all wounds can be seen with the eye. When Ash hugs Gulpin for helping to free him from the band, it slips out of his arms and hides behind Volcanion, scared. Apparently, its Trainer hugged it before it abandoned it. So, Gulpin still carries that emotional scar.

INTERESTING ITEMS

ARCANE SCIENCE

With a focus on technology, mechanics, and the future, Arcane Science was developed to make people and Pokémon happy. Nikola, a master of Arcane Science, felt it was his job to invent things that brought harmony to the world. Nikola was so forward-thinking and precise, the inventions he built 500 years ago are still the cornerstone of Azoth Kingdom. Raleigh, Clemont, and even Alva are big fans of this branch of science. While most use it for good, Alva found a way to twist its purpose.

THE CHARGED CHAINS

Alva and his goons use charged black chains to trap Volcanion, Ash, and their friends. When Alva comes to the plateau in his flying ship, they slither up out of the ground and wrap around a group of Pokémon at the plateau. Levi has his finger on the trigger as he demands that they turn Magearna over to Alva.

Then, while aboard the Floating Fortress, Alva uses them to tie up Kimia, Gardevoir, Greninja, Ash, and Volcanion. The charged chains are released from trap doors in the floor. Eventually, Volcanion is able to channel its anger and break through the chains to free itself and its friends.

MEGA EVOLUTION AND ALVA'S FAUX KEY STONES

Typically, in order to help a Pokémon pal Mega Evolve, a Trainer needs a Key Stone, a Mega Stone, and an incredible bond of trust. It's a relationship that takes time and care to build and a skill that is hard to earn. But Alva doesn't respect this sacred connection. Instead, he manufactured a solution. To control Pokémon and force them to Mega Evolve, Alva has created completely faux Key Stones. To make it work, all he has to do is utter two little words: "Mega Wave."

He keeps his faux Key Stone in a tall golden staff that he carries with him everywhere. Alva also gave them to his goons Levi, Cherie, and even Jessie and James in golden bracelets. However, the second that Alva's staff is smashed, their faux Key Stones are shattered, too.

THE BANDS

In an attempt to capture Volcanion, Alva's goon Levi tosses a couple of bands at the Mythical Pokémon. While one wraps around its leg, it's able to dodge the other. But as Volcanion falls to the ground, it takes the tethered band with it. That loose band winds up right around our hero Ash's waist. Although Volcanion tries to run, toss, and shake him off, nothing works. Through some special glasses, Clemont can see that they're connected by an unbreakable electromagnetic pulse. So, while Volcanion can't stand humans, it soon finds itself spending every second with Ash Ketchum. However, after learning to work together, what seems like a trap turns into a true bond of friendship.

Clemont is eventually able to free them from their chains by combining a small Clemontic Gear saw with Gulpin's metal-melting Acid Spray.

POKÉ PUFFS

These sweet pastries are a favorite snack of Pokémon. Serena is known for baking delicious batches of the Poké Berry-filled treats for her Pokémon friends.

TOTALLY AWESOME TECHNOLOGY

FLAMEL'S COMPUTER

This sophisticated machine fills Flamel's office. She keeps the lights off in the room so she can clearly see all the screens as she conducts her investigation into Alva and his evil plans. Amazingly enough, she doesn't have papers or books lying around. The computer is so powerful that her desk only has a keyboard on it.

KIMIA'S HOLOGRAM WRISTWATCH

This device projects a screen so Kimia can communicate with Flamel and receive her intel no matter where she is.

KIMIA'S CONVERTIBLE POWER CYCLE

Parked in Kimia's garage at the castle is one cool convertible power cycle. It has lots of speed on land and can even transform into a stealth jetpack.

MR. IRON DEFENSE

To protect against Volcanion's attacks...and surly attitude, Clemont built Ash a full-body suit of armor he calls Mr. Iron Defense. This incredible Clemontic Gear outfit comes complete with a helmet. The protective suit was inspired by moves like Defense and Protect.

KIMIA'S FLYING MACHINE

This princess is always on the go protecting her kingdom. And when she needs to transport a lot of Pokémon and people, she can use this flying open-air bus.

THE SOUL-HEART

This small sphere is strong enough to power the Mythical Pokémon Magearna and the entire Floating Fortress. But its true might is the strength of Magearna's character.

"HOLDING BACK IS NOT WHAT I DO!" —CLEMONT

DESIGN DIAGRAM

This previously unknown detailed drawing of the Floating Fortress' inner workings was discovered in Raleigh's room. While it demonstrates Nikola's technologically advanced vision, it was one that was never meant to be realized. Nikola did complete the incredible undertaking of building the mechanized Tower Wall, but when it was finished, the kingdom descended into war over who would have the power to control it. Unfortunately, the answer came 500 years later, but it still was bad news. The design diagram fell into Alva's hands and gave him all the information he needed to use it as a weapon.

POKÉMON PAGE NUMBER INDEX

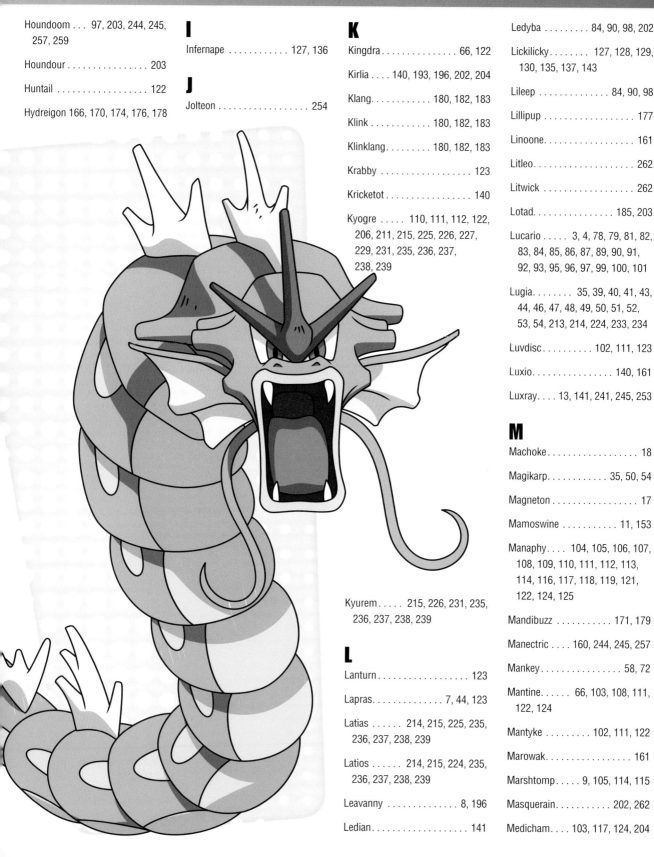

Meditite, Meowth, Mew, Mewtwo, Minccino, Misdreavus, Moltres, Monferno, Mr. Mime, Mudkip, Munchlax, Murkrow

N

Nidoking 17, 160

Nidoqueen 21, 160

Nidoran.............. 161, 203

Nidorina 84, 90, 98, 161, 203

Nidorino 84, 90, 98, 161

Ninetales................ 98

Ninjask 160

Noctowl 7, 58, 61, 68, 72

Noivern............ 8, 245, 252

Nosepass 161

O

P

Q

R

S

THE PERFECT COMPANION
TO THE POKÉMON ANIMATED SERIES

This updated and expanded volume puts the Pokémon world at your fingertips with amazing artwork, fascinating facts, and comical anecdotes. It is the definitive reference for every Pokémon fan!

- The ultimate reference to key **CHARACTERS**, famous **BATTLES**, and important **PLACES!**

- **EVERY REGION** up through **KALOS** is covered, including **EVENTS**, **PEOPLE**, and **POKÉMON!**

- Trace **ASH**'s journey and get to know his Pokémon, friends, and travel companions, as well as **VILLAINS** and **RIVALS** throughout the Pokémon world!

- Learn the powerful **LIFE LESSONS** that Pokémon teaches!

Pokémon™

MOVIE COMPANION

Written by Simcha Whitehill

Published by DK/Prima Games, a division of
Penguin Random House LLC. Prima Games® is a
registered trademark of Penguin Random House
LLC. All rights reserved, including the right of
reproduction in whole or in part in any form.

The Prima Games logo and Primagames.com are
registered trademarks of Penguin Random House
LLC, registered in the United States. Prima Games
is an imprint of DK, a division of Penguin Random
House LLC, New York.

DK/Prima Games, a division of Penguin Random
House LLC
6081 East 82nd Street, Suite #400
Indianapolis, IN 46250

ISBN: 9780744018455

Printing Code: The rightmost double-digit number is the year of the book's printing; the rightmost
single-digit number is the number of the book's printing. For example, 17-1 shows that the first
printing of the book occurred in 2017.

20 19 18 17   4 3 2 1

001-307939-Nov/2017

Printed in Canada.

Prima Games Staff

VP & Publisher
Mike Degler

Editorial Manager
Tim Fitzpatrick

Design and Layout Manager
Tracy Wehmeyer

Licensing
Paul Giacomotto

Digital Publishing
Julie Asbury
Shaida Boroumand

Operations Manager
Stacey Ginther

Credits

Title Manager
Jennifer Sims

Copy Editor
Angie Griffin

Book Designers
Brent Gann
Dan Caparo
Tim Amrhein
Carol Stamile
Jeff Weissenberger

Senior Production Designer
Areva

Production
Beth Guzman

www.primagames.com
INDIANAPOLIS, INDIANA